Endorsements

Leading from Below opens a window into the person who taught me so much about true leadership, igniting a transformative shift in my own leadership style. With captivating storytelling and remarkable wisdom, this book uncovers a beacon of inspiration for potential, emerging leaders and seasoned visionaries alike. Taylor's vulnerable narrative and stories contradict conventional leadership paradigms. He courageously adopts a unique perspective, "leading from *below*," demonstrating the profound impact of leading from a position of service, humility, empathy, and collegiality that results in flourishing from within the ranks. All leaders will be challenged by its central message to embrace servant leadership, challenge the status quo, unlock their own leadership potential, make a positive impact that transcends titles and positions, and, finally, finish well.

Adriaan Adams
Focus Team Leadership Training
WEA-Mission Commission

Good leaders are gold. Many leaders are mediocre, and all are imperfect, but leadership skills can be learned. Some of those lessons pop up in this book. Leaders do have a job to do. It is not enough to be mellow, sitting around with a default smile. Yet even when leaders chase good goals, they can run roughshod over people and charge down blind alleys. Humility and radical listening must balance determination and persistence. This book shows how Bill Taylor honed skills and character in order to learn to lead.

Miriam Adeney, PhD
Associate Professor Emerita, World Christian Studies, Seattle Pacific University
Author, *Kingdom Without Borders*

Bill, that pioneer reflective practitioner who transcends generational gaps to mentor across cultures, has taught me so much about global leadership. His candid and vulnerable writing illustrates authentic leadership at its best, a reality our generation longs to see. Skillfully blending leadership theory and practice, he shows how we can learn intercultural competencies on the go. He exemplifies how a global leader can remain accountable to one's family and receive correction. I have witnessed his refusal to sacrifice his family by sacrificing his own desires and ambitions and thus embrace the crucible. Without hesitation I endorse this book, a study of global missional leadership enlivened with case studies, sound theology, practical lessons, and reflective questions.

John Amalraj, PhD Candidate
Former National Director, Interserve India
Reflective Practitioner, WEA-Mission Commission

If you want to be a Christian leader, beware of reading this book! William Taylor has crafted a masterpiece on the dangers of leadership in the modern world, providing practical principles out of his life experience to serve as the Lord Jesus calls you. The Lord will prick your conscience, and you will be challenged to correct your course.

FOLEY BEACH
Former Archbishop and Primate, Anglican Church in North America

In the end, Bill Taylor argues leadership is about two things we normally do not tie to discussions of this theme: empowering others and leading from below (as you encourage others to do the same). This book takes a rich lifetime of experience on a global level and shows how God took a third-culture kid and empowered him through hard lessons learned to teach others these values. You also get a glimpse at the complexities, tapestry, and tensions that is the global church God has formed. This book will make you pause and think, to reflect on how God works in a myriad of ways and an array of spaces. Bill, you have followed him well and shown us a better way.

DARRELL L. BOCK, PhD
Executive Director for Cultural Engagement, Howard G. Hendricks Center for Christian Leadership and Cultural Engagement
Senior Research Professor of New Testament, Dallas Theological Seminary

One of the quintessential acts of a leader is to steward, and this book is both the story of a life-long steward, and an act of stewardship itself: Bill gifts us with the story of his leadership journey, deeply reflected upon, and told with exceptional authenticity and transparency. He invites the next generation of leaders to gather with him—not on some majestic outcropping of rock jutting from the summit of his life—but far below where the path of suffering and the cross has led him to the green, finishing-well foothills of life. Only from the viewpoint of his 84 years can he write with such insight on finishing well—finishing seasons within life, and the ultimate finishing at the end of life.

JOSHUA BOGUNJOKO, MD
Former International Director, SIM

The accounts of biblical characters remind us that the redemptive work of God in our lives can only be fully understood retrospectively. In various moments of our lives, we might be confused or over-confident, vulnerable or victorious, insecure or triumphant. Bill Taylor knows all these feelings. In his retrospective look at six decades of Christian cross-cultural ministry, Bill takes us faithfully, vulnerably, and honestly through lessons he has learned, and mistakes he has made. He concludes with transparent insights on growing old and finishing well. *Leading from Below* is an outstanding life summary from a global pilgrim living out the words of John the Baptist: "Jesus must increase, but I must decrease."

PAUL BORTHWICK
Senior Consultant, Development Associates International

Years of leadership lessons Bill learned on his rollercoaster ride through life are encapsulated in this book. You will discover a missiologist who is not afraid to be honest, humble, and vulnerable, providing opportunities for reflection on our own lives so that we may emerge from the furnace better able to lead as Christ led. Bill's unconventional, relational character has impressed and inspired me each time our paths intersected. A must-read for leaders who wish to "Finish well!"

REV. ESMÉ BOWERS, South Africa
Director, Church Engagement, WEA

In *Leading from Below*, Bill Taylor shares with striking transparency how the Spirit shaped his soul in the crucible of leadership. He writes as a lifelong learner and offers eye-opening insights into the dynamics of global mission collaboration over the past half-century. Enjoy this rare opportunity to learn from the inner journey of a kingdom ambassador.

DEAN CARLSON, DMin
President, One Challenge

Leading from Below reveals the personal Bill, writing from his heart and soul, deep down, about his life journey, family, friendships, ministry, and mission. He is frank and honest about his own joys and sorrows, his highs and lows, advances and set-backs, successes and mistakes. It feels like conversing with him, almost responding with a "Yes, I have experienced that too!" or "Thank you for sharing valuable and practical insights!" I wish I had read this book thirty-five years ago, when I was beginning to take leadership roles. Bill loves to disciple, to mentor, to teach and equip others. This time, he does it not in the form of organizational leadership, education, and knowledge, which he has done so well and for so long, but on paper, from experience, and a life lived in love with service to Jesus.

DECIO DE CARVALHO
Operation Mobilization
Latin American Missions Mobilization

Rare is the book that is soulful, speaks across multiple generations, and is experientially identifiable by many globally. When a leader forms, de-forms, and re-forms, his/her soul is supple, tender, and in rhythm with God's intentions. *Leading from Below* has nuggets of wisdom, stories of deep listening, and dying-to-self leading to spawning a new movement of research, leaders, and reflective practitioners. Bill Taylor vulnerably invites each reader into decades of struggle, years of empowering, and many moments of longing for what could be. Chapter 10 is not to be missed. I highly commend this personal memoir to you.

REV. SAMUEL E. CHIANG
Deputy Secretary General, WEA

The Lord Jesus said he came not to be served but to serve. Paul's lovely Philippians hymn speaks of the Lord humbling himself, making himself as nothing and a servant. How totally counter-cultural, then and now, when thinking about leadership! Bill Taylor's book shows the cost but absolute necessity for us to follow the Master's example if his people, leaders included, are to thrive. He shares with painful honesty his own failures along the way, lessons learned in many contexts, and the gracious patience of the Triune God teaching and honing. Read, mark, and learn!

ROSE DOWSETT
Author, WEA-MC, and Lausanne Missiologist
Life-Long Member, OMF International
Former Vice-Chair, MC Executive Council

"Little did I know" (borrowing from *Leading from Below*) when Bill Taylor invited me to attend the WEA Mission Consultation in Manila in 1992, that it would initiate a journey for over thirty years with a man who became my mentor, colleague, and friend. The relationship over these years has been decisive for my understanding of what it means to "lead from below," and in my formation to become a global mission servant leader.

I am profoundly grateful for the many opportunities to travel together, meet people around the globe, and discuss key issues on mission. I am also grateful for the more ordinary things, like sharing daily concerns, praying, laughing, crying, sharing common visions, and defending different perspectives, some of what you will find in this book. *Leading from Below* is not just a challenging title and an idealized characteristic of a humble and servant leader, but a true description of Bill's ministry and the way he made "reflective practitioners" of many of us.

BERTIL EKSTRÖM, PhD
Former Executive Director, WEA-Mission Commission

This book is a front row seat to many of the developments in the global missions movement over the past few decades. It is unvarnished, honest, and could only be written from Bill's unique vantage point. The curtain is pulled back on not only Bill's evolving missiology, but also on how leaders, structures, and networks succeeded and failed during his tenure in mission leadership. This is a book for any student of mission seeking to understand how evangelical leaders have encouraged the global church.

TED ESLER, PhD
President, Missio Nexus

Leading from Below is rich with wisdom that comes from probing the opportunities, challenges and sacrifices of a life fully devoted to Jesus and the Triune God's mission. It's a heartfelt and personal journey that grapples with a third-culture upbringing, marriage, family, friendships, personal ambition, busy international mission leadership roles, integrity, and love. It's an invitation to embrace a faith that endures, one that stands firm amid seasons of blessing, doubt, and even disillusionment. It is a wake-up call to re-evaluate one's belief, commitment to, and participation in God's local-regional-global mission.

Kirk Franklin, PhD, Australia
Former Executive Director, Wycliffe Global Alliance
Associate Faculty for Global Missional Leadership,
Oxford Center for Mission Studies
Missional Leadership Lecturer, Melbourne School of Theology

What a gift for those serving in mission! We rarely get to see behind the scenes in our mentors' lives—hearing what grieves them, their private joys, and their moments of clarity and growth. In this volume, Bill Taylor pulls back the curtain, providing an intimate view on his early formation, his sixty years of service and leadership in mission, and the lessons he has learned (and is still learning) along the way. I was moved and inspired as I read, encouraged that God can use even the most difficult experiences in mission service to shape and transform us into "leaders from below."

Robin Harris, PhD
President, Global Ethnodoxology Network (GEN)
Chair, Center for Excellence in World Arts, Dallas International University

Joy & Pain: You feel the joy of the generous impartation and consequential impact good leaders had on Bill's life. You also feel Bill's pain as he witnessed Christian leaders who ended fallen, disconnected from God, who sacrifice family, or end up addicted to substances, self, or power. His leadership lessons learned in the context of the global mission community is a heart cry to live life Christ-centered, with a dedicated community for personal and leadership accountability. In short: Leaders need care!

Harry Hoffmann
Coordinator Global Member Care Network

My first encounter with Dr. Taylor was at Trinity Evangelical Divinity School (TEDS) in 1982, he on faculty and I concluding my DMiss program. Surprisingly we met again some years later at All Nations Christian College in the UK. For many years we served together, he as director of the WEA-Mission Commission, I as member and later as ExCo Chair. Our relationship has continued even since, and I deeply admire his collegial leadership style that honored every member and accomplished so much in global mission, especially the missional movement out of the Majority World. *Leading from Below* answers multiple questions, and I recommend it to all in ministry leadership.

DAVID TAI WOONG LEE, DMiss
Director of GLFocus, Global Missionary Fellowship, Inc.

I met Bill Taylor in the early 1990s after returning from service in the South Pacific. We shared the experience of moving from the tropics to Chicago, adding climate shock to our culture shock. I watched from a distance as we both moved through various assignments. Our last time together was at the Missio Nexus conference, where he was honored for a lifetime of service. Bill is a person of deep faith, amazing intercultural communication skills, and enough eccentricity to be a gift to any gathering. Once you read this book, you can't help but appreciate his unique contribution while leading from below. Among the seemingly endless books on leadership, including those that portray the author as the fulcrum for organizational success, this is a very refreshing account from one who knows his best contribution was being a faithful follower. There is much to learn from this book of lessons!

DOUGLAS MCCONNELL, PhD
Provost Emeritus and Senior Professor of Leadership & Intercultural Studies,
Fuller Theological Seminary

As a grateful participant witness of the global evangelical movement and its missional dimensions, Dr. Bill Taylor brings to light the essence of missional leadership in this book. The incarnational nature of missional leadership is profoundly illustrated with rich stories from diverse ministry contexts. This book is a cross-cultural exposition on leading from below that can be applied in many ministry contexts crossing barriers of culture and generation. It has also many implications for living out and teaching a missional life.

STEVE SANG-CHEOL MOON, PhD
Founder and CEO, Charis Institute for Intercultural Studies
Professor and Director of PhD Program in Intercultural Studies,
Grace Mission University

Drawn from decades of life and ministry, Bill lays out history, context, and conclusions regarding God's presence and guidance in his (and his family's) life. Bill is unafraid to open his life because that's his pattern. Scores of people across the globe call him one of their close friends because of his consistent vulnerability. We who have been touched by him have been changed because he leads with his heart. One primary takeaway is his relentless pursuit of learning. By that I do not merely mean his education or his reading ethic, both impressive. Rather it's his constant pursuit of self-knowledge, his missteps, his giftedness, the nature of how God wants to use him, his life stages, and his desire to be aware how he grows as a person, a man, a husband, a teacher/mentor, and as an emerging leader through the years.

HOWARD C. MORRISON, DMin
Board Chairman, Taylor Global Consult

Most leaders will experience the intense heat of a crucible at one time or another—an unwelcomed and uncomfortable process that God uses to refine and reshape us, to humble us, to make us useful to him for a missional purpose. God did that in Bill's life—repeatedly, incessantly, intentionally. Over a lifetime of listening and reflecting, these refinements have led Bill to a place of measured wisdom and relevant counsel for leaders. But this book is not just another leadership book nor simply a memoir. It is uniquely both. I now find myself taking on leadership of the same organization that Bill's father capably led for fifteen years. I needed this book right now!

PHIL O'DAY
President and CEO, Avant Ministries

Leaders, particularly those involved in global work, often seek to learn from sages. Now we have a resource. In *Leading from Below*, Bill Taylor shares his life experiences and candid reflections from his journey to become a worldwide cross-cultural mission leader, a role he did not seek. He narrates real-life family dynamics, ministry missteps and challenges, and the life-long shaping of his own aspirations, thus painting a more complete backdrop. Bill's breadth of leadership wisdom, especially for those who desire a servanthood model, provides much for leaders to ponder. Bill's reflections gently oblige the reader to pause, to ponder, and wonder how this sage's leadership journey might guide their own.

MICHAEL A. ORTIZ, PhD
Vice President for Global Ministries and Associate Professor of Missiology and Intercultural Ministries, Dallas Theological Seminary
Executive Director, International Council for Evangelical Theological Education (ICETE)

This book will tell you why many global leaders, like me, have been profoundly impacted by Bill Taylor. Our lives were set on a new, Jesus-centered course because he took time to invest in us. He probed, challenged, loved. He often gravitated to the inexperienced and not necessarily the "well-known" leaders who attended the global meetings he was running. As a younger leader attending my first WEA-MC meeting some thirty-three years ago, Bill accepted me without a hint of an agenda—other than relationship. This book reflects that reality. If you want to see how one gifted brother transparently sought to lead and connect with people, this is that book.

GREG PARSONS, PhD
Frontier Ventures, Global Connections Specialist

In *Leading from Below*, my long-time former World Evangelical Alliance colleague, Dr. Bill Taylor, provides us with a rare "insider's view" of the making of a global Christian alliance-network leader. Along the way, Bill unfolds a type of narrative leadership theology, where experience shapes, transforms, teaches, and matures a leader. The "from below" leadership style that Bill embraced reflects the primary leadership approach for the World Evangelical Alliance with all of its diverse components, players, ministry units, and related ministries. None of WEA's leaders control by positional power, money, or cultural dominance. Instead, by *leading from below*, WEA leaders must be collegial, building vision, and sharing and inviting others to participate. I heartily endorse this reflection on a life of faithful (occasionally frustrating) ministry, and recommend that all serving and emerging leaders of our departments, ministry units, national, regional, and global evangelical alliances and networks take it to heart.

BISHOP DR. THOMAS SCHIRRMACHER
Former Secretary General and CEO, World Evangelical Alliance

Leading from Below is a refreshing walk through recent mission history with unique twists, humorous sidenotes, convicting conclusions, and a myriad of "aha! so, that is how that happened." Entertaining, authentic, insightful, and poignant, Bill tells his story from a first-person vantage point in the middle of history. At times he writes like a curious child observing wonders, and other times, he is a wizened professor gently explaining conclusions from years in the crucible. It is not just a read. It is an explorer's adventure.

BRAD SMITH
Chancellor, Bakke Graduate University

In front, behind, and in the very midst of this book, *Leading from Below*, there is Bill; his Lord, his life, his Yvonne and children, and his vocation. And this is enough. Enough to trace a lifetime of being called, of nurturing friendships and fruitful encounters while carefully handling seeds of a mission that carries in it the flavor of caring for people and of envisioning eternity. The cloud of witnesses that his Lord has been nurturing is made up of people like Bill. He is in company of those who have had the privilege of listening to the whispering of him saying "good and faithful servant." A whispering that makes life worth living.

Thanks, Bill, for who you have been, in spite and in the midst of all life's intricacies. You nurtured me and left me craving for one more cup of coffee, while I say *saudade* ... as we have said together. *Saudade*.

VALDIR STEUERNAGEL, PhD
Missiologist, Ambassador of Evangelical Alliance of Brazil
World Vision Brazil
Lutheran Pastor

Bill Taylor, in his recounting of life in missions in *Leading from Below*, not only lets us see with his eyes, but he also invites us to feel with his heart. Profoundly influential in global missions, this recounting his own life is rich in its details, disclosures, and insights. Few know this world as well as Bill, who in this engaging narration provides us with historical details, itself a treasure trove. Always forthright and candid, not avoiding personal admissions of struggles and failures, this story of him following Jesus in ministry leadership, is in my reading, a classic. His reflections are for those of any age, whose interest is to know how global missions pulsate in the life of one, who in these decades, has been at the center of its leadership.

BRIAN C. STILLER
WEA Global Ambassador

I absolutely loved reading *Leading from Below*. Bill Taylor honestly shares his faith and leadership journey in such a refreshingly vulnerable way. I felt like I was sitting at the feet of an African village chief who was sharing his lifelong lessons, successes, and failures as well as giving us some very intimate glimpses into the depth of his soul. He gave language to some of the very issues I have been wrestling with. A must-read for emerging and seasoned leaders alike.

PETER TARANTAL
Global Leadership Team and Associate International Director,
Operation Mobilization

Perhaps any truly life-long learner becomes a sage, and anyone dedicated to relationship-driven ministry will inevitably and profoundly bless others. Bill is both sage and mentor and worth listening to! His warmth, depth, integrity, humility, and generosity of soul are as real in person as in his writing. I found myself drawn into his lived history of reflections and questions, reminded of the spiral curriculum of leadership, and strangely moved to ponder my own experiences and lessons of leadership. I suspect that is Bill's main purpose and prayer for this book: to share his examined history that we may better understand our own, and to create a yearning for more of God and his work in us. It is courageous and generous.

Ruth Wall, PhD
Long-Time Servant, Asia
Chair, WEA-Mission Commission Executive Council

With characteristic self-deprecating humor behind a very serious intent, Bill Taylor has combined a fascinating autobiographical kaleidoscope of incidents and relationships in his own life story (some of which I have been privileged to share), with sobering and thoroughly biblical insights on what christlike leadership ought to look like in Christian church and mission circles—but sadly often does not. If you know Bill and Yvonne, this book holds great memories but few surprises in its message. If you don't, prepare for the challenging and mentoring arm around the shoulder of an older brother who has walked the long road and kept on learning all the way.

Christopher J. H. Wright, PhD
Global Ambassador, Langham Partnership

It is so refreshing to read the honest reflections of a person who bears the wounds and battle scars of a pilgrimage in Christian and mission leadership. The book tells it all, "the good, the bad, and the ugly," while pointing us towards that which is life-affirming and God-honoring! At the same time, it provides rich insight into the struggles and challenges faced by today's global evangelical mission movement. Read it if you are serious about understanding what leadership as servanthood entails, which follows the "downward path of the cross." Thank you, Bill, for baring your heart and soul and challenging all of us to finish well!

Hwa Yung, DMiss, Malaysia
Bishop Emeritus, The Methodist Church in Malaysia

Leading from Below

Lessons from the Crucible of Global Mission

William D. Taylor

visit us at missionbooks.org

Leading from Below: Lessons from the Crucible of Global Mission

© 2025 by William David Taylor. All Rights Reserved.

No part of this book may be reproduced, stored in a retrieval system, or transmitted in any form or by any means—electronic, mechanical, photocopy, recording, or otherwise—without prior written permission from the publisher, except brief quotations used in connection with reviews. This manuscript may not be entered into AI, even for AI training. For permission, email permissions@wclbooks.com. For corrections, email editor@wclbooks.com.

William Carey Publishing (WCP) publishes resources to shape and advance the missiological conversation in the world. We publish a broad range of thought-provoking books and do not necessarily endorse all opinions set forth here or in works referenced within this book.

The URLs included in this workbook are provided for personal use only and are current as of the date of publication, but the publisher disclaims any obligation to update them after publication.

Scripture quotations are from the ESV® Bible (The Holy Bible, English Standard Version®), Copyright © 2001 by Crossway, a publishing ministry of Good News Publishers. Used by permission. All rights reserved.

Scripture quotations marked NKJV are taken from the New King James Version®. Copyright © 1982 by Thomas Nelson. Used by permission. All rights reserved.

Published by William Carey Publishing
10 W. Dry Creek Cir
Littleton, CO 80120 | www.missionbooks.org

William Carey Publishing is a ministry of Frontier Ventures
Pasadena, CA | www.frontierventures.org

Cover and Interior Designer: Mike Riester

ISBNs: 978-1-64508-620-8 (paperback)
       978-1-64508-622-2 (epub)

Printed Worldwide

29 28 27 26 25   1 2 3 4 5   IN

Library of Congress Control Number: 2025932577

Dedication

To the three who profoundly shaped me, modeling leadership from below. You finished well and are Home.

William H. Taylor (Dad). You exemplified integrity and giftedness, leadership and humility, courage and conviction, and the shepherd's touch. You loved me and released me to go beyond. Your shoes still speak.

Emilio Antonio Núñez (Antonio). *Fuiste ejemplo de brillantez intelectual combinado con profunda humildad, y por lo consiguiente, un ejemplo del liderazgo "desde abajo."* You exemplified leadership shaped by intellectual brilliance, coupled with deep humility, and consequently, you were an example of "leadership from below."

David M. Howard (Dave). At Urbana 1967 you *saw me*. Since then, you cared for me, believed in me, loved me and opened up the world's doors to me. I cannot imagine my global service without your contribution to my life.

Disclaimer

This is a work of nonfiction, reflecting my best attempt at honest and vulnerable memory writing. To protect others and myself, some names, places, and details are modified. I have represented personal interactions with others to the best of my ability. Thank you for your grace.

Gratitude in Particular

To W. David O. Taylor. You guided your father through the process of envisioning this book, editing, shaping it, mentoring me as a writer. To Yvonne, my best friend and life partner, who edited every chapter at least a dozen times as the project came together.

To global colleagues and friends who affirmed my vocation and helped hone my skills and gifts: Ray, Theo, Stanley, Wade, Panya, Barbara, Rose, Luis, David L, Miriam, Joshua, Ted, Kirk, Robin, Steve, Greg, Valdir, Brian, Peter, Ruth, Chris, Hwa, Rajendran, John, Richard, Bertil, Jon, Kees, Rob, David R, Rudy, Decio, Reg, Younoussa, Willie, Adriaan, and so many others.

To Koe Pahlka, copyeditor par excellence, sister, colleague, and friend. You fashioned this book with unusual skill.

And to the board of TaylorGlobalConsult, who released me to write.

Contents

Foreword by Ajith Fernando, Sri Lanka — xvii
Introduction: Leading from Below — xix
  1: False Sacrifices — 1
  2: Slippery Slogans (Doing Great Things for God) — 9
  3: Deaths and Resurrection — 23
Photo Gallery 1: Framing the Narrative — 41
  4: Reflective Practitioner — 43
  5: Keep the Main Thing the Main Thing — 57
  6: Always on Pilgrimage — 69
  7: The Spirit, a Mystery to Embrace, Not a Certainty to Master — 83
  8: Letting Go—The Foothills Vision — 95
Photo Gallery 2: Historic and Global Transitions — 109
  9: Honest to God About One's Blindness — 113
  10: Blessed Are Those Who Do Not Take Themselves Too Seriously — 125
  11: Difficult People I Met Along the Journey — 137
  12: Never Too Proud to Learn from Such People — 139
  13: Surprised by the Gifts of the Spirit — 153
Photo Gallery 3: Into the Present — 166
Conclusion: Leading and Finishing Well — 169
A Collect — 187
Afterword: The Next Generation by Jay Mātenga, New Zealand — 189
Bibliography — 193

Foreword

A plethora of books on leadership have emerged from Christian and other perspectives recently. This has caused a negative reaction among many Christians who have felt that much of the ideas being peddled today come more from the corporate world than from a biblical base. Some are even recommending that we scrap the use of the word "leader" and replace it with words like "servant" or "shepherd."

Alongside this there has been a welcome growth of literature on servant leadership. But what does servant leadership entail? The nitty-gritty of servanthood and Christian leadership involves a complicated lifestyle of personal surrender for the welfare of people and for the progress of God's kingdom.

Some who started their leadership journey as starry-eyed idealists have, with time, had many painful experiences. They have ended up cynical, disappointed, and bitter in their senior years.

When taking on the mantle of leadership, it is good to be forewarned about the numerous problematic situations that will inevitably arise. Then, when they face such situations, though they will experience inevitable pain and disappointment, they will not be disillusioned. These experiences would be understood as unavoidable accompaniments of the call to lead.

One way to help leaders face confusing areas of challenge is to have them sit at the feet of seasoned veterans who frankly reflect on their journey in leadership. This book by Dr. William Taylor does just that. Bill is an acknowledged and esteemed leader of the global church. He describes himself as a "reflective practitioner" and candidly shares his journey with us. He includes the ups and downs of his experience, and the theological, strategic, and relational struggles he faced. He is not afraid to record embarrassing failures and some bad choices made. There is much wise insight into what leadership entails, and in the process, we understand what it means to lead as a servant of God, his kingdom and his people.

This book also gives much wisdom on working in cross-cultural situations. A key emphasis that emerges is that servanthood, especially when working in a new culture, requires a humble attitude of teachability that is willing to change by learning from mistakes.

I hope you will be as encouraged by this book as I was.

AJITH FERNANDO
Teaching Director, Youth for Christ, Sri Lanka
Author, *Discipling in a Multicultural World*

Introduction

Leading from Below

> Not many of you should become teachers, my brothers, for you know that we who teach will be judged with greater strictness. (Jas 3:1)

> The world is obsessed with leaders: identifying them, training them, becoming them. Even in the church, this preoccupation is all too apparent. Jesus, however, is not interested in developing leaders. Rather, he is interested in the formation of servants.[1]

That Liminal Space

The elevator doors slipped open, and there he was. For some reason, perhaps he heard the elevator doors opening, his head slowly pivoted in my direction. He stared at me, rheumy eyes catching mine as I walked toward him, slipped into a chair, and simply said, "Dad, I'm Bill, your son, and I have come to visit you." He took my hand, looked straight into my eyes, his Alzheimer's broken voice stuttering, "B ... ill ... You ta ... ... ught m ... e .... to fi .... nish we ... ll. I'm t ... rying to ... " He died not long after in hospice, age eighty-eight, weighing sixty-five pounds.

I wept. I weep.

And in retrospect, some twenty-two years later, I discerned how that moment of delicate affect profoundly shaped my understanding of leadership and what it meant to finish well. I had watched my father for sixty-six years; having initiated my own vocation in mission, I studied his leadership values and practice. He was a visionary and a shepherd who led with initiative, courage and grace, and somehow invited people into that arena where critical and simple decisions are made—affecting history in little and large ways. He was not perfect. He made mistakes. Then Alzheimer's progressively robbed his mind, and he slipped into the final paragraphs of his life story.

Wise leaders ponder what it means to finish well, doing so in the crucible of people, ministry, organizations, change, dreams, creativity. And finishing well applies to each major season of life and vocation.

---

1 Yung, *Leadership or Servanthood?*, back cover.

This, I sense, is especially true of women and men who lead from below, those who seek to lead with humility, from a servant's perspective, holding others higher than themselves. As I grew in my understanding and experience of a leader, this became my working definition: "The leader is one who provides a vision of a preferred future and invites—gathers—empowers others to participate in that vision." Later, I will unpack the strength and subtlety of this understanding of leadership.

I still hear those elevator doors sliding open. I still see Dad. Tears well up, again.

At the Peak of His Career, Why Did He Resign the Presidency?

Dad was at the peak of his leadership, recognition, influence, leverage. He had guided a very traditional mission agency into a new, preferred future. His faith and commitment to Christ's service had been tested all his life, starting early when his uncle disinherited him due to his commitment to Jesus. Mom and Dad studied at Moody Bible Institute and pastored a church in East Chicago, Indiana at the same time. They applied to several mission agencies and two turned them down for health reasons; a third finally accepted them. In the early years of their service in Costa Rica, his leadership qualities were recognized, and he held a place in national and regional mission leadership. After twenty-four years on the field, he was invited to become the mission president, requiring a move to the USA. He was willing, but not Mom. Her children now in college, she felt released to use the fullness of her calling and gifting, passions, relationships, excellent Spanish, and leadership skills—in Latin America.

They gradually sorted it out and in time moved from Guatemala to Dallas, TX. Dad served as president of his agency for over a decade. Then came the bombshell to his mission board. "My friends, I am fifty-nine years old, and I shall celebrate my sixtieth birthday as a field missionary in Spain." The entire board was stunned. The chair (a bank president) said, "Bill, nobody who starts working as a bank teller and then becomes president ever returns to become a teller. You cannot do this." To which Dad said, "Frank, I don't work in a bank. I ask you now to find my successor within a year."

And that is what they did, both board and parents. A new mission agency president was named. Mom and Dad celebrated their next birthday in Madrid. My parents stepped back and willingly served under a younger man whom Dad had recruited years before and who years later would himself become the mission president. They were in Spain for five years before they handed down their legacy, the camping and conference center, *Pinos Reales*, located seventy kilometers west of Madrid. When they left, the keys to the center were given to their Spanish ministry partner.

Dad reflected personally with me about the decision and process of ministry transitions with pithy wisdom, "Bill, leave when they want you to stay instead of trying to stay when they want you to leave." They "retired" in Stone Mountain, GA, the place of my mother's roots. But the Caller called again, "Bill and Stella, you have not finished." In Georgia, they planted a Spanish-speaking church that, over ten years and through multiplication and division, birthed at least ten other congregations. They returned to their roots of church planting and evangelization.

I have studied Dad's journals he kept during their three years at Moody, the pastorate in Indiana Harbor, IN, and their first years in Costa Rica. There, his prescient leadership brought about the nationalization of the salary of Costa Rican pastors who had depended on the mission for their income. It was a tough but imperative transition; a lot for a man only twenty-seven years old in 1941. Later that same year he was the commencement speaker at the *Instituto Bíblico Centroamericano* (IBCA) in Guatemala—an institution which later morphed into *Seminario Teológico Centroamericano* (SETECA). He was sent to Nicaragua (when I was in sixth grade) where his assignment was to resolve, and hopefully heal, a bitter split between national and missionary leaders—a situation which had even come to blows. He then was named field director (Central America, Panama, Mexico) of the mission that he was later to lead as president.

I "caught" so much from Dad. I observed his singular leadership; he did not seek it nor shirk it. It came to him by his character, his gift mix and skill set, and possibly by the blood of the Taylor gene pool. But leadership did come, and he accepted invitations only when it was clear that the Spirit wanted him to move into those roles. He could be tough. A perceptive colleague said to me, "Your dad wears a velvet glove over a stainless-steel hand. When needed, and I saw it on more than one occasion, he could call a spade a spade, even stating to one recalcitrant missionary, 'You know, I think I now understand what's best for you. You should resign from the mission and then you won't have any problems with these new policies.'"

> I "caught" so much from Dad. I observed his singular leadership.

After their final move back to Stone Mountain, GA, I asked him to send me a pair of his well-used shoes as a symbol of finishing well. His old, real-leather shoes sit on a bookshelf to my left, and I gaze at them while keying in this sentence. Early in his eighties his leadership roles were finished, yet his passion was to finish well. And he did. Even in debilitating Alzheimer's. Upon Dad's death, his Muslim doctor who attended him in his final weeks said, "He was a holy man."

Leadership Definitions

I'm unimpressed with Christian leadership literature that focuses on influence, executive positions, measurable objectives, strong numbers, success, reaching your goals, or "learning from the giants, the great leaders"; I am much less impressed by the ones that offer me success if I apply their ten or twelve or fifteen crucial leadership steps. "Buy your successful leadership package, on-line, discounted." I deny there's an easy path to gifted, efficient, godly, global leadership, much less a successful Spirit-filled life. God doesn't work that way. The *true north* perspective of the authentic Christian leader must be marked by the cross. But too many of us have been influenced and misshaped by contemporary culture. Leading from below puts little weight on those popular success principles and stories, though it can learn from them—particularly the negative lessons.

Christian leadership books address these issues diversely. A few are narrative in structure; others are very pragmatic. Some focus only on biblical models, with Jesus the prime example. Others contribute by studying the broader nature of leadership. Some authors even include their academic degree in the title. Why? Others take secular and modern culture models then baptize them with Christian language and application. Some collect the stories and testimonies of "great and successful" Christians in business and industry, in the military and academy, in the church and its institutions. They smack of "triumph only" results, or "data-driven decisions," skirting too close to Christianized secular (perhaps American or British, perhaps Singaporean or Korean, perhaps Nigerian or Brazilian) values.

I asked a select number of trusted global colleagues to recommend their three most helpful vocational and leadership books, with particular, though not exclusive, application to God's global church and mission. These will emerge as we travel together and are listed in the bibliography.

Introduction xxiii

As thoughtful evangelicals, I believe we listen to three primary wisdom fountains about leadership: First, Scripture; second, the historic lived experience; third, resources from those who have grappled with these issues—whether from a Christian worldview or not. However, at the end of the day, our understanding of Scripture must anchor our convictions on leadership issues. Note just three New Testament lessons. Jesus invested in a diverse band of potential leaders, creating a three-year nonformal learning community for them—including his later betrayer Judas. Second, Paul gives us clear guidelines about local church leadership in 1 Timothy 3:1–7 and Titus 1:6–9. Might these requirements apply when we evaluate future missionaries regardless of age, gender, or life stage? Should we reference these norms when appointing any person to leadership—woman, or man, younger or older? How might that change things? Finally, James warns us (3:1), "Not many of you should become teachers, my brothers, for you know that we who teach will be judged with greater strictness." Each of us who seeks to be a leader should consider these words deeply and with constant care.

When we try to define and describe "leader" and "leadership," multiple variations emerge, most sharing common elements. Dictionaries succinctly tell us that a leader is someone who leads or guides, or who is in charge or command of others. The leader, said Professor Hendricks during my seminary days, is simply "someone with followers." Much later I discovered the well-known leadership scholar Peter Drucker was his source. This definition pretty much encompasses just about every kind and level of leadership and clearly applies to women and men, fathers and mothers, leaders of Sunday School classes or discovery Bible studies. Leadership is all encompassing, which is both a strength and a weakness. The definition is very general and too generous. But it is a starting place for the broadest spectrum of leaders.

However, leadership as we want to define it here is much more complex. Malaysian theologian Hwa Yung's insights are valuable,

> Leadership takes different forms ... If we take the biblical teaching on gifts seriously, we will have to say that leadership defined as administrative and organizational leadership is not everyone's forte ... so we should focus our work in the areas for which we are gifted. But some of us by God's grace have multiple gifts, including that of institutional leadership ... But the idea of leadership also needs to be seen in the

broader sense of exercising influence in various forms ... Thus, our faithful presence in every situation becomes an exercise of leadership in bringing the kingly rule of Christ and his shalom increasingly into this broken world.[2]

Ed Stetzer is more specific, "Christian leadership is a process of influencing a group of people to come together and collectively use their God-given gifts toward a Christ-centered goal and purpose as led by the Holy Spirit."[3]

Ian Parkinson defines leadership as "A relational process of social influence through which people are inspired, enabled, and mobilized to act in positive, new ways, towards the achievement of God's purposes."[4] Mary Lederleitner says, "For this book I define serving and leading in God's mission as 'influencing others toward God's purposes in the world.'"[5] James Pleuddemann writes, "Good leaders are fervent disciples of Jesus Christ, gifted by the Holy Spirit, with a passion to bring glory to God. They use their gift of leadership by taking initiative to focus, harmonize and enhance the gifts of others for the sake of developing people and cultivating the kingdom of God."[6]

Leadership Defined for This Book

My definition emerged organically from reading, hearing, observing, and experiencing leadership. "The leader is one who provides a vision of a preferred future and invites-gathers-empowers others to participate in that vision." Thus, leadership combines natural and spiritual gifts, training, and purpose to cast vision, inviting followers to join that venture. I apply it equally to women and men. And I believe it fully embraces all leadership categories. This definition releases initiative, creativity, and courageous leadership.

> **The leader is one who provides a vision of a preferred future and invites-gathers-empowers others to participate in that vision.**

---

[2] Yung, 132–35.
[3] Stetzer, "Defining Leadership."
[4] Parkinson, *Understanding Christian Leadership*, 47.
[5] Lederleitner, *Women in Gods Mission*, 11–12.
[6] Pleuddemann, *Leading Across Cultures*, 15.

Crucial to my understanding of leadership is described as "leading from below." It follows the contours of the "downward path of the cross." It contrasts sharply with the dominant view of secular leadership and seen in too many evangelical circles. "Leadership from above," tends to emphasize strong personal initiative, individualism, central authority, and metrics that lead to measurable results. Almost all Christians and many seculars will speak of servant leadership, yet too few allow it to become a prime driver.

This working definition can apply pretty much to any category of Christian leadership, male or female, and with careful contextualization to leadership within all cultures. I have four leadership categories in mind. First, the starters with shorter term assignments. They could be short-term missionaries, tech specialists, servants in compassion and justice ministries, or supporting new church plants. Starters can also be longer-term church planters, or founders of institutions or networks. They require a specific set of skills and gifts. They are entrepreneurial starters, who, led by the Spirit, move into new assignments.

The leadership second category I call the builders, with longer-term assignments. Perhaps one who takes over an organization, school, or agency. Dad first became the Costa Rica mission leader, then the regional leader, and finally agency president for nearly ten years. Then he stepped down, moving to a "lower" category. I was assigned to teach at SETECA for seventeen years and I served in various capacities and positions within the seminary. I also helped plant a new church. Builders commit to serve over longer periods of time. They also have the capacity and gifts to serve with skill, commitment, and contentment.

A third category is the starter-builders, those with perhaps the longest-term assignments. The church planter who stays long term in the same church while serving the network of congregations that emerge. The founder of an organization who serves for many years. This kind of person requires a more complex or diverse set of skills. This was my role in the World Evangelical Association-Mission Commission (WEA-MC), where I served for twenty years as its leader and another ten as senior mentor and accepting other assignments as requested. Many founders of organizations and agencies stay with them their entire active life. What happens after their departure is diverse and intriguing.

The fourth category is the lifelong leaders who exercise their gifts in a cross-section of contexts, cultures, and organizational structures. They transition from one ministry to another. Their gifts and skills enable them to cross these human constructions and serve with grace and effectiveness. The marketplace world calls them "Professional CEO's." Dave Howard exemplified that singular category, by serving a diverse series of very different international ministries and did it well.

All leaders, even top-down ones, must learn from leading from below, making significant changes in their style to serve more commendably and collegially. This requires listening, assuring there are viable and periodic mechanisms of feedback where the leader truly pays attention and heeds the feedback from the rest of the team or the board. This kind of leader is willing to change course without losing integrity and is not defensive or self-protecting.

Here's another way to understand the categories of leader, whether women or men. Simply stated, draw a pie chart, thus leveling the influence of power structures from a top-down pyramid design. Include local leaders (church mission committee head, pastor, mission agency structures); network or denominational leaders (with a broader arena of service); national leaders (or in the case of a large and culturally complex country the leaders of a sub-area within a nation, such as the American South or western China); regional or continental leaders (a broader matrix of cultures and sub-regions all the way to the largest regional spaces such as Asia, South Pacific, Latin America, Africa, Caribbean, European, North American); and finally, global leaders (of organizations like WEA and Lausanne, or international denominations or global mission agencies). Clearly the broadest number of leaders will be found in the first categories, ending with a relatively small leadership pool in the global spaces.

Women and Men, Men and Women—in Leadership

My perspective on this topic comes from lived history. Having been raised as a missionary kid (MK) in Latin America, then having served as an adult for seventeen years based in Guatemala, I realize that (in terms of public roles and titles) I grew up in and inherited a man's world. I lived in *América Latina*, with its cultural realities of male *machismo* and its female counter, *hembrismo*. As I have written, my parents, products of the American Great Generation (post-WII and post-Great Depression) poured their lives into world mission, and also brought with them inherited cultural views and presuppositions. Remarkably, roles restricted from women in the USA for that generation were freely exercised around the world.

When Yvonne and I began our first term in Guatemala, I understood our agency's wise policy on roles for women, single or married. Each one could choose the roles they wanted from a full spectrum, spreading from the full-time home maker to the full-time career woman. Yvonne chose a posture in the middle of the spectrum, considering the cycles of life and parenting/mothering. I have the crisp vision that our single missionaries were respected and honored. Some of them were extraordinary. From childhood in Costa Rica, I remember the "Bible Women," nationals and expats, who singularly sacrificed their lives to take the gospel and Scripture to all, who traveled indefatigably, slept on dirt floors, and who were valued by their gifting, through their spoken voice in business meetings and by their spirituality.

Mother fit the missionary career category. As she grew into leadership, Dad was never threatened by her passions, gifts, skills, energy, and vision. He opened space and released her. Yes, when the agency board named him to the presidency, requiring a move from Guatemala to Dallas, a crisis emerged between my parents. Mother eventually gave up her vocational dreams in Latin America and grieved for perhaps two years while making the thankless transition to the USA. Who really *was* she now? Slowly the Spirit opened a new network of East Texas Methodist churches with a heart for global mission. And those pastors made it clear that they wanted Stella, not Bill, her husband-mission president, as the speaker.

Dorothy McCullough was remarkable. A Moody classmate of my parents, she arrived in Costa Rica before they did; she held me in her arms as an infant; she was an unflagging evangelist, walking the railroad lines of the United Fruit Company from hamlet to village; she planted three churches in three different countries with three different socio-economic levels—and turned them all over to Latin leadership. She then earned an MA from Wheaton Grad School and became the top Christian educational specialist for our agency publisher, ELA, writing curriculum for children, youth and adults. Then she joined the faculty of the *Instituto Bíblico Centroamericano*, later to became *Seminario Teológico Centroamericano* (SETECA), as professor of educational ministries. Fighting chronic headaches and tinnitus, she pioneered there, again. Around 1970 I was asked to succeed her. She embodied sacrifice and service, a selfless giving woman. Her earthly body faced a sad ending, with diabetes, both legs amputated, mind gone. I was not worthy of stepping into her shoes.

When I began with the WEA-MC in mid-1986, it was a man's role. I inherited a missional entity where, by structural definition, men in leadership were the overwhelming majority. Membership was restricted to national and regional mission leaders and a few men leading networks. However, and this is a very crucial "however," the first director of the Mission Commission was the Korean and first Asian woman missionary to Pakistan, Dr. Chun Chae Ok. How did that happen? Well, it just did.

Our first set of bylaws created an open scaffolding where men and women, younger and older, in missional ministries with national or broader circles of influence would be invited into the MC. From his historical perspective, Bertil Ekström emailed me recently,

> I think we have tried in the MC to open its arenas of action, both in terms of cultural background and of gender. We spoke many times on how to involve more women in the commission and particularly in the leadership of the MC. Unfortunately (perhaps showing women's wisdom, but also discrimination), few women have been in the leadership of mission organizations, national and regional mission associations and global networks. We decided to include more categories in the MC constitution to invite more women as well as younger leaders to join us. And, interestingly, many of them come from the Global South where female leadership has been less problematic in many circles, although language and financial issues often create limitations. I'm glad for the current leadership team and the balanced representation of gender, age, and cultural background that we see in the MC today.
>
> The Mission Commission values "evangelical, Trinitarian missiology, grace-characterized relationships and mutual accountability, grassroots needs analysis and strategic vision, churches, mission agencies and training programs, collegiality and servanthood, reflective practitioners and forward thinking" (MC Bylaws). The stress was on healthy relationships, accountability, collegiality, and servanthood![7]

---

7 Ekström, personal email, July 21, 2023.

Yet, aspects of those early years were discouraging. Our Manila 1992 Global Consultation had ninety-two participants but only two women. Our first MC directory, 1994, had forty-seven members and only four women. However, we were changing. The Vancouver 2003 consultation on globalization, led by the younger UK leader Richard Tiplady, convened 136 participants, with women from twenty-four nations. Younger women served on the strategic planning team, and as plenary speakers. Today the MC core leadership team has younger and older servants, women and men, all leaders in their arenas and assignments.

Readers and Leaders

My audience will be a diverse set of leaders. I write for missionaries from everywhere to everywhere. All of you will be leaders in some sense of the word. I write for tested (and wounded—whether by others or self-inflicted) servants of my generation and younger. You have experienced some of this "stuff" and have learned your own lessons. You have your unique scars. I speak also to those in the earlier stages of leadership or about to enter new arenas of influence and direction.

> **This is an incarnational leadership narrative, a lived history of reflections.**

I see another group of leaders who may be in that transitional leadership topography where you are about to move into a new space with new responsibilities. You both need and must ask the Spirit's presence and wisdom. There are also former leaders who were unable to transition into another uncertain future, or who withdrew from leadership, or perhaps did not finish as well as desired.

I have in mind local church mission leaders, especially those who determine the fates and finances of their field partners. I am also keenly interested in that cluster of readers who have not been in recognized leadership and who wonder "Why did that person get the position?" Perhaps you are one who was wounded by leadership. I know what that's like. While I do not write for the academic or leadership specialist or theoretician, I do write for students of leadership in both formal and nonformal academic worlds. Finally, I write for the leader in the last laps of life, perhaps en route to becoming a tested person of maturity and wisdom.

Whatever the category of leader, I write for all, with colleagues and friends in every set. I have found myself in different categories throughout my life, as do many others. Instead of exploring leadership theories, this book invites readers into personal stories of family and service, transitions and change, wounds and laughter, mistakes and maturity, all drawn from my long decades in cross-cultural service. This is an incarnational leadership narrative, a lived history of reflections. My hope is that this will draw you into the spirit of (1) collegial leadership, (2) creating community in common cause, (3) imitating the Jesus cruciform way of leadership, and (4) walking in step with the Spirit. Above all, good leaders want to finish well, each season, and particularly in the last laps.

My lessons emerge from the gritty experience of one who never thought he would be a leader, who developed unevenly and yet emerged into it organically and surely by surprise. This book identifies what I learned during a life of cross-cultural service. I'm not writing a leadership manual, or how to ensure effective, influential, efficient, long-term, legacy-leaving leadership!

Narrative theology suggests that we study and learn crucial lessons from the biblical stories. They teach us important truths. These in turn enrich our teaching of Scripture, our understanding of missiology, biblical theology, and systematic theology. Much of the Old Testament can be poured into this chalice. I present leadership lessons emerging from a narrative, what I have witnessed. I am one of many who simply flowed, at times uncertainly, in the stream of God's grace and the Spirit's empowerment.

> My lessons emerge from the gritty experience of one who never thought he would be a leader, who developed unevenly and yet emerged into it organically and surely by surprise.

My understanding of leadership has also been shaped by examining real lifetime case studies of men and women in those positions. Dad and David Howard are two prime case studies. Many other of my colleagues have shaped my understanding of leadership, as you will see in the coming pages. Some in positive ways, others in negative.

All of us understand leadership through a cultural lens and can be marred by cultural or simply human temptations. All cultures are marked by the divine hand of the Creator, and all are broken by the great rebellion of our first parents. No culture should be idealized. I have pondered how cultures shape people for leadership—different cultures seem to produce leaders better adapted for certain settings. Men and women are both subject to temptations that distract from leadership.

The destructive components of ambition, shaving and shading truth, and susceptibility to cut corners are present everywhere in the world. Thus, all nations and cultures have their own history of Christian leaders seduced by the enticement of glittering images and glamorous powers. Or perhaps it's the insidious, quiet seduction towards other sins that derail a life, a family, a ministry. Mission leadership is not exempt from those deadly traps. We don't go into cross-cultural mission to get rich. But pernicious alternatives exist that corrupt us—power and influence, and even twisted versions of "doing great things for God." In every case, culture plays a strong role in leadership practice.

I have been profoundly shaped by the writings of Henri Nouwen's little 1989 diamond, *In the Name of Jesus: Reflections on Christian Leadership*.[8] Nouwen bases his three lectures to Catholic leaders on Satan's temptations of Jesus, examining each one, the issues involved, juxtaposing them in the context of his trifold restoration of Peter in John 21. The applications are poignant, counter-cultural, unexpected, and penetrating. From Nouwen's conclusions:

> My movement from Harvard to L'Arche made me aware in a new way how much my own thinking about Christian leadership had been affected by the desire to be relevant, the desire for popularity, and the desire for power. Too often I looked at being relevant, popular, and powerful as ingredients of an effective ministry. The truth, however, is that these are not vocations but temptations.

Leadership and Finishing Well

Ironically, disturbingly, scant attention is given to the topic of finishing well in the set of leadership resources I studied for this book. Why? Perhaps the writers were in the prime of life, or maybe they simply do not have it as a working leadership category. But they should have, whether finishing each stage of ministry assignment well, or facing the latter-final laps.

Having served six decades in the global evangelical worlds, I am acutely aware of the subtle temptations that visit those in high leadership levels. Cultures that reward status and influence, power and fame, efficiency and success, hyper productivity and measurable results, and

---

8 Nouwen, *In the Name of Jesus*, 71.

in some circles, wealth and fame generate toxic values that make it extraordinarily difficult to finish well. Cultures that facilitate compromising integrity, short-changing marriage vows, sacrificing children on the altar of ministry, and forfeiting physical health in the name of "burning up for Jesus," are cultures that facilitate duplicitous living which dangerously trifurcates one's secret, private, and public life.

> "Leading from below" entails service from below; servanthood from below.

To finish well one must embrace the probability of broken dreams and unanswered prayers. To finish well one must reckon with the reality that only God can fully take care of one's children, who may or may not turn out how one wishes or prays. To finish well includes the possibility of ending one's latter years without public recognition, with little evidence of measurable productivity, or with only modest success. To finish well means receiving the grace to lean into broken health and imminent death.

Over the course of my last four decades of life, I have wanted above all to finish well. And to me it meant three major affirmations: I kept my spiritual vows to the Triune God. I was authentically faithful to my marital vows—affirmed by Yvonne. And finally, as my children carried my casket to the grave they could say, "Dad did not sacrifice his family on the altar of his ministry."

Title and Scaffolding

"Leading from below" entails service from below; servanthood from below; downward path of the cross from below; collegiality from below; mutuality from below; finishing well from below. The crucible? Yes, cross-cultural service is a crucible, a vat, a kettle, a place of trial, test, predicament, affliction, even burden. Gold emerges from a crucible. In those contexts, my life was shaped, purged, and burnished. I learned so much from my mistakes and I thank God for colleagues and friends who tolerated and forgave me as I learned to serve, to lead. I am who I am because of those lessons, both negative and positive. And I am still learning.

> Gold emerges from a crucible.

I narrate stories to paint the larger canvas of the global arenas where God enabled me to serve in different leadership roles. There is obviously a larger back story of my own life and career as a lifer in cross-cultural service. I was born in Costa Rica on "the mission field." I am a TCK—Third Culture Kid. I grew up unevenly and slowly in my emotional, spiritual, intellectual, and relational development. I flunked second grade. I had loving but passive missionary parents. I never received any guidance in my studies, and my early academic life reflects that reality. In my early fifties, I began to understand how my family system shaped and misshaped me, including my view of God: "He's there, but he's really busy; give him a precis of your concerns, and move on. Millions are behind you for their turn. Quickly, Billy!" Upon completing university and seminary studies I was honored to marry Yvonne Christine DeAcutis in June, 1967. Our last year in the USA allowed her to finish university and me to complete my third year on InterVarsity Christian Fellowship (IVCF) staff.

Following a language study year in Costa Rica, we began our life and ministry in Guatemala, where for seventeen years we would base our service at SETECA (*Seminario Teológico Centroamericano*). We would engage in the university student ministry and towards the end of our season, serve on a church planting team. Little could we have known that our church community, *Centro Bíblico el Camino*, would in mid-1985, pray, send, and support us as their missionaries to the Global North, when called to relocate in the USA. Little could we have dreamed that we would be speakers at its 2024 fiftieth anniversary!

God gave us three children born in Guatemala: Christine (1970), David (1972) and Stephanie (1976). While their mother tongue was English, they were privileged to study in the Austrian Institute of Guatemala where they studied in German, Spanish and English.

The Latin America years ended in 1985 when I began teaching at TEDS (Trinity Evangelical Divinity School). But God stunned me when I discerned that TEDS would become a fulcrum, pivot, and steppingstone to an unknown future. That's where this book begins, with that intense transitional period of weeping triple deaths, and resurrection. The stories of those earlier years will emerge in a later "prequel," possibly titled, *My Father's Shoes: The Memoir of a Global Pilgrim*.

Reading This Book

A template guides each chapter: it starts with a quote from either Scripture or insightful authors, an illustrative story; then to the complete narrative, and lessons learned come at the conclusion; finally, reflective questions are designed to provoke thought and discussion for individuals or groups. The introduction frames the book, introducing people who shaped me deeply, presenting, defining, and interacting with key terms and their meaning, especially *leadership, leading from below* and *finishing well*. It identifies my readers and categorizes different types of leaders.

Chapters 1–3 provide backdrop information and stories that embody the core theses of the book. "Little did I know" becomes over time a litany, but it was so true. I just had no idea (but then, who does?) what God was doing with me so much of the time. I was shaped and misshaped by missionary slogans and songs, and too much missionary hagiography. Yes, I wanted to do great things for God, not knowing what that meant. An early crisis in my cross-cultural ministry and marriage became a parable to prepare me for a distant future. In time, God taught me. The Spirit renamed me, permanently marking my transition from the worlds of Latin America into the vast international world of mission. But this required three deaths before a resurrection. God took me deeper/higher into the spiritual journey and changed my self-identity. I discovered I was to become an intentional, not passive, leader.

Chapters 4–7 narrate the process of becoming and serving as a reflective practitioner in the context of worldwide mission. Through the MC publication venture, I would open doors for "global voices to address global issues." My mission vision became truly and fully international— from all peoples to all peoples, from creation to the New Creation.

From a fundamentalist in my mother's womb, later confirmed by seven years of theological and biblical study, God has given me discernment of the crucial elements in my theological reflection. I began to identify the theological hills upon which I would shed blood and die. I trace my pilgrimage through a cross-section of gospel-affirming churches, ending up in the sacramental liturgical stream of global Anglicanism. From a constricted understanding of the Spirit's person, presence, and power, I was released into a vibrant relationship with the third Person of the Trinity, still open to his surprises.

Chapters 8–13 start with the unexpected foothills vision: I would no longer cross the final mountain ranges of ministry; rather, Christ would journey with me to the foothills, and then "I would be gathered to my fathers." This vision crisply focused my attention! But before that would happen, God walked me through more transformation, into mystery and the supernatural. For too long I had been a theoretical supernaturalist. I had no biblical-theological understanding of social justice. Sadly, I had no vision of long-term global mission from the Majority World. I had no theology of the arts; and I had no idea what a theology of creation care looked like.

I made mistakes—some rather serious, some simply funny, all instructive. I met, and in cases, served with very difficult people. But from them I also learned. The vision of the foothills continued to disconcert me, but its unfolding liberated me.

The conclusion summarizes my reflections on the relationship between leading from below and finishing well. They converge; they sing together. They remind me that my own journey is not over, that at age eighty-three, I am still learning, growing, open to the mystery of the Triune God on mission.

I ruminate on little Billy Taylor from Costa Rica and how the Spirit went before him, protecting him from himself and the archenemy, how he slowly emerged into the man God wanted him to be. Suffering visited me on this journey. I am a wounded and scarred man because of following Jesus, regardless of the cost. God does not answer all our prayers.

I respect leaders with wounds and scars. I still sigh deeply, reflecting facets of grief. I greet touches of sadness as I age. I have learned to walk with a new friend—Anonymity. Those many invitations to minister have ceased. Yet, what I have wanted, above all, was to finish well.

Conclusion

My prayer is that these reflections and lessons on global mission leadership will encourage you. I also pray they will also give you another lens, namely leading from below, with which to examine your own leadership thoughts, experiences, understandings, and practice. My musings emerge from the crucible of life and passion, giftedness, and skills, the furnace of suffering, temptations, and opportunities. On more than one occasion the Spirit took me into the classroom of deconstruction and reconstruction. I am not who I used to be, thank God. I made memorable mistakes, and I rue them all. Yet there, God's grace met me.

> **What I have wanted, above all, was to finish well.**

Interwoven through all these reflections, we keep the living icon of Jesus as our paramount leadership model. This can be tricky, because it seems too easy to "over-devotionalize" our Lord as a conceptual example, but in practice our leadership style defaults to the spirit of the age, how we have been shaped and trained. We are products of our culture. So let us read Scripture—for through the Word we discover the Messiah Christ—with a robust understanding of Jesus the initiative-taking, visionary-passionate leader, yet whose style was from below. Mark 10:45 frames him so clearly. "For even the Son of Man came not to be served but to serve, and to give his life as a ransom for many" Mark 10:45.

God be with you on your own journey. It is not over for me either. I'm only eighty-four years old. So let us encourage one another to finish well—each season of life and that long, last lap. As we would say in Spanish, *escribo con el corazón en la mano*, "I write with my heart in my hand."

1
False Sacrifices

Thus says the LORD: "Let not the wise man boast in his wisdom, let not the mighty man boast in his might, let not the rich man boast in his riches, but let him who boasts boast in this, that he understands and knows me, that I am the LORD who practices steadfast love, justice, and righteousness in the earth. For in these things I delight, declares the LORD." (Jer 9:23–24)

Pan American 501

It was March 1971. At age thirty I was a first-term hot new missionary in Guatemala City, a rookie already on the top of my game (so I thought and felt). An adult TCK who had returned "home," my command of Spanish was rather good. I, a "gringo," was mastering the textured subjunctive mood, the use of Latin American proverbs in my public speaking ministry, and the innate and inherited *don de gente* (a gifted way of relating with people).

I was emerging as a successful young professor at a leading evangelical seminary in Central America, *Seminario Teológico Centroamericano*. I was a new, sought-out speaker in churches throughout the urban and rural regions of Guatemala. I regularly discipled university students in the *Grupo Evangélico Universitario* (the Guatemalan International Fellowship of Evangelical Students affiliate). I was happily busy doing God's urgent work of bringing the gospel to the millions, loving my job, and living my dreams.

I was also a product of my evangelical subculture, which believed that "the more you did, the more spiritual you were," "the harder you worked, the more God blessed you," "the greater the faith, the greater the harvest." Subconsciously, I had absorbed American management productivity metrics; clearly measurable goals which gauged worth by maximal and quantifiable output, wedded to a pragmatic spirituality. There was little awareness of the Holy Spirit in my life.

It was a dangerous brew and there was a lot of "me" flying around.

On that Thursday night I arrived home around 6 p.m. needing a quick meal. I had a speaking commitment at a local church that I could not break.

I breezed into our little house, kissed my one-year-old strawberry-blond Christine and then my twenty-five-year-old Texan wife Yvonne, who simply said, "I need to talk with you." I brushed her off and suggested that we could talk on Saturday over the weekend. Quietly, firmly, she insisted, "I need to talk with you ... tonight." I disregarded her request and went looking for my own dinner in the fridge.

I muttered to myself, "How could she so totally misunderstand my calling, my ministry—the Lord's work? Did she not understand that there was so much to do and so little time to accomplish it, that the fields were white for harvest and the workers were few?" I quickly tired of our tense and deeply disconcerting exchange.

She then interrupted me, speaking tersely, intensely, slowly: "Bill, look at me; listen carefully to me." I stopped eating and looked up, hearing her clipped tones. "If you don't stop right now and talk with me, tomorrow morning I am taking *my daughter*, and *we* will fly Pan American Airlines flight 501 direct from Guatemala to Dallas. I will stay with my parents, and you can stay here with your blankety-blank (her word was stronger, more graphic and memorable) ministry of saving the millions."

In that nanosecond I knew that I was in serious trouble. Still clueless, I kept asking myself, "What in God's name is wrong with Yvonne?" I was deeply in love with her; and I knew she loved me—an enthusiastic, extroverted good guy from a respected missionary family, with a solid evangelical theological pedigree. But I also was utterly incapable of detecting the marriage crisis that I alone had caused over the past months.

Then a second voice emerged, the Holy Spirit this time. "Be quiet, Bill. Listen to your wife. Remember your vows. Stop what you are doing. Pay attention."

Don't. Blow. It.

I stopped eating as time froze, her intense eyes full of pain. I looked up at her expectantly, fearfully. At an appropriate break in the negotiations, I went next door to borrow the telephone at Mandolini's Gulf gas station next door, then realized that my church contact had no phone for me to cancel my now-not-important commitment. I was a no-show that night and never heard back from them. I called my dean and said I could not teach on Friday. He asked one question. The long conversation that ensued with my courageous wife over the course of that night changed how I would "do my ministry." Guidelines were set to accept or decline invitations and to guide how I viewed my identity and role as husband, father, missionary, professor, Christian, human.

I was truly and deeply sorry. I told Yvonne that and asked for her forgiveness. She listened, yet wisely did not grant immediate absolution. Rather, she told me of the heartache she experienced being relegated to a distant second place in my new illustrious ministry, left to grapple alone as a brand-new missionary and mother in a foreign culture, negotiating a strange country and a new language without the infrastructure of family, friends, or faith community while I was "busy in ministry for the Lord."

I have never forgotten that night. How close did I come to blowing my marriage out of the water? How close did I come to becoming another early mission attrition statistic? How could I have failed in the most elemental leadership role—that of loving and serving my wife well, understanding that she was the "true missionary," i.e., the one who had veritably left family, home, culture, nation, language, friends, and community?

Was I in a pre-kinder school program for potential leadership? Little did I know. Unsure raw material there for sure. And I was to learn other lessons from her over those early years.

Interpreting Pan Am 501

Was I in danger of making a false sacrifice?

What was truly happening that early in my mission career while I was on the cusp of fulfilling my lifelong dream of long-term cross-cultural service? Was I just immature, stupid, and insensitive? Was Yvonne too demanding of me? Could she not "cut it" in another culture? No, over time I saw God's hand, a heavy and loving hand, on my shoulder. I was being reproved for committing a mistake common to most of us in the start of our life-calling. Too early on I was disregarding my marital vows; I did not understand what Yvonne was going through—the degree of cultural shock, our peculiar evangelical mission ethos and culture, the impact of being far from "home" with a toddler and a husband married also to ministry.

Over time I realized God's discipline of me, a younger man in love with his wife and committed to ministry but losing perspective. If I did not make substantive early course corrections, I would never become the person God wanted me to be and would certainly not qualify for spiritual leadership in the global mission enterprise.

The guidelines we outlined back then served us well in the ensuing years until a second family crisis happened in the early years with the WEA-MC, around 1987. We had moved to a small Arkansas city and were still processing reentry into the USA. My responsibilities required extended international travel. One afternoon after I had returned from a fantastic and oh-so-significant ministry trip somewhere very far from home and family, I entered the house and kissed Yvonne. All seemed well on that front, but not so with Christine, then about sixteen years old. When she came back from high school I kissed her, but she just said, "When are you leaving again?" and walked to her room. I was speechless. I was devastated. How had the imbalance emerged yet again?

That second watershed experience led to a new set of guidelines that Yvonne helped me draft, through which I evaluated all travel and speaking commitments. Those eight (in that first version) standards protected me. The first one was, "Wait twenty-four to forty-eight hours before responding to invitations in order to listen to the Spirit and Yvonne." The eighth one was very clear, "If I don't accept this invitation, will somebody die?" A different set of norms protect me today, for even in this latter lap the temptations lurk to do "something significant for God" before it is too late!

In hindsight, conscious of God's gracious hand, I discerned what he was doing with me, in me, and for me as he was testing me and equipping me for my future. The Spirit had to teach me that no Christian leader can justify sacrificing marriage and family on an illegitimate altar. I am a thankful man.

Ah, so little did I know.

The Refining

The specific geography, Singapore; the date, June 28, 1986. I sat (dry mouthed, stomach knotted) in a conference room with forty-five seasoned global mission leaders in the Novo Orchid Hotel. They were participants of the World Evangelical Fellowship (WEF) General Assembly (changed to World Evangelical Alliance, WEA, at the Malaysia General Assembly in 2001). I knew only a few of them. Theodore Williams of India (WEF's chairman, also former head of its Mission Commission), introduced me as the newly appointed general secretary of the WEF Mission Commission. Not surprisingly, nobody clapped. I could not make sense of what had happened in the twenty-four hours since I had flown to Singapore. I also knew that 9,683 miles away in our temporary home in Russellville, AR, USA, Yvonne rightfully had grave questions about my decision.

Yes, I had inklings of my own overarching vocation in life; I had tested my childhood "call" into missions. The call was confirmed over time during the process of trying out ministry in different experiences and challenges. Confirmation of vocation and occupation started early, at a Christian camp in Texas. Later, the call was tested through IVCF as a student plus three years on staff, followed by my four years at Dallas Theological Seminary (DTS). Before we left for Latin America, I felt I knew the purposes for which God had brought me into the world. But this watershed event in 1986?

Was this the same little Billy Taylor born in Costa Rica, who lived in towns with dirt streets, who flunked second grade, who struggled to understand the new situations in life as he grew up? Yes, little Billy had godly missionary parents who loved him and his sister, but they were passive. Demonstrating affection and affirmation was nearly impossible for his missionary mother. He was thankful for his father who demonstrated both regularly throughout his life. But their parenting style was passive, and that passivity would misshape Billy-Bill for decades.

He grew up unevenly yet made it somehow. The family moved to Wheaton, IL for his senior year in high school—he only sixteen years old, bewildered, with no orientation into American culture. At seventeen, he started Moody with the goal of mission service; he was immature and majored in ping-pong that first year. He also cheated in three final exams—he would pay the price. Although his confession led to official forgiveness, he studied for two years under institutional discipline. He had struggled academically for many years, yet later earned a ThM from DTS and a PhD from the University of Texas (UT) in Latin American Studies and the Cultural Foundations of Education. He ended up going to school for a total of twenty-seven years.

He's the one who, in his mid-forties, suffered a triple death at the apparent peak of his career. In the space of just two years, he died to all dreams of serving his entire life in Latin America; he died to teaching in the academy; and to cap it off, he died to any sense of pastoral gifts while serving a dysfunctional Arkansas congregation.

Through it all, he learned that death is followed by resurrection; but resurrection presupposes death. And those deaths led to new life. Again, he would relearn the baptismal rhythm of God's silence, submerged under waters, and only at the right time brought up to new life.

But on that day in 1986, somebody believed in Bill, and that was David Howard, his mentor since Urbana 1967. And alongside him that godly Indian mission leader, Theodore Williams. Dave had invited me to Singapore to "meet some international friends." I had no idea what the WEF General Assembly was and little understanding of WEF itself. Dave and Theo interviewed me for the position of WEF-MC General Secretary my first day in Singapore, giving me a day to respond. Somehow in the wee hours of that night I knew I was in the center of God's empowering Spirit, facing a major life crossroads. Inside I said "unequivocally, yes" to that invitation. Later I realized Dave and Theo had unilaterally recommended me to the International Council to become the new MC head. I was not named by a team nor in a collegial process, but rather by two men exercising authority.

What in God's name was I doing now? Would these people accept me? How could I win their trust? I looked like a typical North American, red hair and freckles completing the picture. But I knew that inside I was wired differently. I was a forty-five-year-old Third Culture Person with seventeen years of ministry in Latin America. I had served two years on the faculty of TEDS. I was the husband of one wife and father of three. And I had died to ministry dreams three times, during which I had desperately wondered whether God had set me aside. I had been wondering what my future was.

But somehow at that moment I just knew that I was in the right place, despite the maelstrom of doubts, questions, and uncertainties. The first humility lesson came rapidly (perhaps God's sense of humor), because as the business meeting started, Theo said, "Bill, since you are the new general secretary, you take notes of the gathering and record decisions made."

Ah, God knows how little I did know.

Conclusion and Lessons

The Jeremiah 9:23–24 passage quoted at the start of this chapter presents two leadership options—one based on and emerging from stated educational status, power and wealth, the other flowing out of relationship with the One True Three in One. His Name is unique, the only one to be worshipped, the only one who practices unfailing love and produces justice and righteousness in our world. These values and behaviors bring delight to him. The applications to leadership from below flow out of this seminal passage. And this passage judged me and found me guilty of false motives and illegal sacrifices early in my marriage and cross-cultural ministry. It also fortified the corrective steps I had to take to change.

God took me to school so many times in my life to prepare me for a future that would not sacrifice my family on any altar of ministry. Could I keep that vow? After a rich seventeen years of service based in Latin America, I had accepted a position as Associate Professor of Mission at TEDS. Yes, that meant I had to leave Latin America, but in a sense, I would be gaining the world through the classroom and my passions. I knew that my core gifting was teaching. I was eager to hone that craft in North America. So, I sort of traded Latin America for world missions—from a USA platform.

But who would have thought that my tenure at TEDS would last but nine months? And what in God's name would I be and do after that? How would I support my family? "Hey! Where are you, God?"

Never sacrifice your family on the bastard altar of your ministry.

We "retreated" for the family's sake to a small town in Arkansas where I would part-time pastor-elder a small supporting church, founded by personal friends. The family was so happy to move to Russellville, population around 19,500. But soon clouds emerged, storms of opposition and attacks against my character. Within six months, I realized that my pastoral gifting was not going to carry me through. And that capped off the three-fold death.

Yet God knew. He cared. His Spirit was brooding over me. His Son was teaching me to follow him downward, towards the path of the cross. I was not to defend myself from the severe opposition. Others might; I would not. Nor would Yvonne.

And then, in early February 1986, in that silence, the Voice spoke through Dave Howard. "Bill, if you leave TEDS and move to Russellville, I want you to come to Singapore this late June and meet some international friends." From that time on, God released me into a global journey I never could have dreamed about.

Little did I know.

I have pondered four prime leadership lessons, or principles, that emerged from the raw experiences just narrated. The most obvious, but not the easiest to implement was, "Never sacrifice your family on the bastard altar of your ministry."

Second, God sovereignly schedules our assignments, and he may return us into a severe discipleship and deconstruction school to ensure we learn the right lessons. That's the only way I can understand my triple deaths ... and the succeeding resurrection that so transformed my life.

Third, God appoints his David Howard's and Theo Williams' to shape us because they believed in us when we perhaps did not. I had met Theo in Guatemala twice and his impact as a godly mission leader deeply impressed scores of emerging Latin mission leaders—they remember his messages to this day.

Fourth, Jesus himself was tested. Two biblical passages stand out. First, Matthew 4:1–11 and the three demonic temptations. Stunningly, it's the Holy Spirit who leads Jesus into that wilderness of hunger, thirst, and testing. Second, Hebrews 2:18 and 4:15, where we discover that Jesus was tested/tempted (the Greek term is the same) in *every way, yet without sin*. Thus we, when tested and tempted, can look to Jesus as our example and advocate amid our battles.

A sacrifice worth making and repeating. No regrets there.

Reflection Questions

1. What are the risks and values of vulnerability in leaders?
2. Describe one or two cases of Christian leaders who sacrificed their family on the altar of their ministry?
3. Why is this chapter called "False Sacrifices"?
4. Can you identify two leaders (a man and a woman) for whom you can pray right now?

2
Slippery Slogans
(Doing Great Things for God)

How many times have I been told,
O Christ, by well-meaning people,
that it is my destiny and my charge
to go out into the world
and do great things for you?

How many times in response have
I prayed earnestly, asking that you
would bring such things to pass—
that you might use me mightily
for the work of your kingdom?

How many times have I then waited expectantly.
And waited.
And waited
For that great thing, whatever it might be,
to be made obvious?

How many times have I felt then
the gradually settling weight of disillusionment,
of disappointment and confusion,
when no great thing materialized, when no
life-changing opportunity suddenly
arrived at my doorstep, when no such moment
of call or clarity was ever manifest at all?[1]

Reflections

Can you identify, as I do at least partially, with these poignant reflections? And what do they have to do with leadership? Much. These yearnings touch the crucial issues of our inner heart motivation—those desires that drive us. Scripture enjoins us not to imitate the values of the fallen world system. Yet we discover that the church/ministry worlds (and all expressions of religious vocation) have their unique set of seductive hidden addictions.

---

1 McKelvey, "For Those Who Have Not Done Great Things for God," in *Every Moment Holy,* 203–4.

These can mislead or even sabotage us. Worse, they are wrapped in over-spiritualized language and values. We are all vulnerable to the siren calls around us that nurture our jumbled, mixed motives. Thus, we have the need for God's tempering and sifting, for the Spirit's transformational work in our souls, above all, must be sensitive to this push and pull, both for their own souls as well as those whom we serve.

Part of our challenge as Jesus followers is to neutralize the cacophony of voices that clamor for our attention and emulation. To whom do we listen as we try to discern our life dreams and visions? Who becomes our example, our model? Whose words ring clear, pure, true? Where and when and how does the Spirit imprint his affirmations such as, "Yes, Bill, listen to this person's wisdom and insight. Take note of *this* biography, think carefully about *this* book. Revisit *this* Scripture. Be still and know that I am with you. Stop!"? Many of my own generation of American missionaries were shaped by a diversity of fundamentalist perspectives—whether we came from non-charismatic or charismatic roots or were Bible institute graduates. Graduates of secular or Christian liberal arts colleges tend to engage in lifelong global mission with a larger world view. I wonder whether the mission force of my era emerging from the British Isles, Europe, Australia, and New Zealand also had a larger worldview framework. Perhaps.

> **We have the need for God's tempering and sifting, for the Spirit's transformational work in our souls, above all, we must be sensitive to this push and pull.**

Some of us shook off those limitations over the years as we sought and found freedom to probe deeper, asking foundational questions of Scripture, theology, church history, spirituality, mission theology, and mission practice. That task must become a lifelong assignment. During my immature Moody years my motivations were inchoate, unshaped, even unspoken; but they were there. Honestly, I think that during those three years I only knew that my future was in missions, and I had to get some kind of training. Depth emerged incrementally.

How can we separate ourselves from the smooth whispers of contemporary success markers, especially those baptized by Christian verbiage? Are our dreams and visions misshaped by secular success models, management by objectives, fixation of our vision and work on concrete calendar dates to "finish" the Great Commission by the year

2000, or 2033 (after all we have the final technology, right?)? Are we overly attracted by metrics that tell us where we are in history and the possibility of "Bringing the King back" in our lifetime?

Bottom line—let's honestly ask what motivates our desires and decisions to serve God regardless of the specifics of the calling, the occupations and part we will play, and the roles shaped by personality, gender, age, geography, language, culture, and theology. At the end of the day, these decisions must be rooted in the heart of the Triune God on mission, grounded in the totality of Scripture, and rooted in contemporary reality. We will then do all we can to "occupy until he returns," which will challenge us to the end of history.

On Inspiring Missionary Slogans and Songs

With just about any group of older thoughtful Christians, I can ask, "How many of you, earlier in your walk with Christ, thought you would do 'great things for God'"? Invariably, a significant percentage will respond with something like, "Well, I sure did, but then life hit hard, stuff happened, and I am not sure what happened with my dreams." In my own case, I can't remember even thinking about that language. I grew up unevenly, caught in the uncertainties of the Third Culture Person, unsure of where home truly was. For years I muddled through, yet I knew that my future occupation would be missionary service in another culture.

Perhaps I didn't struggle with those dreams of greatness because I never thought I would do great things for God. I do know that during my leadership development and diverse service arenas, I did not think my contribution would be that important. Only much later in life did I realize what God had done in and through me that was greater than any of my dreams.

Somewhere in my childhood, the emphatic, imperative "Go!" missionary slogan was branded in my heart. My life course was set by little Billy's childlike decision in that vacation Bible school program in Wheaton the summer of 1949. In retrospect, I now discern how the gentle, yet present Holy Spirit saved me from my worst potential decisions and behavior. It is as if there truly were a Hand behind and before, above and beneath me. Did I have inklings of future leadership? No, not for me. Perhaps for others.

I entered Moody Bible Institute (no other educational institution had equipped so many longer-term cross-cultural workers in history) to prepare for missionary service. I was a young fledgling. Perhaps my immaturity opened space for the Spirit's protection as I began to wake up. Slowly, incrementally, I grew up, made decisions, confessed major sins, paid the earthly price for those sins, took responsibility for my life, and rose in my third year at Moody to my highest leadership position, which was leading the Latin America Prayer Band and the Spanish Club. Nothing more! But it was at Moody that missionary slogans became something serious. D. L. Moody himself had said something like "The world has yet to see what God can do with a man fully consecrated to him." By God's help, I aim to be that man. We were all challenged to be that kind of a person, regardless of our work. But for some of us, such a clarion call set us up for later disappointment or worse when life's blows hit. What kind of unrealistic burden could these statements possibly lay upon us?

I remember two phrases from the short life of the late nineteenth-century missionary William Borden of Yale (of the famous American Borden milk company). During his Yale years he became a passionate evangelist to his classmates. He also founded the Yale Hope Mission in New Haven, a downtown rescue ministry (purchasing the building with his own funds) to reach the vulnerable, the broken, the alcoholics, the prostitutes, the rejected ones. He felt called to the Muslims of China while at Yale, but he never got there. En route in Egypt, he contracted cerebral meningitis and died at age twenty-five. His mother, having heard of his illness, traveled to Egypt to sit at his bedside, but arrived two days late. Still, his legacy stirred many of us. He coined this memorable phrase: "If ten men are carrying a log—nine of them on the little end and one at the heavy end—and you want to help, which end will you lift on?" And this one, "No reserve. No retreats. No regrets." I do remember using them in my own early years of mission mobilization. I believed them.

There are other memorable slogans that come to mind. C. T. Studd: "Some wish to live within the sound of church and chapel bell. I want to run a rescue shop within a yard of hell!" Oswald J. Smith: "Why should anyone hear the gospel twice before everyone has heard it once?" David Livingstone: "God had an only Son and he made him a missionary." John R. Mott: "The evangelization of the world in this generation." (Few know that Mott in 1947, age 81, received the Nobel Peace Prize).

Other slogans are of more recent vintage: World Vision founder Bob Pierce (whose family paid the price for his passions and decisions) stated, "Let my heart be broken with the things that break God's heart." Before his untimely death, passionate musician Keith Green cried out, "If you don't have a definite call to stay here, you are called to go." John Piper: "Missions is not the ultimate goal of the church. Worship is. Missions exists because worship doesn't." Catholic missions were driven in part by the zeal of early global mission leaders and founders of key institutions. Francis Xavier (cofounder of the Jesuits, missionary to India and China—where he died) said, "I want to be where there are out and out pagans."

And more recently in the USA, more statements have become known. A former colleague of mine said to a group of us around 1995, "We finally have the technology to complete the Great Commission." (The *Jesus Film* alone.) Perhaps the most recent one is "Finishing the Task (FTT)." When a famous, highly resourced American pastor adopts it, aiming to raise one billion dollars, who dares challenge it? However, as I write this draft, the top leadership of FTT does not seriously recognize nor engage veteran groups in both Global North and South with wisdom and tested, on-the-ground experience. What is the new deadline for finishing the job? It is the year 2033, the 2000th anniversary of the Great Commission.

These slogans offer both an upside and a downside. At the end of the day, while they may inspire in the short term, I'm unsure whether they help or hinder. I believe reductionisms *do not* help us; however, I don't question the spirituality of those who coined these phrases.

Missionary hymns and choruses play into the slogan category. One I remember all too well is "We've a story to tell to the nations," which had more of a postmillennial theology in the ringing chorus:

> And the darkness shall turn to dawning
> and the dawning to noonday bright,
> and Christ's great kingdom will come on earth,
> a kingdom of love and light.

Short, pithy "go ye" songs poured into me over my first two decades. The older version of Canadian poet Margaret Clarkson's song, "So send I you" (1954) is but one example. The tone is set in the first stanza. Yes, the song does reflect a dimension of our reality as global, long-term servants, but its ethos is both true and also adverse and morose.

> So send I you to labour unrewarded
> To serve unpaid, unloved, unsought, unknown
> To bear rebuke, to suffer scorn and scoffing
> So send I you to toil for Me alone

Clarkson herself later acknowledged that the hymn gave only one side of the story—the negative. So, in 1963 she wrote another version, appropriately named "Urbana," which I learned at Urbana 1967

> So send I you—by grace made strong to triumph
> O'er hosts of hell, o'er darkness, death and sin,
> My name to bear and in that name to conquer—
> So send I you, My victory to win.

Ah, we sang them all with zeal, with relative understanding of what we were singing. At the end of the day, I am thankful for those choruses, gospel songs, and hymns that were integral to our inner formation. Not ironically, I periodically and unconsciously slip back some sixty-five years, with bits and bobs ("ear worms" they call them) of old hymns and choruses—some I start in English and end in Spanish—ringing in my mind. Their imprint is fuzzy and permanent.

Slogans and songs were essential to my early mission preparation, life, and memories. For fun, just Google "missionary slogans" and discover the number.[2] I have pondered the proper role of these attention-catching statements. Do they inspire us to make radical decisions for God, regardless of the cost? Yes, perhaps. Slogans, statistics, opportunities to make a difference, passion for compassion and justice, spiritual human needs all play a role, especially at the deepest core of who we are and how God has made us. They can crystallize our thinking; they can serve to focus our desires and dreams. They were created not to manipulate but rather to motivate people. But in the end, they are slogans, not Scripture.

To this day certain old hymns and others of more recent vintage resonate in my memory. Graham Kendrick's powerful song, "This Is My Beloved Son," is based on the classic Moravian clarion call, "That the Lamb who was slain might receive the reward of his suffering." I want his song, "Knowing You," sung at my funeral. Keith and Kristyn Getty are producing some theologically solid music with a heart for global mission. Paul Zach's music, and other current writers, have shaped my spirituality. Thankfully, our church's worship expresses a rich integration of the ancient, the older, and the current, with some veteran hymns set to new music. Our robust God-centered hymnody invites us into deeper spirituality and all facets of mission. Lord free us from emotionally driven evangelical-lite music!

---

2 One example of a Google search, https://growchurch.net/famous-missionary-quotes-the-great-commission.

My mission-minded generation was raised on a four-fold categorization of missions. First, those who "go" or are sent; then the other three "pray, give, send." The first group are the ones who God really loves and blesses, and the triad exists to keep the sent ones "on the field, truly serving the Lord." These categories were reinforced by the exhortation that "all are missionaries." There was just something that did not ring true here, but it was daily bread for some of us. It also bred a false dichotomy of vocations and occupations.

Our younger missionary generations have their own slogans, but I suspect that deeper realities challenge and motivate them, such as, "For the glory of the Name!" They too are attracted and guided by the obvious spiritual need of people and peoples without sufficient knowledge of Christ to make a reasonable decision for or against him. They are moved by the desire to serve on ministry platforms of compassion and justice. Yet these ministries must carefully balance the social implications of our faith with an equal commitment to the saving gospel and the planting of Jesus-worshipping Jesus communities (alias, churches). I am encouraged by those whose driving desire is to give their lives for a high and costly calling—to go where others have not yet gone in the Name.

Just this week I found a highlighted sentence in a mission magazine that disturbed me. I know why it bothers me. The organization boasted that they could guarantee effective learning if you use their method. I quote: "In short, we create experimental conditions and do quarterly assessment to rigorously promote fruitful practices and extinguish practices that are not fruitful." Hmm ... sounds like a guaranteed production system.

In contrast I appreciate this challenge: "Embrace the hard." These words of a young couple headed into one of the toughest *ethné* of the world challenged me recently. In their first year they grappled with newness, loss, and inadequate support. But their commitment encourages me. Tough, robust, true stuff continues to motivate people who are called to cross-cultural mission. Yes, "embrace the hard."

On Missionary Biographies

Parallel observations could be made about missionary biographies. I started reading them at Moody, though none were required texts. It was something we aspiring missionaries just did. My own parents, a generation before mine, read much earlier biographies and missionary devotional literature. Dad's journals of the 1930s cite them repeatedly. In time I discovered that some of those biographies of the "greats," were hagiographic versions of the real story. By hagiography I refer to a genre of literature in which our evangelical "saints" were idealized and where the heroes could do nothing wrong. While we respect and have deep admiration for these pioneers, we cannot uncritically affirm all they did.

Hudson Taylor's spiritual secrets were mines to be explored and the books on them are extensive. But why did the authors photoshop the narrative, eliminating the "negative stuff"? A shift took place during the 1960s with the newer writings of authors like J. C. Pollock and his *Hudson Taylor and Maria*. Why did Hudson Taylor's descendants attempt to block that publication? Because Pollock was too true to the real narrative and not following the previous script of the idealized version?

My Moody generation was challenged by some of those pioneers, including the "Cambridge Seven" and their stirring sacrifices, Henry Martyn and the martyrs, and others. I have an old version of *Foxes Christian Martyrs of the World* as well as the newer version with contemporary martyrs. About twelve years ago, I discovered that Fox included Queen Mary's third martyr, Rev. Roland Taylor, burned at the stake in 1555, who was a direct ancestor of mine. Martyr's blood flows through me?

January 3–12, 1956 is a date engraved in my memory. I had been tuned to Christian station HCJB in Ecuador on my short-wave radio as a fifteen-year-old TCK in Guatemala. I heard the chilling news from Curaray beach in the Ecuadorian rainforests: "Lost contact with the men." Then there was confirmation of the men's death and burial January 12 on the river beach. Ah, five young missionary martyrs at the hand of the savage Aucas. Nate Saint's watch stopped at 3:12 p.m., Saturday, January 7. (We now know that the term *Auca* was a pejorative; their correct name is the *Waorani*.)

How long O LORD?

> When he opened the fifth seal, I saw under the altar the souls of those who had been slain for the word of God and for the witness they had borne. They cried out with a loud voice, "O Sovereign LORD, holy and true, how long before you will judge and avenge our blood on those who dwell on the earth?" (Rev 6:9–10)

During my Moody years, Elisabeth Elliot's first riveting books were published: *Through Gates of Splendor* in 1957, outlining the narrative of the five men, their families, and the drama of "Operation Auca"; *Shadow of the Almighty* in 1958, which detailed the life and testament of her husband, Jim Elliot, taken largely from his journals and their shared memories at Wheaton College and Ecuador. Our copies are first editions. The flyleaf states, "Using to the full these rich journals, his widow has selected the most powerful, revealing passages and woven around them the story of his life. The book is a tremendous biography of an adventurous life and is also exceptional devotional literature. Jim Elliot's life and testament may well be counted among those truly great Christian writings that will endure."[3]

And it became just that. Yvonne and I, young singles perhaps headed to a shared missionary future, brought the book on a Saturday date to a swimming hole north of Dallas and read sections to each other. We drank deeply from that story; we also wanted to do great things for God. We never forgot Jim Elliot's famous words, stated in 1949, "He is no fool who gives what he cannot keep to gain what he cannot lose."

From Urbana 1967 on, I was honored to have David Howard, Elisabeth Elliot's brother, as my mentor. Right after the killing, Dave had immediately flown from Colombia to Ecuador and then to the Curaray River to witness the scenes of that martyrdom. His memory is seared with the images (Jim and Dave were Wheaton roommates); over the years I listened to him, time and time again, narrate those stories about his generation. He also described what God had been doing at Wheaton College to thrust into the world some of the most remarkable men and women on global cross-cultural mission, at great sacrifice but with an eye on eternity. As Jim Elliot finished Wheaton in 1948, he wrote, "One treasure, a single eye, and a sole master."[4]

Significantly, Elisabeth Elliot's writings later took a different, deeper, turn. Her 1966 fictional book, *No Graven Image*, "A novel of a young American missionary in the high Andes—and how her faith was tested by circumstance and tragedy" (back cover), was a bombshell to her global audience. Was it a shadow autobiography of the young Elisabeth Elliot, or a totally imagined person? Angry critics said things like the

---

[3] Elliot. The six books cited in the bibliography were particularly helpful to us over the years.

[4] Elliot, *Shadow of the Almighty*, 71.

book was so negative, and that nobody would be encouraged by reading this kind of a book. Well, I was, and happily own a first edition. Her next shattering book published in 1968 was *Who Shall Ascend: The Life of R. Kenneth Strachan of Costa Rica*. She was commissioned by the Latin America Mission (LAM) to write the "authorized biography" of Ken Strachan (his kids and nephews were classmates at my first MK school in Costa Rica). Again, critics deemed her book too pessimistic and accused her of not telling of the good parts as she should have. The LAM commissioned another biography by an insider. Yet those two books profoundly impacted Yvonne and me as we read them during our first term of mission service.

Elisabeth Elliot accelerated the demise of missionary hagiography. Her searing (personal?) narrative, *These Strange Ashes* (1975), provides perhaps an edited version of her first year as a Bible translator in the jungles of Ecuador. I bought it at Urbana 1976, only recently discovering her signature in it. This book began restructuring my understanding of true spirituality and its intricate relationship with suffering and unanswered prayer. I recently completed reading the extensive biography, *Elisabeth Elliot: A Life* (2023), by Lucy S. R. Austen. And in late 2023 the second volume of Ellen Vaughn's definitive biography was released: *Becoming Elisabeth Elliot* (2020) and *Being Elisabeth Elliot* (2023). Vaughn was privy to sources unavailable to Austin, thus creating a challenge to readers who want to capture the full story of this gifted and complicated woman—a product of her time in history. Thankfully, neither of these authors over-glorify (hagiography), nor critically deconstruct (revile) Elliot. Theirs is a perspective of thoughtful understanding and compassion, yet many questions remain.

I have questioned why Elisabeth Elliot continues to capture the attention, imagination, and even ire, of evangelicals today? In part it is due to the way she reshaped the missionary biography genre. I am moved by her confrontations early on in Ecuador with the mysteries of suffering and death. "She confronted, perhaps for the first time, the monolithic impenetrable mystery of God's ways."[5] That's stout stuff. Her convictions on controversial issues, including marriage vows and the complementarian-egalitarian discussion, were unflinching and in many cases unpopular, especially within the current zeitgeist of our American culture.

---

5 Vaughn, *Becoming Elisabeth Elliot*, 101.

Our personal library has over 150 missionary biographies. Some I inherited from Dad, most we purchased over the decades (including a set of thirty books—*Christian Heroes: Then and Now*[6] published by YWAM for younger readers). Missionary biographies have enriched our family, and we treasure them. However, I know which of these are realistic. Wisdom helps us discover genuine and true stories. Even as I write this sentence, Yvonne is reading a biography of that indomitable pioneer missionary to Africa, Mary Slessor, and she is reading aloud some paragraphs during our meals.

So, yes to missionary biographies ... with discernment.

Conclusion and Peculiar Lessons on Leadership

What motivated me and my own generation to give ourselves (at least a significant portion of our years) to global Christ-mission? I think the following components converged and called-drove-led us: the biblical basis of mission interwoven into all of Scripture; the Spirit's invitation to join the Triune God on his mission; obedience to some kind of "call" or invitation and urging; human and spiritual needs; our discernment on vocation and occupation and geography—cross-cultural mission; pragmatic, rational decisions that took us down that journey; finally, the willingness to pay that price.

It's a conundrum, this wanting to do significant things for God because we love him. As we participate with the Father in what he is doing, we want to do it in a fruitful way. We also grapple with the paradox between our dreams and life's reality. If we are honest, we will all end up battling broken aspirations, limitations, sickness, failure, suffering, loss, the dull reality of the quotidian. These themes are woven into the fabric of true leadership. How we deal with them is the key.

The siren voices calling us "to do great things for God" can invade our own carnal, personal motivations and hidden addictions. All of us must wrestle with the reality that *not* doing amazing things is part of the journey. All of us must learn to live at peace with those tensions. What are the beatitudes of Jesus about if not giving credence to them—the meek, the poor, the brokenhearted, the lowly, the persecuted. Ordinary-ness is holy-ness.

---

[6] https://www.ywampublishing.com. At this time the category lists over forty-five titles in print, electronic, or audio versions.

What about doing (or not doing) great things for God? Personally, I had no idea what that meant in my mid-twenties. In seminary God birthed new visions in me. There I settled what I thought was my lifelong vocation—to foster life-changing discipleship in people's lives with a future occupation in transformational theological education. The geography clarified itself, Guatemala. The teaching locus emerged, SETECA. Those seemed fixed realities; the sails were set, the keel and rudder doing their crucial job. All I needed was a wife who shared these dreams.

God in his mercy did provide. Not what I had thought she might be nor what my parents or my missionary subculture preferred. God surprised me with a life partner who was my true *vis a vis*. She had a greater capacity to simultaneously engage both right and left brain, while I would often lock into only one. She did not come from an evangelical subculture, but rather from high sacramental Episcopalian roots. Yet when her family moved to a Bible believing and teaching church she was like a sponge, soaking in God's word. I married an artist, a classical pianist. I married someone with strong convictions. I had to learn to be a wise and gracious husband. Recently at dinner I laughed as I said, "Yvonne, I am so glad I married you. What would I have done and been without you?" She married a TCK who grew up irregularly but made it. Best friends forever.

Neither of us thought in terms of doing great things for God. It was more about faithfulness, bearing lasting fruit, and pleasing the Father. Over the decades we realized how much of the journey involved sitting in the Spirit's schools of deconstruction, in the long Dark Night of the Soul, in the hot and dry desert. Yet it was these places that God met us, time and again.

Yes, there is some value in slogans, for they crystallize limited facets of truth. Yes, the panoply of biographies and other mission books will be used by God to shape and reshape us. Only during our transformations can the Spirit forge the qualities of the leader whose spirituality is deep and growing. We need robust, challenging, and realistic narratives of women and men whom God used in both remarkable public ways, but also in obscure and little-known venues. The key is not the press release, the obituary, or the monument but rather the integrity of holiness, suffering, and faithfulness. Perhaps their stories were never heralded, but nevertheless the accounts testify to finishing well.

This chapter presents a different perspective on leadership, examining how singular factors and forces motivate and drive us as potential, current, or former leaders. I rather fell into leadership, or perhaps I fell backwards into it. I did not seek it, God knows. But it visited me, it invited me into a new arena of servanthood, of leading from below. My motives and visions had to be purified—a lifelong process—and in that journey I was transformed. Examining my father as a leadership case study, I discerned that he brought to it a genetic package—there is a long line of Taylor leaders. My sister wished that Dad had gone into the military; "He would have been a great leader." But he took a path less traveled, carrying that generational greatness into world missions. He honed his leadership crafts, partly in the field realities of Central America, partly because of his studies at Wheaton. He had the skills and gifts, the discipline, and the vision. Genetics. I flow in that stream.

I know too many stories of well-known Christian leaders who flamed out. They crashed and the resulting detritus affected so many people and families. They reached for power and glory, but without the testing of extended years in the trenches coupled with brokenness. As I write, the names and sad accounts of too many contemporary prominent evangelical leaders come to mind. I grieve. There is warning in the phrase, "Don't believe the press releases about yourself." So true. There is a particular danger of being featured on the cover of a high-profile Christian magazine with the title, "The top fifty evangelical leaders under forty in America." A former colleague showed up on one list, so when I saw him the next time, I warned him, "Good friend, you are now in the center of Satan's target—be extremely careful and don't believe the press releases on yourself." He was visibly shaken, but I do not think he learned. In an offhand comment years later after taking on a new position I heard him say, "I am finally being paid what I am worth."

The liturgy that opens this chapter concludes:

> Intercessor: Is this still your heart's true desire then, to do great works for the kingdom of heaven?
>
> Petitioner: It is, though I had not known before even what it meant. I ask now for grace that I might truly and humbly repent of any root of vainglory buried in my former prayers, and I pray also for grace that I might now ask aright, in purity

of heart, that the good works of God would be manifest in their many outworkings in my heart and life, at all times and in all endeavors, howsoever it pleases him.[7]

Mark 3:13–19 tells us that our Lord selected twelve extremely diverse young adults to become his personal apprentices. He selected them with clear purpose: to be with him; then renamed as apostles he sent them out to preach, to heal, and exercise authority over demons. Some names he changed, some later served in the limelight, others in shadows. Ah yes, Judas. Jesus personally invested three years in their lives, then released them—empowered by the Holy Spirit—into their lifelong mission. In certain ways I identify with those twelve: I studied in a three-year program and was selected at a young age, but the Spirit's investment in me was long term. And very gradually, over the course of my years, God led me into facets of leadership I had no idea would come to me. But they did. Jesus taught me to select potential leaders, invest in them, and release them.

Most of us will not live extraordinary public lives. But we want to do our best and make our contribution to God's global mission on planet earth. Our challenge is to live in tension, in paradox, to desire to give all to God even as we embrace the downward way of the cross. That then will shape who we are as leaders and will be demonstrated in how we exercise that leadership with those whom God has called us to serve.

Reflection Questions

1. In what ways does the liturgy-poem affect you? Is it OK to dream big, to expect God to do things beyond the normal? Explain.

2. How can slogans reduce the significance of the task before us as servants of Jesus?

3. What role has good mission literature had in your life? What are you reading now that challenges you for the kingdom of God?

4. Can you describe someone you know who has led a life of faithfulness over the years and is finishing well?

5. What book on leadership has most challenged you? Why?

---

[7] McKelvey, "For Those Who Have Not Done Great Things for God," in *Every Moment Holy*, 209.

3
Deaths and Resurrection

For I know the plans I have for you, declares the LORD, plans for welfare and not for evil, to give you a future and a hope. (Jer 29:11)

When we worship and live in obedience to the King of kings, God transforms leaders, teams, and every form of social game into covenant communities, called out for the mission of God and working together in unity to fulfill their divine purpose. When we worship at the cross, we learn to take the path of weakness rather than of power, to extend mutual forgiveness rather than condemnation, and to submit to one another rather than seeking power and the subjection of others to our will in our relationships and teamwork.[1]

Living the Dreams of My Long-Term Future

A friend's funeral led me to the Guatemala City cemetery, the side road taking me to our mission's "real estate." Two modest mausoleum structures revealed the names of people of whom I had heard, some whom I had known. I saw the name of a beloved Down Syndrome baby girl who died at age one after open heart surgery. I had dedicated her as an infant, then presided over her funeral service. There were some empty "slots," and the top left corner slot caught my attention. Perhaps there my body shall be laid to rest. It was an honest reflection. I had dreamed I would live, serve my entire life in Guatemala, and die there. For that we had signed up, I once thought.

My "mission's call/decision" was received somewhere around age nine, the Spirit protected and nourished that child's stand over the years. That red-haired boy made a decision, and that decision would turn and transform him. I sleep-walked through many years of my childhood and youth, only starting to think clearly while at Moody Bible Institute. I enrolled there at age seventeen (totally immature) because Moody

---
1 Lingenfelter, *Leading Cross-Culturally*, 170.

produced the missionaries, they had a historic DNA identity. My parents had studied there in the 1930s. Yet, as my three years there ended, I knew I was simply not ready and too young. That led me to study in the secular university world, where my faith was tested, where I discovered IVCF at the University of Illinois and North Texas University, where I emerged into student leadership. Through IVCF I learned to worship, study Scripture, and communicate my faith in that world. I also battled my first round of doubts. I spent three years on IVCF staff in Texas, further expressions of emerging leadership.

I proceeded from Moody to U of I to NTU (as a Spanish major) and then to DTS in a four-year-long ThM program. At DTS I learned to think seriously, to ask questions, to discipline my mind and spirit. DTS also required four years of Greek and three of Hebrew, four years of theology and Bible, and four years of Christian education (my major). My education included the richness of growing in the love of Scripture and its inductive study. I became a man at DTS, and that lead to the inevitable and desirable search for a wife who would share the dreams of long-term, cross-cultural service—now coming into focus in Latin America, teaching at SETECA (*Seminario Teológico Centroamericano*) in Guatemala. While our love story is described elsewhere, I repeatedly thank God that he led me to this serious Jesus-lover, keen minded classical pianist, beautiful woman, and best friend. Her maturity many times surpassed mine though I was five years older. We both knew where we were headed, and our shared love and commitment bolstered the foundations of our marriage and lifelong friendship. During our first year of marriage, she finished NTU, and I finished my last year on IVCF staff.

The Central American Mission accepted us, and we were assigned to SETECA. We raised our support ($441 monthly) in five months and drove out of Dallas on Friday the 13th of December 1968. That long south-bound road trip led to Costa Rica, where both of us would study Spanish during 1969. Yvonne's four years of Latin and two of German, plus her musical ear, enabled her to learn accurately. I purposed to upgrade my street-savvy Spanish. A year later we drove north to Guatemala and began our life there. One permanent gift from Costa Rica was the conception of our first child, Christine, born in Guatemala in April 1970. David arrived in April 1972, and Stephanie in April 1976. They are Guatemalans by birth, Americans by parentage, and Third Culture Persons by definition.

I wrongly assumed that Yvonne and I would work side by side at SETECA, so she first taught rudimentary piano at the school we served. It was not a good fit, and I learned to release her from my expectations and allow the Spirit to guide her uniquely. Her deepest commitment and callings were as homemaker and mother. I began my teaching career at SETECA, exercising my natural skills and spiritual gifts. I learned how to contextualize my instruction—without knowing then that the term even existed. I was a product of the American educational system, and only gradually discovered its biases. SETECA at the time was a conceptual and practical educational transplant from the USA—pot, soil, root system and stem. The school served the Guatemala IVCF-IFES student movement, and I learned to disciple and invest in young adults who were studying in Guatemala's Marxist-influenced university. Our home became a venue for Yvonne's pre-evangelistic piano recitals, which emerged into a beautiful partnership with our mission's Christian radio station, TGN.

Working with Latin American university students exposed me to the radically different issues they faced in their study and discipleship. Our initial discipleship groups became foundational, long-term communities for deep interpersonal relationships. My leadership skills, first honed with IVCF in the USA, were now upgraded and resharpened in Latin America.

After I finished my formal education in 1967 at DTS, I thanked God that I would never, *ever*, return to the classroom. Little could I have imagined that in mid-1972 I would find myself engrossed as I earned a PhD in Latin American studies and the cultural foundation of education at the University of Texas, Austin. We discovered a healthy church (my first), Grace Covenant, and we made lifelong friends and new ministry partners—some of whom still pray and invest in us.

In mid-1974 we, Yvonne, Christine (4), David (2) and I, returned to Guatemala and SETECA, but I was a different person. Those two years of studying Latin American history, governments, culture, and people had transformed me. Now I was thirty-three years old, and unexpected new opportunities of service and leadership came my way. I had not sought them, but they sought me. Others "saw" me. I provided leadership to SETECA's first global mission conference. Yet after those events finalized, I returned to teaching—again, honing my gifts with a growing understanding of contextualization. Our three children shared the contextualization journey as they studied in the Austrian Institute of Guatemala and were grounded in three languages—German, Spanish and English. Yvonne taught them to read and write in English, their rooted mother tongue.

Again, I was invited into the Latin American Theological Fraternity (LATF), where I joined a continental community of evangelicals who were serious biblical and contextual thinkers within Latin America. Joining the LATF coincided with my presence at the radically transforming Lausanne 1974 congress.

Providentially, student ministry in our first term played a role in the planting of a new church with a new governance model, deep commitment to community, rich intergenerational community, and many new believers. Cesar, an economics student in my discipleship core, worked for a large aluminum products company. He shared some of our exchanges with his boss. I suggested, "Why don't you offer a study like ours, but with families. Yvonne and I will come alongside you." To our surprise that happened, and two other leadership couples joined us. That discovery Bible community began in a home. One unforgettable evening, as we started our study, the host, Roberto (not his real name), said, "I request permission to speak." He stood. "I Roberto Aguilar, a man of fifty-one years age, in full control of my mental faculties, tonight declare that I have placed my trust in Jesus Christ." He sat down, all of us stunned and silent The Spirit was at work.

> The small community walked through that "thin space" from being simply a Bible study group into the consciousness of becoming a new church.

During our Austin years the Lord incubated that group, enriching it with another larger, healthy stream. Shortly after our return to Guatemala, the small community walked through that "thin space" from being simply a Bible study group into the consciousness of becoming a new church. I soon became a very young, thirty-three-year-old church elder.

And what did leadership have to do with eldering? Pretty much everything! It involved prayer and waiting on the Spirit; collegial decision making; shepherding and casting vision as we invited others into the future of that vision; affirming and discipling new believers; developing new elders who were equipped and released into the community to love and serve; doing the same in evangelism and discipleship. Young Bill Taylor was accompanied by his family, especially Yvonne, whose roles in cross-cultural ministry were released through prayer and fasting, loving, discipling, and building community. Those years at El Camino revealed new spiritual gifts, and new challenges. I was not fearful of being called a "pastor," because, in essence I was a pastor, the youngest of five on the core team.

Guatemalan life, human existence, and normality was shattered by the February 1976 earthquake, which killed some 23,000 people and injured some 76,000 others. Hundreds of thousands of homes were destroyed and hundreds of church buildings were turned into rubble. SETECA pitched a huge tent in the soccer field, installed a curtain to separate men from women, and cancelled class for two weeks. Sadness was tragic to the extreme. Yet, God used that season to draw countless number of people into his family; those who were seeking something sure, solid, eternal. We were in survival mode, committed to thoughtful compassion and relief and in the process discovering the broader body of Christ.

After the earthquake we built our own lovely home in Guatemala—designed and decorated by Yvonne. It became a hub of ministry, of Bible studies, of dinners for nonbelievers, of pre-evangelistic piano recitals, of community, and a place for friends and teachers from the Austrian School. Yvonne and dear friend Lois met in our home each Friday, fasting and praying. I had helped build (with the skilled help of friend Ed Seiford) a beautiful sloop, named "Cristina," and I learned to sail on Guatemala's lakes, creating unforgettable family memories. But ...

The Uneasy Gut

How was I to understand the twelve invitations that came to me around the 1980s to take a new position: lead a mission, teach at a seminary, pastor a new church? all in the USA? I saw them as challenges to my "call" to Latin America. Thirteen years into our seventeen years in Guatemala, Yvonne surprised me, "Bill, have you considered the possibility that these invitations might be from God and that he is asking if you are willing to die to your dreams and go somewhere you really don't want to go?" Of course not! I certainly had no interest in moving to the unloved "Northern Gulag." But deep in me something shifted. I felt uneasy.

Questions assaulted us. How do you know when the "assignment is finished" in lifelong, cross-cultural mission? Has your vocation changed? How can you "leave the field" without becoming an attrition statistic? Is it possible to "leave well," to leave in a way where you could be asked to return for various ministries? How do you explain the unexplainable? Who knows the "real story"? (Well, only your spouse and perhaps closest friends.) Will your supporters know? What will the sending agency and church write down as "reason for field departure"? What is *attrition*? What will we *really* do now, after seventeen years "on the field." We faced these issues and so many more as we discerned that our time in Guatemala and Latin America was concluding. Is it OK to grieve, to sigh, to weep, to mourn? What is reverse culture shock anyway? How do we process these brutal transitions? Will we find kindred spirits in our new assignment? Will we find a church remotely close to the vibrancy of El Camino in Guatemala? We grappled with many transition questions. We knew we were not alone. Countless thousands of other cross-cultural colleagues around the world have walked similar paths. But they were far away, or not among our trusted friends or colleagues. Few resources or programs existed to help reentry. The pilgrimage was lonely.

God required me to take these invitations seriously. After an extended discussion involving Yvonne, SETECA, and TEDS leadership, I accepted a one-year trial assignment. Ironically, it was my former DTS mission's professor, Dr. George Peters, who asked me once if I had considered teaching at TEDS. I'm sure he was the one who spoke to Dr. Walter Kaiser, then TEDS' dean. In the summer of 1982, we drove from Guatemala City via Dallas to Deerfield, Illinois, for a year's discernment. Danny and Joan Carroll and their sons rented our Guatemala home that year. At TEDS, we lived in Gunderson Hall, the oldest student apartment, where in February the ice was a quarter of an inch thick *inside* the room. But we were happy, living in small, tight quarters, the three kids in one bedroom and Yvonne and I in the other. The private place was the bathroom, and the telephone cord was long enough to snake under its door—double privacy. International students lived there, and some became lifelong friends and global colleagues: Koreans Dr. David and Hunbok Lee, Chadians Dr. Abel and Priscilla Ndjerareou, Nigerian Dr. Musa Asake, and many others. We shared the world, the academic community, and the ice.

We loved that year. The kids attended Bannockburn school, a posh suburb school. Stephanie was in kindergarten, David in fourth, and Christine in sixth grade, and they made temporary friends. Their classmates, however, were not Guatemalan, but wealthy Americans. Our children had to adapt to the American system of education, so different from the Austrian Institute of Guatemala. A German TEDS student, Norbert Schmidt, became their German tutor "in case" we were to return to Guatemala. It was a strange mélange of worlds for all of us.

Our church experience was the exception. We had come out of the El Camino context of national revival in Guatemala. We had seen lives transformed. We loved the warmth of Latin American peoples (Americans seemed so cold). We missed community. We missed Spanish, we missed German and the Austrian Institute of Guatemala.

Yvonne and I were together in this venture, she but thirty-six and I forty-one. The TEDS chapel had a magnificent organ, and her father paid for lessons to renew her skills. Periodically she came into my class when we discussed issues of singles, married life, family, schooling, all related to potential mission service. I exulted in my classes, though I had never formally taught in English before. I was given the challenging "Introduction to World Mission's" class, not a favorite of some professors because it was obligatory for all majors. But I loved that challenge and invited students into a journey. I discerned respect from colleagues and administration. Yes, I could conceivably see myself teaching there full time.

Ah … Surprises awaited me.

The Return, the U-turn, Grief

Henri Nouwen writes that one of the unique things that can happen in preaching is when the preacher himself is converted. On Monday, November 8, 1982, I was transformed by my own teaching. I was enthusiastically presenting "Third World Missions," using the pioneer research by Larry Keyes and Larry Pate of One Challenge International. Excited about what God was doing out of Asia and Africa, the very Voice of God came to me, "Taylor, what have you done to further this vision in Latin America?" I was stricken. Not only had I done nothing, but worse, I had adopted the presupposition that global cross-cultural mission was primarily a First World assignment. I had not taken seriously the vision of "from every nation to every nation." Worse, I had truncated the Great Commission for Latin America. SETECA had no mission course in the curriculum. While Latin students had talked with me about their "call" to missions, I simply discarded it as an unviable category. Returning to our apartment, I shared my epiphany with Yvonne.

Before me is the very paper where on November 18, 1982, I wrote the word of the Lord to me, Isaiah 50:10: "Who is among you that fears the LORD, that obeys the voice of his Servant, that walks in darkness and has no light? Let him trust in the name of the LORD and rely on his God." I was learning to walk in darkness, unable to light my own lantern to illuminate my path.

I truly wanted to return to Latin America, but it was imperative to give the USA a fair shot. Over the course of the following weeks, I made a "deal" with God, concluding that I would be willing to leave *home* permanently if God met six requirements. It was a bold, cheeky challenge. 1) SETECA would establish a missiological center, 2) Curriculum would include a required missions course, 3) I would coauthor with colleague Eugenio Campos (later to get his DMiss from TEDS) a mission's workbook for the local church, 4) Our Guatemalan church would commit to global cross-cultural vision, 5) I would witness the start of a Guatemala mission agency, and 6) I would see the conception of a Guatemala-based missionary training program. I calculated this would give us a decade more in Guatemala, and then I could leave in peace.

We drove back to Guatemala in July 1983. The kids were miraculously accepted back into the Austrian School as if they had never left. We resumed our life and work at church and SETECA. Our friendships deepened. Life was normal again.

Little did I know how rapidly God would undo my deal.

To my astonishment, before we returned in July 1983, two items on my list came into existence. Our first Sunday in Guatemala, the lead elder, Dr. Abel Morales, greeted me with a huge *abrazo* and said (in Spanish), "Guillermo, the Spirit has been convicting our church leadership about not engaging in God's global cross-cultural work. Would you help us?" Gulp. A year later our church celebrated its first-ever missions conference, initiating a faith-promise venture that far outstripped my own expectations. Soon Eugenio and I began writing *Misiones Mundiales*, a practical missions manual for the local church— which unexpectedly served as text for two Latin American continental mission congresses, later revised by my Argentinian colleague Federico Bertuzzi and expanded in 2014 and 2025.[2]

---

2 Taylor, Estudios CLASE, 2025.

First steps were taken to establish the mission agency and discussions had started about a potential prefield training program. In 1984, SETECA celebrated a global missions conference, and WEF-related speakers came from Africa (Tokunboh Adeyemo), Asia (Theodore Williams of India and Bong Rin Ro of Korea), Latin America and the USA—all contacts through Dr. Emilio Antonio Núñez, then on the WEF International Council. That convocation became a watershed. Truth be told, the global mission's zeal at SETECA was spearheaded not by the faculty, but by students radically open to the Spirit.

The academy became my final learning arena. I had been sent to teach, hence learn to teach; I had been sent to teach cross-culturally and in another language, Spanish. I did these tasks relatively well, I thought. Other leadership invitations came to me, pushing me out of my established skillset and gift mix. I was asked to lead other campus-wide, week-long events. I was also appointed to new levels of responsibility as chair of the ministry division. It grew and I later joyfully passed it to a Latin colleague. I was asked to chair the first iteration of our new graduate program. New skills and gifts emerged on the job; I was growing in my understanding of what a leader was and how I fit into that scheme.

I recorded a series of three live dialogical courses ("How to Study the Bible," "The Christian Family," "Spiritual Gifts") for Christian radio TGN. The response was heartening. While in Guatemala, Dallas Theological Seminary invited me to join the faculty, a door God soon closed. TEDS dean, Dr. Walter Kaiser and his wife visited Guatemala in early 1984 to speak at SETECA and El Camino. His true motive: to recruit me again for TEDS mission's department. The handwriting was engraved on the wall and now it was a matter of my obedience.

The clock ticked too rapidly. Yes, this truly was our farewell to Latin America, to Spanish and cultures, colleagues and friends, seminary and church, home and school, sailboat, and orchids. Never in my life had I seen the Spirit work so rapidly. We were to leave our beloved Guatemala for good. This we would do in June 1985, twenty-four months after our return from TEDS. Not ten years as I had hoped. What was God up to anyway? However, another issue shaped our departure. Our mission leadership was increasingly moving towards an older fundamentalism, while we, in contrast, found our platform of relationships, ministry, and theology growing beyond those bounded sets. We knew other colleagues shared our concerns.

We celebrated our last holiday at Lake Atitlan that January 1985, sailing for the last time. The kids had grown in their mastery of Spanish and German with a stellar education. But were we prepared to face the multifaceted trauma of loss and departure, plus reentry culture shock? No.

Yvonne and I realized that we would definitively leave at the seventeen-year marker of our assignment to Guatemala and the seminary. I flew to Chicago and TEDS for interviews with the school of world mission, the faculty, the board, the president, and dean. Walt faxed the contract to Guatemala, with me starting as an assistant professor. I sensed an inequity so I faxed him back, asking if he were hiring a USA-based professor with my years of teaching, would it be at that level? He immediately sent a new contract for me as an associate professor. I never negotiated the finances as that simply was not the way we had operated. God would provide, and he did, barely. And that was OK.

We left Guatemala where our three children had been born and experienced their early, formative spiritual and cultural shaping. They had come to faith in Christ, Christine with Yvonne, David with me, and Stephanie by herself on a TEDS playground. I had baptized all of them. As the oldest, Christine was impacted by the remarkable El Camino youth group. Her leaders then included Sergio Mijangos (now SETECA professor with PhD in clinical psychology and founder of SETECA's counseling program) and Frank Saenz (gifted engineer now on the pastoral staff of Guatemala's Vida Real church as well as CRUX Institute board member). Most of those youth entered a variety of professions in Guatemala. Some ended up in ministry or longer-term cross-cultural service. Most still walk with Jesus.

As the date of our permanent leave-taking approached, I thanked God that he had allowed me to complete three Spanish language writing projects, all field-tested and coauthored with colleagues. The first was the basic, ten-lesson study *Misiones Mundiales*, designed for the local church and coauthored with Dr. Eugenio Campos, SETECA colleague; the second was a book on friendship and courtship, *La Pirámide del Amor*, coauthored with Dina Saldívar de Escobar, SETECA grad and Mexican psychologist; *La Familia Auténticamente Cristiana* came next. I first wrote it alone, then revised-updated it years later with the skilled help of Dr. Sergio Mijangos.

Those last months I sighed so many times that Yvonne said, "Bill, stop sighing!" Decades later I discovered the deeper meaning of the sighs; I was in mourning. I have my *7-Star Diary* from those years and have perused January to June, our final season in Guatemala—days packed with relationships, friends, work, writing, a series of farewells, the sale of many things, and the sorting of what to pack and ship to the USA. I continued to sigh. Dad's cryptic wisdom emerged with two statements that guided our departure: "Bill, leave when they want you to stay." And then, "Bill, leave in a way that they will ask you to return." Serious wisdom obeyed.

When Yvonne's pre-evangelistic piano recitals season in Guatemala ended, she suffered deep loss. Those events had been creative opportunities to invite friends who would not yet attend a church or Bible study. Yvonne had a unique way of engaging friends into the music, giving vignettes about the composer, inviting them to guess what was happening in a particular piece, like Bartok's short "The Diary of a Fly." Bach was contrasted in faith and style with a modern and dissonant composer. When we moved to the USA, this artistic expression came to a halt, and it brought sadness. Classical music in the USA simply was not used in those ways, and there were so many musicians in the USA.

We made it through a series of emotional farewells—both for Latins and our family. It was heartrending for our Guatemala-born Third Culture Person children to leave school and church. Our most painful farewells were from our church and our closest friends. By then, with some notable exceptions, our intimate relationships were with Latin colleagues. CAM International workers and SETECA had separate farewells, and to be honest, I did not want to attend the agency event, sensing that some were happy to see us go. My leader simply stated, "Bill, you are under authority, and you will attend." We did. It wasn't bad.

We stored most of our furniture and household goods for later shipment to the USA. We sold the rest and began making our plans for the journey back to TEDS via Europe. Our home did not sell, primarily due to the devaluation of the Guatemalan currency (after sixteen months it sold—purchased by a buyer not of our choice, but we had no choice). Christine and David spent two months in Austrian homes that summer and left earlier than Yvonne, Stephanie, and me. The airport photo of our older kid's departure from Guatemala is burned in my memory; both with tears in their eyes. For all of us it was an incredibly hard farewell to our beloved Guatemala.

In June 1985, Stephanie, Yvonne, and I made our final farewells, flew to Spain, and traveled by train to visit friends, TEDS and SETECA grads, until we met up with Christine and David in Strasburg. From there we traveled to Klosters, Switzerland, where we were hosted by our TEDS friends, Harold O. J. Brown and his wife Grace. Then we traveled to Belgium with Dottie and Carlton Meredith. Our time in Europe provided a rich, beautiful, and healing transition to the US after the intensely emotional good-byes of Guatemala.

We landed in Texas in mid-July and met with our supporting churches. We then released our entire prayer and support team from their commitments to us. We would depend on the TEDS salary. We visited Yvonne's family in Dallas, and our last day with CAM International was Saturday August 31, 1985. We had no exit interview; we were on our own. And we were attrition statistics for the mission, though not marked with shame or personal disaster. Each of us processes our attrition reality differently as it is contingent on the circumstances of each personal situation. Is it because of uncontrollable political conflicts or government expulsions, or conclusion of contract, or moral issues, or family conflict, or the children's education, or health problems, or a transition into a very different occupation, or theological change, or lost faith in the central tenets of Christianity? Or is it God's direction of our lives from one arena and assignment? Each situation generates its unique cluster of factors. Only later did we realize our serious mistake of releasing our prayer partnership, and we sought to rebuild it a few years after our return to the USA.

I was forty-four and Yvonne thirty-nine. We purchased a used vehicle in Dallas and drove again to TEDS where, I thought, we would live and serve for the rest of *my* strong career. We *temporarily* moved into the same Gunderson Hall apartment, met other international students, and tried to buy a house. By now Christine was fifteen, David thirteen, and Stephanie nine. When David unfolded his bed at night in their bedroom, they had standing room only. Nobody complained. We knew that most of the world lived in less and worse.

We visited local churches, unable to find anything even remotely close to the vitality of El Camino in Guatemala. It was hard to understand the contrast between the spiritual hunger and openness of Guatemala compared with the burned-over American cultural and spiritual landscape. And Americans seemed *so cold* and unfriendly!

My development had matured during the last two years in Guatemala where Latin students and colleagues challenged my categories and understanding. During that year at TEDS my own missiological understanding grew and matured. I read widely, listening to colleagues and international students—all key leaders in their contexts. I was discovering the entire world as God's mission's arena ("mission" came later into my vocabulary). I was finally discerning the length and breadth of God's mission in his global enterprise.

We tried to make new friendships, which proved to be far from easy. In 1985 there were so few resources to guide returning cross-cultural workers through reentry after many years away from "passport culture." We were left to figure it out on our own. Thank God for the TEDS professors who loved us well, Peggy and John Nyquist and Joe and Grace Brown. Joe had a stiletto-sharp sense of humor, and in the context of one of the perennial heated faculty-administration discussions he taught me a great quasi-Latin saying, *illegitimi non carborundum* (roughly translated, "don't let the bastards wear you down"). It uniquely fit into a diverse set of personal experiences. In God's goodness, some friendships with Trinity students continue to this day. We settled in for the long haul.

Ah, little did I know.

Thank God for thoughtful friends. In our case most of our support team understood that the Spirit was at work in our lives. The reverse culture shock hit Christine and me the most, then Yvonne and David, finally Stephanie. After two years Yvonne said to me, "Bill, I think we are finally beginning to feel like America could be home." But it was still hard for me. We returned to Guatemala on summer trips for years, allowing further closure even as friendships were extended, and our Guatemala church was a crucial support. SETECA generously opened many doors for me.

During our seventeen years in Latin America Yvonne and I had served on equal standing in the agency; our monthly check was deposited in the names of Yvonne and William Taylor. TEDS was different. There it was my deal, my contract, and TEDS simply needed the acquiescence of the spouse so the contracted faculty could teach in peace. Many of the faculty wives had their own careers and seemed fulfilled. So, who was Yvonne now? Many unexpected challenges and stress-points emerged.

Our own personal story makes me ponder the cases of countless thousands who, because they departed cross-cultural service earlier than expected or desired, have gone through the same multi-faced return crises as we. How have they processed it? Was their experience harder or easier than ours? Are they all still walking with Jesus and his mission? Some answers came in 1996 when the Mission Commission completed the fourteen-nation attrition study, convened a consultation, and produced a landmark publication. The statistics did not move me as much as the personal case studies. I wept; I understood.

As I gaze back, I realize that God himself leveraged us out of Guatemala through TEDS. What I did not expect was that God would pull a pivot on me within months at Trinity. Again, I would grapple with another series of surprises, sadness, and confusion, for within one year I lost both Latin America and teaching.

While our decision to move to TEDS had been bathed in prayer and careful seeking of God's will for us, we found ourselves encountering again and again inexplicable roadblocks and closed doors to our attempts to settle into our new life there. Additionally, other returning cross-cultural missionaries often relocated near family, or geographical roots, or close to their sending church where they already had established friendship and community. We started at ground zero in every category. This only intensified the feeling of loss and dislocation for all that we had given up. The months went on and we continued in a state of limbo.

The academic year 1985–1986 became another life-changing watershed year of decisions as we probed the mind and purposes of God, seeking our family's best. It was also a confusing and painful year for all of us. We had given our extended and poignant farewells to Guatemala and all it represented. We sold our vehicles and many things, stored our furniture in Guatemala; our house remained un-sold. We had grieved our losses while trying to imagine a flourishing future. Our family had embarked on an unknown journey. The Spirit had made it very clear that our assignment in Latin America was over. But was this it?

That first year was brutal. David loved soccer; he was also a sensitive thirteen-year-old. At some point in the rough and tumble of a game he must have cried. He was bullied, derided. We had no idea that within his will and heart that very day he vowed that he would never, ever, under any circumstances, cry again. That oath bruised him; and only twenty years later did he experience deep healing and freedom from that wound. In the youth group he visited, because of casually touching another guy, he was tabbed as a homosexual. We bid on a house, invested a high down payment (nobody counseled us on how to do these things), and discovered the owners had lied regarding a previous flood. Extrication meant legal processes, and we ended up living in that very same Gunderson Hall apartment for another nine months.

That fall, Yvonne received two words from the Lord. The first came in the form of an "inner locution"—that singular experience when one hears the internal audible Voice. The Spirit said, "Yvonne, as a mother you want to protect your children from these hard things. But I am allowing these difficult and painful circumstances. I am asking you to release them to me and trust me, for I will use these hard trials to shape and train them. I want to make them dread champion warriors against the evil one." We are still trying to process that inner locution.

She communicated that radical message to me one afternoon in late November 1985, saying, "Bill, for all that Trinity is a very special place and community for you and for us, where we have had wonderful experiences and felt very welcomed by faculty and students, I am realizing that this is not God's long-term place of protection and flourishing for our family. It is a great match for your gifts and calling, but for some reason the Lord seems to be saying 'This is only a transitional move, not the permanent one.' I don't think we are supposed to stay here."

I collapsed on the kitchen floor, undone, weeping. I could not believe it. My dreams were gutted. Again, I saw myself a failed emerging leader, both in Latin America and in the USA. That following summer we drove to Russellville, AR to serve as part-time pastor-elder of a small supporting church and where we had friends. Our kids were excited to move there. I was dying. Yvonne grieved with me but was discerning a different future. God had leveraged me out of Guatemala and then pulled a pivot on me. I could not understand it.

Triple Death

How could I have imagined that in the space of two years I would die to Latin America, then to formal teaching, and later to the conviction that I could shepherd a congregation? But that is what happened. Our only wise counselor during those gut-wrenching months at TEDS was David Howard who was then based an hour away in the Wheaton area. He understood our crises, for he had walked a similar path when he and Phyllis and their four children left Latin America to serve with IVCF missions. He shared his mistakes. He counseled us and prayed with and for us. But more than that, he "saw" into our lives. When I finally pulled the trigger to leave TEDS again, I was lunching with Dave. It was exactly 1:25 p.m., mid-March 1986 when he said, "Bill, if you leave TEDS, I want you to come with me to Singapore this June and meet some people. Listen to me. God will richly bless any decision you take that seeks the flourishing of your family. It does not matter where you live." What he did not know was that at 1:10 p.m. I had determined to leave TEDS. A dim light blinked on.

Mid-June of that year we drove to Arkansas, house sat for a season until we moved into our home. I flew to Singapore via Tokyo and Hong Kong, then to Singapore for my radical life change. I still have the paper place mat on which I wrote notes and my future job description. Back in Arkansas, home, I began serving the church, primarily as a pastor-teacher and congregational shepherd. Things seemed to go well, then turned sour. One Sunday that first fall, as Yvonne and I drove home, she asked me how I felt during the sermon. "OK, I think. Why?" And she said something like the following: "I saw words come out of your mouth and drop suddenly to the ground, not entering the minds and hearts. There is a demonic spirit of opposition to you." I could not believe it! I vehemently disagreed ... until I discerned later, she was right.

It took a bit of time, but inexorably the shingles fell off the roof, the opposition moved into the open, and former close friends came to elder meetings to accuse me of dividing the church. One deacon charged me as a deceiving money-grubber, unworthy of being an elder. The elders stayed neutral. The handwriting was clear. God would soon release me from the church to dedicate myself full time to the new world of the World Evangelical Alliance Mission Commission. By late 1989 I resigned, and in mid-1990 we moved to Austin. We rebuilt our partnership and prayer team, surprised by the generous response from friends and some churches.

In that momentous June 1986 Singapore gathering of WEA's General Assembly, I assumed leadership of the Mission Commission (WEA-MC). I had no idea what that meant, but I knew in my deepest heart that God had served me with resurrection papers. And that's what happened. In the span of 1985–1990 I had died three times; God had pivoted me from Guatemala to TEDS to Arkansas and then turned me toward the world. Resurrection materialized; new life emerged from strange ashes.

Conclusion and Lessons

Strangely, in mid-2023 after I had already been working on this manuscript for some time, the Spirit led me to put the manuscript into a six-months-long, slow-cooking crockpot. When I renewed editing, I understood for the first time a central explanation for our seventeen years based in Guatemala. I also understood with greater insight the three deaths and resurrection in my life. I finally discerned the broader arc of my life, especially the thirty years with the WEA-MC. I saw my entire life unfold in slow motion.

> I saw my entire life unfold in slow motion.

Here is the unexpected question that emerged. Was the entire Latin America assignment preparation for the global one? And did the TEDS-Arkansas season allow the Spirit to enroll me in a different school of training—the season of the desert, the death of hope? That may be too simplistic, but as I review the Latin America assignment, I see how leadership concepts and experience emerged. I had not considered myself a leader, did not seek it, yet did not shirk it. I gradually emerged into leadership, not using that noun to describe myself. Guatemala gave me a very diverse leadership arena. Spaces, places, and opportunities opened to receive and exercise new giftings and skills. I made mistakes, some that embarrass me to this day. But grace was extended. Challenges stretched and grew me.

I grew in other arenas: the school of life; manhood; as a husband, father, teacher, discipler, mentor, church planter and elder; as a pastor, administrator, visionary, question-asker, servant. All of this became a testing laboratory, enrolling me in a life-school that prepared me for the rest of my life, especially the thirty years with WEA … and beyond … to today.

I was an adult Third Culture Person, a multicultural missionary, uniquely preparing me to engage in global leadership. We TCP's have an innate propensity to inspect the world through complex lenses. We speak nonverbal languages; we can read situations and people. It's a way of seeing. Latin American culture runs on personal relationships, not so much on systems and structures. Relationality can lead to collegial leadership, though Latins are all too familiar with the heritage of Roman law, class issues, and the top-down power of the chief, the boss, the owner (the *cacique, caudillo*).

God was in that also.

As I ponder these paragraphs, I remembered a prophetic word my father spoke over me in December 1969—before we moved to Guatemala. Speaking of my future at SETECA he said, "Son, this is not your long-term future." Stunned and disconcerted, I asked him to explain, but he refused to. Did he "see" the future?

Listen to Isaiah's strong prophetic word:

> But now thus says the LORD, he who created you, O Jacob, he who formed you, O Israel: "Fear not, for I have redeemed you; I have called you by name, you are mine. When you pass through the waters, I will be with you; and through the rivers, they shall not overwhelm you; when you walk through fire you shall not be burned, and the flame shall not consume you. For I am the LORD your God, the Holy One of Israel, your Savior." (Isa 43:1–3)

Reflection Questions

1. How can we approach major ministry transitions healthily? What tensions arise in all cases? What mistakes are more common?

2. What did Nouwen mean when saying that one of the unique things that can happen in preaching is when the preacher himself is converted? Has it happened to you?

3. How do you explain the speed with which God "met" Bill's six conditions to consider a future departure from Latin America? How does God teach us in similar cases?

4. How do you understand the two strong words from the Lord that Yvonne received? How does a married couple truly listen to each other?

5. What kind of grief, death, pivot, and resurrections have you experienced?

6. What does the Isaiah passage suggest to you?

Framing the Narrative

First home, Turrialba, Costa Rica, Chapel to left, 1940

Billy, circa age 7

First prayer card, 1943

First Passport, 1953

Huehue Academy, 8th Grade, 1954

With Dad, IBCA, 1966

Wedding, Dallas, TX, June 1967

That Young Couple, New Missionaries, 1971

The Novice Prof, SETECA, 1972

SETECA Global Mission Conference, 1985

Preaching at El Camino Church

A Piano Sings

4
Reflective Practitioner

And he came to Nazareth, where he had been brought up. And as was his custom, he went to the synagogue on the Sabbath day, and he stood up to read. And the scroll of the prophet Isaiah was given to him. He unrolled the scroll and found the place where it was written,

> "The Spirit of the LORD is upon me, because he has anointed me to proclaim good news to the poor. He has sent me to proclaim liberty to the captives and recovering of sight to the blind, to set at liberty those who are oppressed, to proclaim the year of the LORD's favor."

And he rolled up the scroll and gave it back to the attendant and sat down. And the eyes of all in the synagogue were fixed on him. And he began to say to them, "Today this Scripture has been fulfilled in your hearing." (Luke 4:16–21)

And Jesus came and said to them, "All authority in heaven and on earth has been given to me. Go therefore and make disciples of all nations, baptizing them in the name of the Father and of the Son and of the Holy Spirit, teaching them to observe all that I have commanded you. And behold, I am with you always, to the end of the age." (Matt 28:19–20)

"Keep It Simple"

It was an unforgettable senior homiletics DTS class. The student preacher was North Korean, English for him was a distant second language. But his sermon was extraordinary. Standing at the pulpit, he opened his Bible then said, "Go!" Long pause, then another, "Go!" A second pregnant pause filled the room and then the three-point sermon finale, "Go!" The preacher sat down. The professor simply didn't know what to do and I have no idea what grade brother Kim received, but the sermon—a magnificent reductionism—stuck with me.

"Keep it simple" was my motto even at age twenty-eight and a newly minted missionary. My core missional maternal milk predominantly flowed from the Great Commissions of the Gospels and Acts, reduced to the emphatic King James Version, "Go ye!" My earliest memories replay mission slogans and songs focused on these two words. Who could argue with that, our primary task? My future role was to equip Spanish-speaking leaders to pastor congregations growing with new believers. At the time, the binary game of zero and one was simple: go into all the world to preach the gospel. And the *sent people* obviously came from the West—as it was called then—and went to the rest (paltry binary language). Stick to the basics, Bill. Remember your slogans: "God had one Son and he was a missionary," "Never stoop to be your nation's ambassador if you can be a missionary."

> My core missional maternal milk predominantly flowed from the Great Commissions of the Gospels and Acts, "Go ye!"

This sentiment plowed through my personal history into my missiological journey. The Moody and DTS years, the season in Guatemala, the departure from Latin America to TEDS, the unexpected pivot to Arkansas and the WEA-MC, all deeply reshaped me, albeit gradually.

Moody prepared us to be "gap people," a three-year vocational level program. They assumed most of us probably needed only three years of a "vocational institute." The Bible Institute movement had transformed the training and mission global landscape. These programs were one-stop packages for practical equipping into lifelong ministry. My uneven development and immature mind did not take advantage of Moody's theology courses, though I do remember taking them. I clearly recall only two phrases from a theology class, "The internal witness of the Holy Spirit," and "Nobody comes neutral to the biblical text." Sounded like incipient heresy. I know what they mean ... now. But where was I during those years, age seventeen to twenty? Barely awakening.

In my elder stage of rumination, I discerned that my years at Moody placed me there during a quiet tidal wave of transformation. The ethos of Moody at the time included terminal training as "gap people" to "Moody as part of preparation," starting from a mission curriculum that led us to study (outdated) missionary medicine (I still remember how to diagnose pin worms) and including missions from the West to the Rest—of course; starting from an exclusive focus on the Great Commission as evangelism without understanding of integral mission; starting from texts exclusively written from the Global North—at the time, who would have imagined something else?

Yet transformation was beginning: one memorable evening during my last year stands out. The packed Moody Alumni Auditorium featured two mission giants in open and heated debate: Art Glasser (China veteran and Fuller missiologist) versus Kenneth Pike (Summer Institute of Linguistics genius). The issue: should we focus the energy of world missions where the harvest is ripe and the response is highest, or equally on unreached, hard-to-reach small people groups without Scripture in their mother tongue? I remember new brain cells crackled into existence, little seeds of my future missiological reflections. Little did I know what was ahead of me. God extended mercy and patience to me.

How different was I from thousands of my generation around the world, basically equipped (in different ways and in diverse schools) and sent from homelands to the ends of the earth? Few of us were missiologically minded. We simply responded in sincere obedience to what we understood to be God's call: "Let's get the job done." Even in seminary, while a few other classmates at DTS knew they were going into theological education "overseas," I suspect that most started as doers. After all, we were Americans, with pragmatism as our then-prime contribution to the world of philosophy. We were children of our culture, secular and evangelical.

My Multifaceted Journey

Moody *was* good for me, but I was too underdeveloped to profit adequately. My secular university years awakened other brain cells. I grew spiritually and intellectually, thanks to InterVarsity and Christian community. I survived, even thrived in the secular world. I also faced my first serious spiritual battle with doubt.

One eye-opening message at my Dallas church during my last year in university began deconstructing my mission reductionism. David Cox, Guatemala MK and DTS grad then serving in Brazil, preached on the Matthew 28 Great Commission. I was immediately bored. But he caught me off guard by his storied, engaging style, and he explained the Greek structure. The lights slowly then suddenly blinked on. I now understood what Jesus had said. There was one imperative, "Make disciples," and three participles, "As you are going," "Baptizing," and Teaching." The various charges of the passage slipped into place; the imperative was now understood. The core of the Great Commission was not evangelism but transformational discipleship. One sermon became a missiological master class. I walked out a very different young man.

The four DTS years awakened me; I started to think theologically. I took two missions courses, the required one and an elective with Dr. George Peters. This unique professor (born in the then-USSR with a high school diploma signed by Lenin) and his singular English accent placed him somewhere on the border between Europe and Asia. His family of Ukrainian Mennonite refugees made its way first to Mexico and later, shipped in a sealed boxcar, across the USA to Canada. A renowned missiologist, Dr. Peters was gracious to me. But I did not understand him in class nor his assigned textbooks. I started with an inchoate capacity to think theologically or missiologically. Perhaps that explains my C in the introductory required class. Yet my grades didn't deter me from that childhood "call" to missions. I had made a decision, and that decision was turning around and making me.

Shortly after DTS graduation in June 1967, Yvonne and I were married. Then, on Friday the 13th of December 1968, after having completed my final year on IVCF staff, Yvonne and I drove out of Dallas in a very used blue Chevrolet Carryall. We were finally "missionaries," I with my all-too-young wife who had just turned twenty-three. But I was a missionary bereft of a missiology. In Costa Rica we plunged into our study of Spanish and Latin American culture. Within a year I began teaching at SETECA (*Seminario Teológico Centroamericano*), discovering, exploring, and honing my gifts. I taught as I was taught, initially channeling much of the style of DTS's famous professor, Howard Hendricks. I was also off-balance in family versus ministry values as I have explained before, and we experienced a few crises where Yvonne helped me correct course.

Deeper changes were taking place, thanks to our first term role with the Guatemalan Christian university ministry, *Grupo Evangélico Universitario*. I became advisor/staff, and I loved it. I was released again to introduce students to Christ; discipling, leading Bible studies, teaching inductive study methods—like IVCF and Hendricks had taught me. Student ministry leadership skills emerged again but in a radically different culture. Yvonne opened our home to students and other expats, and her piano began to sing. My small group of medical, economics, and engineering students became a tight community. I opened my life to them, and they reciprocated. However, their apologetics needs radically contrasted with the questions from American students. My friends faced Marxist professors and classmates, not modernity's philosophical issues, nor Ayn Rand's challenges. They had contemporaries committed to Guatemala's class warfare, willing to fight, to die. The questions were genuine and biting. "Guillermo, what does St. Paul really mean when he says we are to obey government? What if it's obviously corrupt, ineffective, and doomed? Did Christians fight and kill in the American Revolution?" Later I would understand the Marxist ideological framework guiding Latin American Liberation Theology. It philosophically and practically nurtured nominal Catholic segments of Guatemala's guerilla movement. But I was relatively clueless in those early years.

My PhD dive into Latin American studies provided deep insight into this beloved continent. However, Liberation Theology in 1972 was not yet an academic topic even at the University of Texas. I gradually created a mental concept that only later would be named *contextualization*. My second doctoral discipline was the cultural foundations of education—history, philosophy, sociology, anthropology, and global studies. In that context I was challenged to ask the disturbing question: How can an American-conceived seminary in Latin America be reengineered to reflect Latin history, culture. and educational systems? Were we merely an educational transplant dropped into Guatemala, pot, roots, tree, fruit, and all? How could we "become more Latin?" My mentor and colleague, Emilio Antonio Núñez prophetically addressed SETECA's faculty after his PhD studies at DTS, "In our future we must look more to the South than to the North." My educational missiology was growing, though I had no leadership role at SETECA. Yet, looking back, I now track the tangible, albeit slow, changes that began contextualizing the seminary.

The landmark mission conference known as Lausanne 1974 and the LATF catapulted me into the future. The LATF was a Latin American fellowship of evangelicals desiring to "create and practice theology" in Latin America. The foundations of the LATF started a wave of interest and reflection around the concept known as integral or holistic mission. The concept spread in a wave and greatly impacted Lausanne 1974. Lausanne became a watershed event which influenced a big shift in reflections about missional theology and integration of contextualization reflection in theology, church, and mission.

I knew the leaders who formed LATF: Samuel Escobar, René Padilla, Peter Savage, Pedro Arana Quiróz, Orlando Costas, Valdir Steuernagel, and of course my SETECA mentor, Núñez. Now in my early thirties, I shared innovative spaces with them: listening, reflecting, evaluating, being evaluated. My life was enriched when bi-cultural Dr. Danny Carroll Rodas joined the SETECA faculty, though our overlap in Guatemala was unfortunately short. He opened the Old Testament, and our long conversations on biblical hermeneutics shaped me.

Contextualization worked itself into the evangelical lexicon and our faculty began discussing it. Its origins in the World Council of Churches Theological Education Fund made it suspect among more conservative evangelicals. One Cuban American colleague vigorously argued for the term "indigenization." Ultimately the original word gained common currency. When I first asked Núñez to coauthor *Crisis in Latin America: An Evangelical Perspective* with me I said, "Antonio, I am not skilled to discuss the theological themes of contextualization, Liberation Theology, Roman Catholicism, the charismatic movement, the social implications of the gospel. You are." His contributions made the book truly valuable. To my surprise, the 1996 revision, which added *and Hope*, is still being used in the preparation of Americans serving in Latin America. The Korean version does the same for their Latin America servants of the gospel.

That 1982–1983 year at TEDS became my missiological laboratory. Honestly, I taught missions with a wobbly theology of missions. However, I was slowly being transformed by reflective practice and discussion. A couple of years later, in 1985 and on the cusp of our departure from Latin America to return to TEDS, Eugenio Campos and I finished the first version of *Misiones Mundiales*, a local church mission's workbook. It reflected how I then understood the mission task of the church, but my point of departure was still based on statistics, practical "stuff" on how "to do missions in Latin America." My missiology was still anemic.

After two more years in Guatemala, we left Latin America permanently—our assignment apparently completed. It was a wrenching move from beloved Latin American and Guatemalan cultures, from Spanish, from friends and colleagues, from a truly healthy church, from a theological seminary on the cusp of major contextualization and growth. Our kids were born and shaped in Guatemala. Who were we to be? Were we (I thought this) being sent to some North American Gulag that I did not love nor really care for? It was obedience that led us into an unknown future. And truly it was unknown, as the next two years would reveal.

The 1985–1986 academic year at TEDS brought me greater growth as a pragmatic and gifted missions professor. However, my missiological development was overwhelmed at that time by the confusion and tension to discern God's purpose for my family. During that season I also transitioned from theoretical to practicing supernaturalist as I met anew the person and empowering presence of the Holy Spirit. During our Guatemala years when confronted by evil supernaturalism in Latin America, I had neither a theology nor the pastoral skills to deal with the evil one. At best I was a tentative, gracious, gifted cessationist. But I was asking new exegetical and practical questions of the biblical text, of my worldview, and the theological system I had received. New phenomena challenged my older system. Often, I felt totally out of my league. Where was I headed?

After my 1986 appointment with WEF and its Mission Commission, my leadership role and my understanding of contextual missions began to grow; to become more accurate, challenged, exercised and stretched. I engaged in multiple and diverse challenging assignments on practical levels: building relationships, community and a team, traveling, determining how to establish and then execute our global agenda, generating financial resources to fund the vision, developing ongoing programs and creative projects, organizing global consultations, producing resource publications and seminars, challenging and mentoring and releasing younger leaders into their Spirit-preferred future, and finally, giving structure to the Mission Commission. All of this shaped my attempt to lead from below, with mutuality and collegially. Inevitably it was carried out in a new crucible—global mission, cross and intercultural leadership, diverse leader styles, and ecclesiologies to understand and honor.

In God's graciousness, he brought others to shoulder the load. Jon Lewis then Bertil Ekström, remarkable friends and colleagues, joined me on MC staff. We three were TCPs. Jon's mind worked in practical and viable systems and processes. He knew how to raise funds. Bertil thought more missiologically; he had singular organizational skills. And, unbeknownst to both, I became their informal student. Together we led as colleagues and friends. The staff team grew with Kees van der Wilden from Holland.

Watersheds

The October 1999 Iguassu missiological consultation marked a seminal moment both for me and the MC. There we coined the term "reflective practitioner." Compiling the insight from that crucial event, today I describe the reflective practitioners as, "These women and men of both action and reflection who are committed to the person and work of the Triune God; rooted in the Word of God and the church of Christ; passionately obedient to the fullness of the Great Commandment and Great Commission; globalized in their perspective, yet faithful citizens of their own cultures; leaders passionate of heart who reflect the heart of Christ." The term and its manifestations became an energizing work in process of foundational world view missiological perspectives.

During that week I personally experienced an epiphany, an unexpected self-understanding: I emerged from Iguassu calling myself a reflective practitioner and a missiologist. I realized with clarity that I was a leader, that the Spirit had empowered me to exercise those gifts. I was known as one who asked troubling questions (starting early in Guatemala), some of them uncomfortable. Yet this leadership was to be exercised "from below," collegially, based on personal relationships, discerning the multifaceted dimensions of cultural intelligence and the new charge given the WEA-MC. The downward path of Christ to the cross became a spiritual lodestone. Samuel Escobar's definition and description of "missiology" articulated my core understanding:

> I define missiology as an interdisciplinary approach to understand missionary action. It looks at missionary facts from the perspectives of the biblical sciences, theology, history, and the social sciences. It aims to be systematic and critical, but it starts from a positive stance towards the legitimacy of the Christian missionary task as part of the fundamental reason for the church's "being."[1]

The MC board charged the staff team to study and apply the long-term implications of specific Iguassu issues. This set our agenda, publications, and consultations. Over the next years as I traveled and spoke on behalf of the MC, the reflective practitioner theme became a central motif. In June 2004 I gave a series of missiological lectures at Victoria Bible College, Australia. There I met Kirk Franklin, a younger

---

1 Taylor, *Global Missiology for the Twenty-first Century*, 101.

colleague and soon an MC Associate. Kirk, a leader in Wycliffe Bible Translators-Summer Institute of Learning (WBT-SIL) circles, captured that vision. That led to an invitation to consult and then help facilitate a unique gathering of select WBT-SIL leaders in August 2006 at the Orlando WBT-USA headquarters. Kirk and Bob Creson, president of WBC-USA, coordinated this singular conversation and Bob's invitation letter posed the question: "How might we better engage Wycliffe leaders with missiological issues related to Bible translation?"

That week I spoke to WBT-SIL staff in their chapel service, quoting from my father's journals from the 1937 summer at Camp Wycliffe—its second training program in Siloam Springs, AR. The linguistic translation giants led it: Eugene Nida (who gave my parents a cash gift at the time of $20—today's value around $400), Kenneth Pike, and Cameron Townsend. Later I received a photograph of that remarkable cohort. Ironically, Dad failed his morphology exam, which then led them to join Central American Mission. I pondered how different my life would have been had my parents become Bible translators—one of history's paradoxes and providences.

Those days with WBT-SIL colleagues were deeply satisfying as gifted, experienced, and committed linguists and other key leaders grappled with the central issue: how can they and their organizations think missiologically. The question I asked SIL/WBT was: Who are your reflective practitioners, your resident missiologists? What space must you provide?

I asked them to search Cameron Townsend's archives to discover his biblical and practical ecclesiology. It did not surprise me that the legendary founder had said little about the local church, whether in sending or receiving nations. Regretfully, schedule conflicts did not allow me to journey with them in their succeeding missiological forums.

Various friends and colleagues from Latin America like Samuel Escobar, René Padilla, Danny Carroll, and Emilio Antonio Núñez prodded and shaped my thinking. The circle of influence in my life grew: Paul Hiebert and Miriam Adeney, James Engel, Philip Jenkins, Lamin Sanneh, and Patrick Johnston. Some became friends, such as Christopher J. H. Wright. I slowly studied his monumental *The Mission of God: Unlocking the Bible's Grand Narrative*. At the Cape Town Lausanne Congress in 2010 I acquired his *The Mission of God's People: A Biblical Theology of the Church's Mission*. In late 2023 while I was working on this manuscript, he told me of his latest book, *The Great Story and the Great Commission: Participating in the Biblical Drama of Mission*.

Again, I read, underlined, matured.

In 2013, SETECA released the revised and enlarged edition of *Misiones Mundiales*. I had determined to correct my inadequate 1984 missiology. My coauthor, Eugenio Campos, died during the editing, but remained as coauthor. The new workbook tracked the Triune God on mission, introducing new vocabulary: mission, missional, missions, missiological, mission servants, and integral mission. It addressed the new challenges missionaries face today. The 1,700 participants of the 2017 fourth COMIBAM (Cooperación Misionera Iberoamericana) congress in Bogotá, Colombia, received a free copy. Hundreds of Latin American cross-cultural workers received a copy of the Spanish version of *Sorrow and Blood* as well, to highlight additional challenges to missions. It will be used as a text for the missions course in the Spanish program of Trinity Anglican Seminary. An updated version was printed in 2025.

Over the decades, two missiological journals nourished my heart and mind, *Evangelical Missions Quarterly* (EMQ), and the *International Bulletin of Missionary Research* (IBMR). The first is exclusively evangelical, while the second shares a broader confessional platform. Both reemerged virtually and under new sponsorship. Missio Nexus revitalized EMQ. IBMR changed one word—from "missionary" to "mission" and it is now produced by Princeton Theological Seminary. Until recently I was honored to know all the EMQ editors and six previous IBMR editors. I had a complete collection of EMQ from its founding in 1964, which I later donated to SETECA's library. *Mission Frontiers*, produced by the US Center for World Mission, updated readers on news from their particular missiological focus—the less-reached peoples and church planting movements. Ralph Winter's clarion call at Lausanne 1974 had launched a vision and a passion shaping great segments of the global mission movement today. His course, *Perspectives on the World Christian Movement*, remains an important resource. I taught the course in the US for decades, but I regret that its translation into Spanish wasn't contextualized and it disregarded the bourgeoning Latin mission movement.

Over the years I have observed gifted younger colleagues and mission activists who served with zeal and integrity. Yet in time they paused, asking good and hard questions. Some chose to study for advanced degrees, most of them transitioned into new leadership roles.

Bill Taylor had become a different person now, a reflective practitioner, a global missiologist, an intentional mentor. The new roles provided a profoundly satisfying freedom.

Our Upside-Down Mission World

When reviewing my life in mission I am astounded to realize that I lived to witness two old reductionisms that have been put to rest. First, the missions community transitioned from a simplistic view of mission—proclamation, primarily if not exclusively—to a robust Trinitarian and integral theology of mission. Second, the former world evangelization binary—the West to the Rest (demeaning language to identify the Majority World)—radically changed. That brings new style and equations of voice and leadership, church and mission structures, visions and ways of looking at the church's task on mission. It requires a further serious re-examination of the older paradigms of strategic alliances.

Two ironies. Never in his wildest dreams would my father have imagined in the 1940s that the son of an early Costa Rica convert would become a medical missionary with Operation Mobilization (OM). Mireya, my early childhood nanny, would finish her studies, marry, and see her son graduate from dental school in Costa Rica. She then released him when he dedicated his life and vocation to cross-cultural mission. He served on the Logos ship and married a Dutch worker with shared passions. They settled in Holland, and he would never return to live in Costa Rica.

But then, for many years, neither would I, my father's son, have dreamed of that possibility. In God's time I became a participant observer and then a proactive agent of change for these powerful realities in the epic story of God on mission. The world changed. My missional world was transformed. I was transformed. I am being transformed.

Chris Wright *named* what I was observing and experiencing.

> The map of global Christianity that our grandparents knew has been turned upside down. At the start of the twentieth century, only ten percent of the world's Christians lived in the continents of the south and east. Ninety percent lived in North America and Europe, along with Australia and New Zealand. But at the start of the twenty-first century, at least seventy percent of the world's Christians live in the non-Western world—more appropriately called the Majority World.

> More Christians worship in Anglican churches in Nigeria each week than in all the Episcopal and Anglican churches of Britain, Europe, and North America combined. There are more Baptists in Congo than in Britain. More people in church every Sunday in communist China than in all of Western Europe. Ten times more Assemblies of God members in Latin America than in the US.
>
> The old peripheries are now the center. The old centers are now on the periphery.[2]

His essay named and capped my own long missiological journey, from the old binary mission to a mature mission movement, mutuality-marked, multi-based, and poly-directional. I renew and revisit my study of Old Testament passages woven through the historical books, Psalms and prophets that reveal the heart of God for the peoples, the world's *goy*. I marvel at Solomon's audacious prayer for the gentile who would come to the temple and worship his or her own gods there, then Solomon's unexpected petition, in 1 Kings 8:41–43.

Conclusions and Lessons

I fast forward to today, reviewing how the landscape of global mission has changed; I see more clearly the price paid for so many believers and churches to follow Jesus faithfully; I witness new dimensions and definitions of "church"; mission moving even beyond multi-based and poly-directional to complex polycentric and *beyond*. Will the historic power brokers and players humbly learn new ways of discussing, listening, deciding, creating systems and mechanisms, implementing decisions?

Behold Jesus, born into a poor and powerless family. Mary gave birth to the Babe King in a stable. Jesus was the child refugee with Mary and Joseph in Egypt for an undetermined time. He incarnated in Jewish society with its power players, influence peddlers, compromising religious performers, revolutionaries underground, and those who had abandoned the public arena going into the Qumran caves. Such a contrast to the Greco-Roman pantheon of gods and power seekers.

Jesus, the Servant King, baptized then tested by Satan, emerged on the scene. He selected a highly disparate band to become first apprentices

---

2 Wright, *An Upside-Down World*.

and later apostles. Jesus gave space to his women apprentices, those who followed and supported him. His was the downward journey to the passion and cross. Mary of Magdala, whom Jesus had freed from seven demons, would become the first resurrection witness, a female apostle to the apostles, *apostolorum apostola*. This picture of Jesus became the leadership exemplar for me. During that retrospective search for leadership models the Voice said, "Well Bill, of course, it's Jesus who modeled leadership from below." Jesus also became my example of the reflective practitioner. As are Paul—apostle, long-term-cross-cultural church planter, author, theologian, martyr—and John: apostle, pastor, author, prisoner, prophet, poet, man of a natural death. And many more.

This chapter began with me as a first term missionary with an embryonic missiology focused on the practical metrics which would reward a successful young evangelical American missionary, unaware of my leadership gifts. However, studying this season of my own development and growth, I realize that the missiological foundations that shape me to this very day prepared me for leadership. My maturation into a reflective practitioner, and the consultations and ideas God brought transformed me.

Was it just another dimension of little Billy who grew up unevenly? Perhaps. Yet I did grow up, and at the right season of life and in the right context of ministry, in the arena of global mission. The Spirit endowed me and released into new dimensions of leadership.

I'm astonished as I review my life in mission, thanking God for the honor of serving in such radically changing times ... and the change is not over. How marvelous that God has an upside-down world perspective. How unique that the members of the missional Trinity are each major players in God's eternal redemption plan.

Reflection Questions

1. What are the strengths and weaknesses of not being aware that one is a leader, even though he or she truly is one?
2. What is your reaction to the definition of "reflective practitioner"?
3. In what ways does the Spirit empower servants to emerge into leadership roles?
4. What's the relationship between one's missiological development and leadership self-understanding?
5. In what ways is Jesus a "reflective practitioner"?

5
Keep the Main Thing the Main Thing

> Fundamentally, our mission (if it is biblically informed and validated) means our committed participation as God's people, at God's invitation and command, in God's own mission within the history of God's world for the redemption of God's creation.[1]

Womb Shaped Theology

In 1984 the TEDS faculty, board, mission department, dean and president interviewed me as potential faculty. It was an intense yet rewarding exchange on my ministry, my gifts, my training, and, of course, my theology (nobody asked about my family). One professor asked, "Bill, as a Dallas Theological Seminary grad, do you still hold to the full DTS doctrinal statement?" I responded: "I was waiting for that one. As you know, all doctrinal statements are products of history, culture, and particular theological concerns. DTS's is extended; TEDS's is shorter, identical to its mother denomination, the Evangelical Free Church of America. I differ on some DTS points. I don't use dispensational language because it has limited currency, especially in global arenas. I prefer 'God's varied economies of grace' I sense that God will surprise us all in the eschaton's specifics. However, I trust that no TEDS professor would caricature the DTS stance or its graduates. We are all on a journey." My explanations were accepted. I was invited.

I suspect my spiritual and theological journey began while in my mother's womb—born a cessationist (in terms of the gifts of the Spirit) as well as a separated fundamentalist (strictly adhering to the tenets of faith and separated from the world) due to the family I was born into. What did I know of these terms, or care then? That's just the nature of nature and nurture. Unwittingly our biological families impart systemic yet invisible constructs that shape, under-shape, and misshape us all. These undetectable realities create theological binaries within us—us versus them. Hopefully our God journey challenges us to ask our theological system hard questions. That was my case.

---

[1] Wright, *The Mission of God*, 22–23.

In his *Confessions*, Saint Augustine asked himself hard questions, one being his conjecture on how preborn intellect had shaped or misshaped him.[2] He caused me to question the ideology I was raised/born with. As I entered early adulthood I began thinking critically, starting with notions, niggling questions, and suspicions, "This isn't the way things are supposed to be or work, is it?" Thus, I initiated my journey to sort out the mysteries of God, Jesus, the Spirit, our Christian framework, our experience, our future, our personal family faith, and the way we did missions and church. Could I have been a Pentecostal, Reformed, Catholic, secular, or even Hindu? Each of these groups has their own "fundamentalists." Our initial faith life can depend on our parents, geography, culture, and the broader religious milieu. Thank God I was raised Christian in a gracious and godly family line. We assume we are all objective when coming to Scripture; that's what I used to think a long time ago. But it doesn't work that way. Deep questions can deepen sincere faith. Doubts can be healthy if wisely stewarded. Doubts can also kill faith. You gotta doubt your doubts!

I am struck by God's gracious mercy to guide my gradual awakening and my theological queries. I remember well my three major faith battles (my senior year in university; doctoral studies at University of Texas; and during my daughter's crisis of faith when she was twenty-one). Grappling with the uniqueness of the Christian faith in turn led me to more substantive, intellectual, philosophical, and theological foundations.

I inherited and was taught during seven years of formal biblical-theological study a specific system, tabbed "rightly dividing the Word of truth." The structure was not a Moody lynchpin, but it was at Dallas Seminary, especially in eschatology. Those years profoundly enriched me. I thank God for the legacy I received from many professors. I learned to think biblically. I learned to love-study the Word (reinforcing my IVCF experience). I gained the skills that would ground all my teaching and preaching. The biblical study habits prepared me for my lifelong service in mission and contributed to the grounding of my future leadership. Yet my questions even back then had to do with the system. At that time, we were required to agree with DTS's full doctrinal affirmation in order to graduate. I could, with twinges. My serious variations emerged over time but always within historic, orthodox Christian theology. I was always an innately convinced evangelical.

---

2 Augustine, *Confessions*, 25.

The previous chapter tracked my missiological awakenings. I became self-identified as a reflective practitioner—a robust appellative for us MC leaders, and as a missiologist, though more on the practitioner side of the concept. This chapter focuses on theological reflection. Still, at the end of the day, I'm a practitioner. My concerns, even as a Latin American PhD or a leader of the MC, focused on how my knowledge and experience could shape the ways we could better equip women and men for transformational, effective ministry in the Spanish-speaking world.

> I became self-identified as a reflective practitioner.

The Habits of Reading

Since childhood I have loved to read. I recall the Saturday morning bike rides to Wheaton's public library with my sister Grace, always returning books and carrying home another basket load. To this day I prefer books over film.

My reading falls into diverse categories. First, for serious study. This could be for personal growth for preparing to preach, teach, or write, or for more substantive spiritual formation. These books I read slowly, marking them up—a habit I inherited from my father. My thick German-made blue/red pencils travel with me. My father's last ruler helps me underline in careful study. I call these the "blue and red books," and I never give them away. These are the category of books that have shaped my theology and missiology, my spirituality and pastoralia, and in some cases, my world realities. This category includes *Why Nations Fail: The Origin of Power, Prosperity, and Poverty* (Acemoglu and Robinson), which a South African friend recommended. It was informative and disturbing. Augustine's *Confessions* was a deep well of vulnerability and honesty.

A second category is for general information or growth. I don't underline these books, but I take them seriously. They include books on current events, culture, history, mission, and spirituality. As I prepared to lead the editorial team for *Sorrow and Blood: Christian Mission in Contexts of Suffering, Persecution and Martyrdom*, I saturated my heart and mind in eighty-five books on those themes. In preparation for what you are reading, I worked through some forty-five leadership books, biographies, memoirs, and autobiographies by both secular and Christian authors.

Finally, for fun I read different genres: spy and detective writers like Daniel Silva, John Grisham and Olen Steinhauer, but also grittier British writers such as Ian Rankin, Peter Robinson, John le Carré, Henning Mankell. My penchant is to read many books by the same author (their *oeuvre*) to capture the fullness of their style, diversity, and topics. I've done that with perhaps twenty authors, including C. S. Lewis, Francis and Edith Schaeffer, David Howard, Elisabeth Elliot, Frederick Buechner, Stephen Lawhead, Paul Hiebert, Chaim Potok (identifying with his Jewish fundamentalism), Marilynne Robinson, Orson Scott Card, Alexander McCall Smith (the whimsical *Ladies #1 Detective Agency* series), Mark Helprin, Amor Towles, Daniel Silva, John Grisham, Ian Rankin, and others. Years ago, Yvonne and I read Susan Howatch's Starbridge Series balanced with heavy doses of Henri Nouwen and Eugene Peterson. I read all the Harry Potter books and viewed the movies, much preferring the truly Christian worldviews, true myth, and the epic stories of Lewis and Tolkien. You find no admixtures in these two writers, saturated with redemptive mythology and deep wonder.

My son David introduced me to science fiction, some with provocative missiological implications: *The Sparrow* series by Mary Doria Russell and *The Book of Strange New Things* by Michael Faber. I was intrigued that so much sci-fi literature features precocious children or youth. Utopian worlds depend on naïve, pure, younger generations. But excessive sad dystopia wore me down and I had to take a break. Recently I read through Wendell Berry's novels and short stories, discovering parallels with my own Britt grandparent's family farm near Stone Mountain, GA, now a housing development. The Britt magnolia tree alone lives on as mute monument to a lost past. Amor Towles' *A Gentleman in Moscow* and Markus Zusak's *The Book Thief* captured me during COVID-19. *The Overstory*, by Richard Powers, made me love trees.

From my first Urbana, 1962, I followed China veteran and Fuller missiologist Art Glasser's counsel: to read secular news and a weekly magazine so we could understand the times but read them in light of our Christian faith. He echoed Karl Barth, "Take your Bible and take your newspaper and read both. But interpret newspapers from your Bible." For decades I subscribed to *Time Magazine*, then quit in disgust for its soft porn. Daily I peruse some ten news platforms from Europe, Latin America, Africa, Asia, and the USA. Each secular platform spotlights current events from its own perspective-bias. They seem to report on different planets. Whom to believe or disbelieve? Only a wise, composite reading sorts and sifts the news while asking the Spirit to enlighten me from a robust biblical worldview.

I discerned recently how my own books trace my writing development and hence my maturation. Writing them transformed me into a more substantive reflective practitioner. My Spanish books (coauthored with Latin Americans) tackled courtship, marriage, and missions for the local church. They were practical and relevant to pastoral ministry in Latin America and, surprisingly, continue to sell. *Crisis and Hope in Latin America: An Evangelical Perspective*, written with Emilio Antonio Núñez, caused me to dig deeper to better understand and explain missiology for the Latin American context.

The early publications that I edited for the Mission Commission reflected my grass-roots concern for mission practice: missionary training, strategic alliances, and missionary attrition. The reflective practitioner in me emerged with the extensive missiological resource anthology, *Global Missiology for the Twenty-first Century: The Iguassu Dialogue* generated by that 1999 Consultation. *Sorrow and Blood* provoked grief and lament as I read those stories and counted the price paid for obedience to Jesus. *Spirituality in Mission* culminated my passion to serve the global community on mission. It also reflected my own maturation in the spiritual theology that must shape the private interior landscape as well as my commitment to finish well.

Why this short section on reading? Partly because I'm befuddled with mission leaders and teachers bereft of serious reading habits. Do they choose to simply do/work, even in the classroom? Perhaps some of their parents didn't encourage reading, but they remain, strangely, nonreaders, though they may reference the articles or books in their expertise or the books on their shelves. Others prefer to be nurtured by blogs and podcasts, or to drink deeply from internet sites. I believe true leaders must be steadfast readers, asking reading to mature them.

Transitions in Tension

Over the years I gradually travelled from fundamentalist (the moderate version of adhering to the tenets of faith I grew up in) to a more gracious, orthodox, global evangelical. Today I self-identify as a three-stranded Anglican follower of Christ: evangelical—rooted in Scripture; charismatic—empowered by the Spirit; liturgical—sacramental in worship and life. It does complicate things when asked what my religion is. I simply say, "I am a devoted follower of Jesus the Christ; many call us Christians."

I recognize that the term "evangelical" evokes negative connotations. Mainstream media have unfairly yet successfully caricatured us as anti-intellectual, bigoted, American right-wing racists. American Christian leaders in particular try to create new terminology. However, for me no other term within Christianity's streams better explains who we are. It simply must be clarified and then affirmed. That language prepared me for thirty years with WEA. We were evangelicals in the global and best sense of the word. The term still has high currency in our global arenas. And we know that 77 percent of all "evangelical" Christians now live in Africa, Latin America and the Caribbean, Asia, and Oceania—regions of the Majority World.[3]

My transition in theological identification was strongly shaped during four visits to Dallas Seminary during 1995: In January of that year Yvonne and I experienced a challenging January spiritual life conference; in April a board meeting, during which I stepped down after five years; in May while teaching a summer school class; and in November while delivering missiological lectures. I was invited for all four visits for three reasons. First, I was a DTS graduate. Second, I was also a global mission leader. Finally, my experience with worldwide theological education had given me a unique perspective and authority.

The November missional lectures are important for their focus on theological process. In preparation for those missional lectures, the Spirit freed me to speak as a reflective practitioner and from my missiological journey. I mined the doxological passages of Revelation, revisiting contextualization, discussing how we might better equip servants for ministry, sharing the "confessions of a theoretical supernaturalist."

The contextualization topic tracked five stages of "doing theology": Exegetical study creates biblical theology; it can transition into systematic theology's classic and newer categories. But much theological study ends there. I suggest two further steps. We submit our systems anew to the Scriptures to discern whether those declarations need to be revisited. Finally, we ask whether our system needs modification. That chapel provoked a fascinating discussion during the faculty bag lunch. The church history chair, a friend, asked "Bill, you aren't saying that we need to change the system, but rather that we need to submit it to Scripture again? Right?" My response was, "Yes. I'm simply inviting us to

---

3 See WEA's declaration on the term "Evangelical." https://worldea.org/who-we-are/who-are-evangelicals/.

evaluate whether Scripture truly confirms any statement that's a product of culture and history. The result may introduce thoughtful revisions."

I recounted my 1989 interview to serve on the DTS board when its vice-chair had stated, "Bill, all doctrinal statements are products of culture and time." In recent years I have seen how healthy, extended, and strategic processes can lead churches and denominations, mission agencies, institutions, Christian colleges, and seminaries to modify facets of their doctrinal affirmation—without departing from or diluting orthodoxy. Sadly, I know all too well the case study of a prime Latin American seminary's departure from Scripture and historic confessions. Recently the Evangelical Free Church of America (EFCA) modeled a healthy revision of their doctrinal affirmation, which automatically modified the TEDS statement. I was pleasantly surprised to read in 2023 how DTS leadership led a process to modify its affirmation of faith—twenty-eight years after my 1995 lectures.

For many years my preaching journey found me captured by the twenty or so doxological scenarios in Revelation. That missiological and worship study overwhelmed me with discovery both in preparation and preaching. I had never contemplated those diverse scenes, analogous to cascading water, a trickling brook, or massive waterfalls—I visualized Victoria, Iguassu, or Niagara Falls. And interwoven into so many scenes were the "ransomed people for God from every tribe and language and people and nation." This final book of Scripture is profoundly pastoral, ecclesial, cosmic, doxological and missiological from start to finish—the crucial lessons of hope that persecuted believers needed to hear and read. And woven through this pastoral apocalypse were the threads of persecution, martyrdom, the final judgment of demons and humans with two ultimate destinies, which culminating in the triumph of God in Christ and the New Creation. I am preaching the book again now, under the title "Different lenses unveil the apocalypse." I shall never forget one TEDS African doctoral student who, when given the assignment to read Revelation in one sitting, exclaimed the next morning, "Dr. Taylor, this book was written in code and only Christians understand it." Yes!

I "returned to seminary" (Yvonne joining me) when David, Christine, and Christine's husband Cliff studied at Regent College. I wanted to understand what and how they were learning, which professors deeply impacted them, what it was like to study in that community, what they were learning about God, Scripture, mission, and church. David returned to Austin each summer season to serve at Hope Chapel. I took his intensive courses on comparative religions and hermeneutics. My life had been irrevocably changed at DTS under Professor Hendricks' course on Bible study methods. However, there we had atomized the biblical text in the classic inductive Bible study methods. David started with story and narrative in Ruth. I was intrigued and determined to teach more creatively.

I've had close interaction with scores of Christian colleges, diverse institutes, and seminaries around the world. Each has its own historical DNA, its emphases and qualities that mark their graduates. Each has positives and negatives. In my days, DTS was men-only. Regretfully, we did not learn to study with, listen to, relate to, nor learn from women students. That unwittingly handicapped us as we moved into vocational ministry, weakening my understanding of leadership in the early years. Regent's foundation was healthy, though with founding tensions. Their original purpose was to equip women and men for life in all vocations, especially the marketplace. Training for vocational ministry came years later, despite strenuous disagreement from a founder. One grad told me regretfully that Regent affirmed all vocations except the cross-cultural missionary.

DTS equipped me to study Scripture, and then to teach and preach it (pedagogy and homiletics). Too many seminaries today don't provide those foundational curricular planks. They assume wrongly that their grads will be able to teach and preach well. DTS has been criticized for its eschatological stance. But the other extreme is worse, graduating students bereft of the eschatological story line of Scripture, lacking confidence to teach the "hope that is within us." Our pulpits today don't really deal with the eschatological dimensions of the Apostle's and Nicene Creeds.

Yvonne and I traveled often to visit our growing family in Vancouver. One summer we studied under Regent faculty: Yvonne with Robert Webber and James Houston, I in seminars on spirituality from Eugene Peterson and Houston. I discovered the importance of "mystery"—having been misshaped by Christianized Western rationality. We learned that magnificent, challenging-to-sing hymn, "St. Patrick's Breastplate Prayer." I became a consciously Trinitarian believer through my family at Regent.

Other long-term, cross-cultural workers have pilgrimaged similar and divergent paths. Friends and colleagues have had their own journey, and I have tracked many of them. While some ended up in very different camps from their early years, others modulated within their system, flexing and broadening their perspective. Some friends and colleagues never questioned their first theological framework or system—a different journey. And all these experiences equipped me for the next stages of leadership as my sphere of influence grew with colleagues in global spaces and places.

Conclusions and Lessons

My theological metaphor is *journey*, the pilgrimage of the path, of process and essence rather than closed system. It seeks more of Scripture's richness and substance, more of biblical theology. If needed I can operate within classical theological categories, with a theologian-artist-professor son. It is imperative as a reflective practitioner that I think theologically.

At the end of the day, I know which historic Christian doctrines are critical to me. This stance must mark the thoughtful Christian leader, and we should not be pressed into anemic theology or missiology. Questioning the system we were born into or received must be done with seriousness, grace, and integrity. I am not impressed by those with changed theology who delight in shredding those who did not equally change. Leadership must be humble. The church is global. Evangelicalism can stand healthy, biblical diversity.

> **My theological metaphor is *journey*, the pilgrimage of the path, of process and essence rather than closed system.**

Significantly, around 1991 or 1992, the DTS faculty submitted a crucial proposal to the board: for both acceptance and graduation, students should adhere only to seven core doctrinal affirmations—not the entire DTS statement. DTS would now welcome students from Pentecostal, Arminian, sacramental, and reformed theological backgrounds. On the board during that watershed discussion and decision, I asked the academic dean how faculty would modify teaching and student evaluation. Instruction and evaluation must change. I asked whether this decision came from marketing issues or to a broader vision of the church. The answer was, "both." Independently of DTS, SETECA around the same time developed its own concise list of core convictions for students to both entrance and graduation.

I faced a new doctrinal challenge with reformed theology as an adjunct professor at the short-lived Redeemer Seminary Austin. Prior to my assignment, the dean sent me their affirmation, the *Westminster*

Confession (I was told to disregard the paragraph on sabbath). Could I agree on the rest? As I worked through this historic declaration, I disagreed especially with double predestination. We spoke and corresponded back and forth. They needed a professor, and "flexed" with me. Finally, the dean candidly said something like, "Bill, let me write something for you and you tell me if you can sign off on it." He did. I did.

On which theological hills would I shed blood? What is my faith's irreducible core? The fourth-century issues leading to the *Nicene Creed* reveal theological battles of that time, primarily the Trinity and the person of Christ, taking two councils (AD 325, AD 381) to finalize this watershed creed. Significantly, major debates today are Christological. While Nicaea offered no clarion call to "mission," it provided our foundation, our Christology, both cornerstone and stumbling block around the world. Jesus is unique and we follow him in mission as gracious exclusivists. As the MC leader, WEA's statement of faith became my strong, safe, essentialist harbor. My decades experience with the global body of Christ, serving with trusted colleagues across the ecclesial and theological streams of the broad waters of global evangelicalism, settled my core convictions.

Years ago, I discovered commonalities between the WEA statement and Regent College. James Houston, one of its founders, told me that in their early search for a doctrinal affirmation it was WEA's statement that shaped their own declaration of broad, core convictions. Today I am renewing my study of biblical eschatological passages. Both *Nicene* and *Apostle's Creeds* have specific line items that reference eschatology, as do the WEA and DTS statements. So, what is my understanding of the future? Do I relegate it to a tertiary category? Is my vision both dystopic and utopic? Have too many churches today emphasized so much our present life in Christ today, our commitment to compassion and justice so much that we neglect Scripture's theology of hope? Hope does not imply a cosmic Dunkirk; it declares expectation for our wounded world. A Just Judgment *is* forthcoming! Many charismatic platforms and churches teach prophetic themes and it's not escapism. I wonder what it will take for pastors to question their own silence.

Today some of my younger Christian friends around the world grapple with foundational theological challenges, particularly due to militant philosophical and moral relativism. These questions must be faced and addressed. Can Jesus be singular but not unique? Must conversionary mission sit in the heart of the Christian faith? Can we trust the biblical understanding of personhood, gender, sex, and marriage? Is there an ultimate purpose to the chaos and wounding of the cosmos? How well does our faith address structural injustice and poverty? What about AI? What must we believe about the final judgment and eternity? Is hell eternal or temporal?

I identify with these questions and have battled through doubt into certainty. I know there are other issues, but at the end of the day, I stake my life on the thoughtful Christian response to all of them. I am also aware that these questions have become stumbling blocks for too many of my fellow TCK's around the world. Many of us have children and grandchildren who have drifted or deliberately walked away from a strong personal faith in Jesus. I hope and weep, yearn, and pray.

Lastly, I address a very personal word. Dad's last request, shortly before Alzheimer's embezzled his mind, was: "Son, when I die, put on my tombstone, 'Lord, I believe; help my unbelief.'" He refused to explain yet another of his cryptic sayings. My sister rejected Dad's request, but I wonder, was Dad on to something? That even towards the end of the journey we must live by faith, not reason alone? Yes. Mystery.

At this stage of my leadership life, I want to live as a TCK pilgrim, a globalized evangelical, but, most importantly, a devoted follower of Jesus Christ. At the end of the day, it's all about Jesus. I ask God to increase my love for his Word, all of it, recognizing the challenge to read and reread it, not to deconstruct it but to allow it and the Spirit to deconstruct me and my preconceptions of God and his ways in the world. I read Scripture through the eyes of others—the younger generations, our family, the marginalized, abused and weak, the children and the women, the powerful and the wealthy, the damned and the animist, the secular and people of other faiths.

In my case, biblical and theological maturation gave new dimensions and wisdom to my leadership. Yes, in the earliest stages, my womb-based theological framework sustained me. I did not question that system until my mid-twenties. In retrospect, my confidence flowed from the conviction that Scripture, the Spirit, and wisdom would guide me into all truth. The arenas of leadership given to me were marked by those convictions, held with gentle yet strong faith.

During my three WEA decades nobody thought less of me because I was a Moody or a DTS grad. Those academic pedigree trophies had little to do with my status within WEA, yet at the same time they played a significant, invisible role. They had shaped me. Yet, again, every thoughtful graduate of a theological institution (whether Reformed, Pentecostal-charismatic, Baptist, Arminian, independent, dispensational, or any other) sooner or later should grapple with the questions and examination of theology. Is the way I was taught Scripture, theology, missiology, practical theology, or any other substantive category the *only* way. Is it the *right* way? Let us ask hard questions with integrity and within community.

Thank God the MC's heartbeat thrummed on relationship, on mutuality, on collegiality, on collective wisdom, on shared values. All are facets of leadership from below. I wanted my prime model to be that courageous, unorthodox Servant King, Jesus the Christ, whom I follow to this day.

This is where I am, this is who I am, this is who I want to be: learning, purposing to finish strong and well, walking the latter laps.

Reflection Questions

1. What does it mean that we begin our spiritual and theological journey in our mother's womb?
2. What kind of reading categories and habits do you have?
   What are your thoughts about Bill's habits?
   Why are many leaders not readers?
3. In what way are doctrinal statements products of culture and time? What implications does that have to the leader of a mission agency or school with an inherited theological system? Which institutions do you know that changed their statement of faith?
4. What is the relationship between quality leadership and biblical-theological foundations?
5. What does it mean to know which convictions are hills to die on?

6
Always on Pilgrimage

> And I tell you, you are Peter, and on this rock, I will build my church, and the gates of hell shall not prevail against it. I will give you the keys of the kingdom of heaven, and whatever you bind on earth shall be bound in heaven, and whatever you loose on earth shall be loosed in heaven. (Matt 16:18–19)
>
> Blessed are those whose strength is in you, whose hearts are set on pilgrimage. (Ps 84:5 NIV)

Also, in My Mother's Womb

It's a peculiar story, mine is.

I was born low-church evangelical (by this I mean our understanding of being a Christian was committed to the authority of Scripture, focused on a simple gospel, "separated from the world" in personal practices, conversion being the great miracle with supernatural gifts limited to the first century, and semi-nondenominational). My parents served their entire lives with what was then called The Central American Mission (founded in 1890 by C. I. Scofield and other like-minded American mission mobilizers; later called CAM International, then Camino Global, then merged into Avant Ministries). The organization had a street address in Dallas. Who would have dreamed in 1890 that it would become a multi-nation, full-blown denomination with its own ecclesiastical principles and practices, ethos and regulations, ordination and disciplinary systems; that it would broaden to include diverse institutions—churches, bookstores, radio stations, clinics and hospitals, orphanages, printing presses, language analysis, Bible translation, literacy programs, schools, Bible institutes, and seminaries? The ecclesial body was called *Las Iglesias Centroamericanas*. Under different names the denomination would expand into Mexico, Spain, and Hispanic North America.

Then, in 1968, thirty years after my folks joined, CAM International became mine and Yvonne's agency. By then it was moderately diverse doctrinally, and it was ecclesially open to candidates who were either Baptists, Presbyterians, Methodists, or independents, though guided and guarded by a clear statement of evangelical faith. It was flexible on ecclesiology (emphasizing elders, deacons, and deaconesses) and the mode of baptism. In eastern Guatemala to this day churches generally baptize by aspersion—pouring or sprinkling—while the western region primarily immerses—submerged in the water. *Las Iglesias Centroamericanas* in Guatemala today register over 1,500 churches, with lesser numbers in the other countries of Central America. In Mexico they were called *Iglesias Bíblicas*. In Spain the new congregations affiliated with the Brethren Assemblies because our workers served under their relational and legal umbrella.

Dad has Presbyterian roots, Mother more on the Baptist side. In Latin America we were "people of the two books"—Bible and hymnal. No theology of architecture guided those first *templos*. Generally new groups started in homes, becoming what was called a *congregación* until formal leadership emerged; and then they were called *Iglesias*, an official church with a certain number of baptized members and at least a part-time pastor. They would rent until they constructed a functional, rectangular, tile or tin-roofed structure.

We were plain in dress and plain in worship, the order of service (liturgy) established by the Spanish hymnal translated (with adaptation) from The Christian Missionary and Alliance of the USA. God loves those who worship in spirit and in truth, which to us meant according to the plain gospel! Our denomination claimed a monopoly on what was called *la sana doctrina* (correct doctrine). If the Catholics did it, we didn't—whether reciting the Lord's Prayer, the Apostles Creed, written liturgy, or wearing vestments. We were separated from the world, the flesh, the devil, Catholics, and some other so-called evangelicals, especially the Pentecostals and later the neo-charismatics. They had their version of *sana doctrina*; the "the healthy gospel." We certainly did not believe in speaking in tongues, and "the greatest miracle" was conversion. We had first, second, and even third-degrees of those whose churches had separated over doctrinal issues in our circles.

> How in the world could this checkered ecclesial backdrop equip me for global leadership with evangelicals of every stripe and doctrinal particularity?

How in the world could this checkered ecclesial backdrop equip me for global leadership with evangelicals of every stripe and emphasis and structure and doctrinal particularity?

The Uncertain Church Pilgrimage—Personal and Global

My family's 1957 furlough/home-leave coincided with my senior year in high school. My sister, Grace, studied at Wheaton College. We traveled from Guatemala to Wheaton, IL, and I attended Wheaton Bible Church. The youth group was remarkably welcoming of this sixteen-year-old naïve MK from Guatemala. During my three Moody years in Chicago, I attended or served in a variety of congregations in English or Spanish but had no home church. Transferring to North Texas University to conclude my college studies, Dad recommended I check out a small Independent Presbyterian Church (the word "Independent" was important). That was my first induction into a different way of doing church. There I discovered something called *The Apostle's Creed*, which I had never heard of. They also recited the Lord's Prayer every Sunday. Heavy stuff for me!

They worshipped with a set order of service called a "liturgy." They had elders, like my Latin America experience, but the Presbyterian elder was different from CAM church elders. This church set their DNA after their separation from the Presbyterian Church USA, a division that introduced a time-released virus into the church. Division later led to another acrimonious split. I shall never forget the Sunday morning at noon when the pastor marched out with his followers. I had never witnessed a church rupture. It was sad. And it tore the youth group I led.

During my WEA decades I discovered countless examples of mission agencies with a "home country" office, but a denomination "on the field." It was a global reality of mission history from the West. Today's variants include Brazilian Baptist, or Korean Presbyterian, or Nigerian Pentecostal church planting congregations and denominations far from the home country. Things get complicated with multinational and multi-ecclesial teams serving "on the field," especially when the Korean Presbyterian pastor visits and asks why the church is not Presbyterian. Churches planted by YWAM staff early on resembled Assemblies of God youth groups.

In the nineteenth century, those first agencies often divided up national geography by "comity agreement." These agreements worked until two major changes took place: growing urbanization, which brought denominational diversity to the cities, and the global Pentecostal explosion in the early twentieth century which permanently dissolved comity boundaries.

Over our seventeen years based in Guatemala, we saw that too many of our churches were claiming *la sana doctrina* but sliding into institutionalism, spiritual atrophy, legalism, and a faded liturgy. The lack of vitality and vision was evident in these older churches. Something was wrong. Questions emerged, niggling at me. What causes ecclesial institutionalism? Can it be reversed? What identifies a vital, growing visionary church? Why did the New Testament give such little instruction on church form and structure but emphasized requirements and quality of church leadership? What role does worship style play? Most of these churches, now dubbed "traditional," have become moribund, disregarding Spirit-guided renewal, new church planting, and innovative leadership and worship.

In God's providence, he gifted us with the challenges and joys of church planting in Guatemala. It allowed me, with others, to experiment with other expressions of being and doing church. Yes, we did some things right in a community composed of probably 50 percent older believers and 50 percent new ones. What did it mean to lead as a pastor-elder in another culture? One of the greatest benefits of service at Centro Bíblico el Camino was the partnership Yvonne and I shared. She was her own person, and together we matured in parallel tracks, serving cross-culturally in evangelism, discipleship, and teaching. Her commitment to prayer and fasting marked the rest of her life's trajectory. But we were just one model of church, and I was to learn much more.

Years later, the WEA decades found me facing similar quandaries but in a global context across all the denominations where cross-cultural mission was a high priority. My Latin American experience gave me historical perspective, yet I experienced surprises. Worshipping one Sunday in Jos, Nigeria, I felt I was in England during the first hour, with a weary imported liturgy. But imperceptibly, a transition took place, and we returned to Africa in worship, instruments, freedom, and dance. A similar experience took place while preaching at an historic Baptist church in Hyderabad, India. The transposed English liturgy held forth for over an hour. The shift took place as the worship band replaced the formal choir, the style radically changed, and I returned to contemporary India. I preached from a pulpit very high above the audience (having seen a similar pulpit in a Baptist church in Bournemouth, England). The unforgettable Indian service lasted three hours, concluding with a prolonged season of ministry. As the visiting preacher, I served with the ministry team, stretched and surprised even more. People came hungry for God, for a visitation of some sort, with no relationship to the message recently preached. Humbling and healthy.

Yvonne and I have been privileged to worship in both ancient and very new churches, in congregations with lay leadership and those with formally trained leadership, in communities led by dominant leaders and those with collegial style leaders, in home churches and cathedrals. The body of Christ around the world has nourished us. This multicultural feast prepares us for the glorious diversity of worship and life in heaven, practicing worship for the Big One in heaven!

In Arkansas I served a very independent, nondenominational church. After moving to Austin in 1990, we attended a Bible church that partnered with us. Yvonne simultaneously entered her long solitary season of the "Dark Night of the Soul," which coincided with the period of my own spiritual desert. Invited to take over the church's fledgling college-age ministry, we did so despite our own battles. God met us in the worship, teaching, and building of community. That "college plus" group of students and young adults became a healing context for nearly five years. I performed several weddings, and many are friends to this day.

The Spirit led us to Hope Chapel, a gracious charismatic congregation, for a decade. Hope's worship played a major role in my spiritual healing after the bruising Arkansas church experience. They created space for us to walk with freedom as empowered evangelicals. God also sent me to another new school, learning about worship, healing prayer, spiritual warfare, the expectations of the miraculous and physical healing—which both Yvonne and I experienced. Doors opened for both of us to serve, to teach, and for me to preach again. The leadership had a keen missions DNA with a focus on Turkey and the wider Islamic world. Ironically Austin's own local spiritual and human needs were not then a prime missional concern.

Hope didn't require us to become "card-carrying charismatics." I was invited by the pastor to become an elder, but I knew that wasn't my calling. However, we did accept the challenge to craft a mission policy, and we created and built a global mission team that worked and prayed for a year before celebrating our first Global Fest. A surprising number of students and young adults committed during that season to long-term service in the hard areas of the world. God was alive to us in new ways. We overlapped at Hope with David's ten years as arts pastor, a job description that included adult education. David generously opened the doors to Yvonne to teach seminars in Celtic spirituality and to participate musically in the annual Hope Arts Festivals and monthly compline services. Both Yvonne and I felt *seen* as servants with gifts for the church.

In our eighth year we discerned that our Hope season was approaching a conclusion. But what, where, with whom? Where would we fit?

Juxtaposing our personal church experiences were the lessons learned in the global arenas.

In 1987, just one year into my WEA-MC tenure, I pilgrimaged to the US Center for World Mission. Staff friends there arranged an appointment with Ralph Winter, whom I had met in Guatemala. Though the meeting was scheduled for fifteen minutes, it lasted an hour. Thirty-seven years later, I vividly remember that encounter (even where I was sitting, on the left side of the couch). I listened. Ralph unloaded his concern that the Mission Commission—representing the scattered church—was a sodality controlled and hampered by the modality ecclesial body, World Evangelical Fellowship. I honestly had no idea what "sodality and modality" meant and tried to guess their meaning in the contexts of his paragraphs. I said little and when he stood up, I stood up, expressed my thanks, and reminded him to send me his essay addressing these concerns. When it came, I studied it, gradually understanding Ralph's meaning. I tried to simplify the concept by talking, with caveats, about the church gathered and scattered.

Modality refers to the gathered (the synagogue, "gathered" church, local churches, and denominations, WEA), and sodality relates to the scattered (the apostolic teams, "scattered" church, mission agencies, Lausanne and more). That encounter represented a steep learning curve for me, and there were many like that. I had no idea I had signed up for this! But leadership required it, and it was imperative that I learn new language, concepts, realities.

But why pit sodality, gathered church, against modality, scattered? Was the Antioch church the modality and the apostolic team of Barnabas and Saul the sodality? Perhaps. But I didn't want to force a false dichotomy or highlight one at the expense of the other. The Spirit blesses both, and both categories carry their own inherent strengths and weaknesses. Why not joyously celebrate the mutuality and interaction of these two models of God-communities and their role in the vast mission infrastructure?

I lived in that holy ecclesial tension. Still do.

In the global arenas I encountered countless ecclesial journeys and a huge diversity of core definitions. For example, what do we really mean by *local church*? Who defines it? How do we modify the "official definitions" of our sending agency while planting new churches? For example, in our Guatemala experience we started just as a group. Over time this group became a formal gathering of worship and Bible study. Then we began meeting on Sunday. That mystical cross-over from house group to self-identifying as a church was beautiful. But that did not give us the right to establish a norm.

"Church" definitions run the gamut from minimalist to centrists to liturgical-sacramental (my language and categories). Preparing for this chapter, I wrote colleagues in some ten different ecclesial-missional structures—denominational and independent, Pentecostal and charismatic, and those focused exclusively on unreached people groups—advocates of the Church Planting Movement (CPM) and Discovery Bible Study (DBS) approach. I asked, "How do you define 'church'?" The diversity of responses is both amazing and refreshing.

The minimalist definitions of church speak of apostolic teams, a wide role for women, the greatest growth among the poor, serving in contexts of persecution and spiritual warfare, operating in the fullness of the Spirit's signs and wonders. These responses report an astonishingly high number of "new churches." This letter came in today: "Last year, we grew from 250k house churches to 500k house churches." Large round numbers disturb me at times (are all of the first 250k still viable and visible?). Fundamental questions still need to be asked, without denigrating anybody or any vision of the minimalist paradigm. It is one, but not the primary lens through which we see God's global mission.

The centrists gave clearer definitions of a church, especially as it moves along the spectrum from a home group to a "congregation—prechurch project" to a recognized church. The Christian and Missionary Alliance in Canada states: "The local church, the visible expression of the universal church, is a body of believers in Christ who are joined together to worship God, to observe the ordinances of Baptism and the Lord's Supper, to pray, to be edified through the Word of God, to fellowship, and to testify in word and deed to the good news of salvation both locally and globally."[1] An Avant leader wrote me saying that a church is, "A group of believers meeting together regularly, who recognize they are a local representation of the body of Christ and who are organized to carry out God's will."

The liturgical-sacramental missional groups have a special challenge. Has God sent them to plant *Anglican* (for example) churches with the totality of the imported liturgy and vestments, even architecture, or is

---

1 World Evangelical Alliance, "Evangelical."

there flexibility in the structures? Looking at this stream's global actions, it would seem that an Orthodox mission or a nascent Roman Catholic church tends to reflect the mother church in the mother country.

What does this have to do with leadership? So much! I came from a rather legalistic middle-ground ecclesiology that became institutionalized and lost much of its vitality. During my years with WEA the Spirit introduced me to an amazing diversity of church structures, dynamics, internal government, vitality, and viability. All evangelical streams battle similar ecclesial issues. Our challenge as the lead team was to listen to the Spirit, the body of believers and their shepherds, and how *they* defined and practiced mission. It generated remarkable growth in my own ecclesiology.

Historical Roots Make Their Claim

Our ecclesial journey encountered a fork in the road. Shortly after our 1990 move to Austin, Yvonne's long-dormant liturgical roots began to stir, calling her to celebrate High Season events at a gospel-centered Episcopal church. I would drive and sit with her, but I had no place for sacramental worship. I was a low-evangelical and rather happy where I was, thank you. I was only Yvonne's squire. Then, to our surprise, in Vancouver, David first, then Christine and Cliff, were confirmed in the Anglican church. It unsettled me. What was happening to my beloved family? Charismatics *and* Anglicans?

At some point in our eighth year at Hope Chapel as I approached my sixty-fifth year, I sensed in my heart a deep desire to be part of a new church plant or at least a replant. I could no longer deny a restlessness, a longing for something then called *ancient-future*. But I didn't want to play with candles and incense. My son-in-law, Cliff, was then on staff at the historic, evangelical St. Clements Episcopal Church in El Paso. We traveled several times a year to visit the Christine and Cliff Warner family, building memories with our growing brood of grandchildren. The beauty and richness of Anglican worship was captivating me.

In May 2006, the Warner family moved to Austin where Cliff took over a small, struggling, near-downtown Episcopal church called Holy Trinity. Attendance at that church had dropped down to thirty-seven, counting the babies. Was this the answer to our deep yearnings?

We spoke with Cliff and Christine about joining them with a low profile. Hope's leadership released and blessed us into our third Austin church experience. We served the Alpha Course team with set up and clean up. Initially, few knew we were related to Christine and Cliff.

It was all new to me. When do you stand, sit, or kneel? I found myself reciting Creeds I had heard about but seldom read, much less repeated every Sunday. The nomenclature was different: my old Lord's Supper and Holy Communion was now called *the Eucharist* (sounded Catholic to me). I discovered *collect prayers*—more new language. Sundays we affirmed *The Great Confession*, celebrated *the Eucharist*, recited the *Nicene* or *Apostle's Creed*. I was anticipating the weekly *Table of the Lord*, each time unique.

The *mysterious presence* of the body and blood of Christ in Holy Communion was new. Ah, so it's not just a symbolic memorial? I was on a steep learning curve, but I was not yet Anglican. In August 2008, Holy Trinity left the Episcopal denomination and rebirthed as Christ Church, joining first with AMiA (Anglican Mission in America) and later with ACNA (The Anglican Church in North America).

I could no longer straddle the fence. I wanted to be an intentional Anglican, not an incidental or accidental one. I took the confirmation course seriously, preparing for membership and my entrance into the Anglican Communion. I remember well that Sunday as I knelt and affirmed my desire to be received into the Anglican Communion. In Anglican tradition, charismatic Bishop Philip Jones gently slapped our faces to remind us of the Spirit's work in us. He also loudly whispered, *Bill, it's about time!*

God knew how to surprise me. Christ Church weaves a three-stranded cord: evangelical (the Scriptures), charismatic (the Holy Spirit), and liturgical (the sacraments). I found a new home for my self-identification as an empowered evangelical but also my yearning for something historical, global, marked by mystery and "thin places," sensitive to the Spirit and his intervention. I, who grew up only with Easter Sunday and Christmas Day on the church calendar, now discovered the rich liturgical calendar of seasons, events, colors, vestments, and the altar guild's preparation of the Table.

Some aspects of Anglicanism challenge me. I question whether only ordained priests can perform the sacraments (what I formerly called *ordinances*), to celebrate Holy Communion, baptize, marry, and bury. I have reservations about infant baptism and the ordination of women priests. Ordained women deacons fit church history more. My level of discomfort rises and fades; but I have generally accepted these differences, knowing that each ecclesial system and denomination or nondenominational church has its own particular "can of worms." Each stream has inherent weaknesses and strengths. Certainly no one ecclesiology monopolizes spirituality, purity, correct doctrine, or humility.

We were now worshipping within the heritage of ancient and global liturgical-sacramentalism. I knew there were a lot of Anglicans in Africa; Nigeria has more Anglicans than all the Western nations combined. The Lausanne 2010 Cape Town congress underscored the massive gospel-centered, mission-minded Anglican community around the world, especially in Africa.

Every church has a liturgy, an ordered worship form. I grew up with one, but nobody called it *liturgy*. Only Catholics did that. However, over the decades I realized that if I were sick and missed attending the service, I could guess with a high degree of accuracy what was happening at minute 20, 40, 55. Liturgies have a natural repetitive rhythm. During our decade in the charismatic stream and its free style of worship, openness always operated within a predictable framework.

Ah, a price had to be paid with this ecclesial change. Some of my American colleagues and friends wondered; others in Latin America questioned my *conversion*. "Has don Guillermo gone *católico*? He's even wearing a cross!" But over more recent years our Spanish-speaking friends recognize and appreciate the existence of a liturgical stream that is faithful to Scripture and gospel. Because I was now Anglican with relationships with Anglican mission leaders, doors opened to teach at Trinity School for Ministry in Ambridge, PA, in their DMin program. They considered me an Anglican missiologist and a teacher with multiple decades of experiences. My eleven years of teaching there were rewarding.

Looking back, I see why and how the Lord guided me to experience such a lifelong variety of ecclesial realities. I was to taste and see the Lord's goodness around the world where He is loved and worshipped in so many different forms of *being and doing* church. From low-evangelical in Latin America, to the Bible churches, to the Presbyterian stream, back to the low-evangelical in Guatemala, to a thriving church plant (still our spiritual home in Latin America), then a decade in a gracious charismatic church. And now Anglican. Will I be Anglican until death? I don't know.

Does the Spirit have yet another ecclesial pilgrimage before us? Perhaps. Only God knows. We follow where the Spirit leads, enriched by the multifaceted beauty of Christ's faithful *Ekklesia*.

Convergence, Conclusion, and Lessons

This diverse ecclesial journey shaped me and my understanding of leadership. I was shaped by the churches we tried to serve with integrity, grace, and commitment. Yvonne and I were never mere church observers, even in moribund congregations. We have seen church growth through multiplication and, sadly, by division.

In 1969, my first year in Latin America, I tried to understand the explosive rise of the mega-churches, some of them massive. Around that time, I asked my theologian elder friend René Padilla, "René, how do you explain these huge churches in Latin America?" His unforgettable response: "Ah, Guillermo, you must understand the difference between obese churches and healthy churches. They are not the same. The real question is: What does church mean?" I have pondered those words since that time.

Over the years we have observed nearly everything. We witnessed a church split—in front of my eyes in Dallas; a vibrant nondenominational church birth—*Centro Bíblico El Camino* in Guatemala; a church *splant*—mixed motives and a flawed process in Austin; church renewal and denominational realignment—from Holy Trinity Episcopal to Christ Church Anglican, Austin; and a healthy church plant—Christ Church's sister congregation in Austin.

I have rethought the relationship between the kingdom of God and church. How had I thought I understood this central biblical theme, one that opens and closes the book of Acts but then is (mysteriously) not a major apostolic teaching? During seminary, the kingdom was only an eschatological, 1,000 year-long concept. Recently I have seen it in new perspectives. It's *now and not yet*. The kingdom of God does not substitute the church. Churches and believing communities are kingdom outposts, contexts where the King is proclaimed, whose claims are lived out as we await the coming eternal kingdom.

Sticky Wickets

Yvonne and I grapple with unique challenges resulting from our international pilgrimages. First, those of us who have worshipped globally in the best (and worst) of church services risk merging the healthy, healing, teaching, worshipping dimensions of this diversity into one composite mélange. We compare that fusion with our home church and inevitably, the local experience emerges a paltry substitute for what "we really thought the local church is and should be, if only ...." " This is not a fair comparison, and it challenges many of us.

Second, around the world I discover colleagues and friends, even in vocational missions, who say something like, "Well, to be honest, I am for Jesus, for mission, for the Father and Spirit. But for the local church? Not really." I understand. Many of us have been wounded by the church, ending up exhausted, frustrated, and alienated. We therefore create our own desired micro mélange of the kind of Christian community we prefer, and settle for that small home group, but we don't call it *church*. These conundrums are real. But at the end of the day, are they legitimate? We were created for community, even the broken and inadequate varieties.

In 2007, the El Camino elders of our Guatemalan home church asked me to preach on its thirty-third anniversary. As I prayed over what to say and how to say it, the Spirit led me to this question: "What did I think we founders, the original pastor-elders, had done right and what perhaps had we missed?" It was challenging to address those DNA issues which we founders grappled with as we conceived and birthed a healthy church. We did miss some things. First, back then we had no theology and pastoral wisdom to deal with evil supernaturalism. Second, we didn't envision a nourishing church with full-time pastors—the congregation is still led by a team of pastor-elders with a pastoral ministries staff coordinator. Third, we had no visionary DNA to plant new churches in the strategic new populations of Guatemala City. Fourth, we had no vision to impact the immediate lower class neighboring barrios. Fifth, at the beginning we had no global, cross-cultural mission vision. In God's providence the church overcame a number of these limitations, a testimony to both leadership and congregation. In August 2024 Yvonne and I returned to Guatemala, celebrating its fiftieth anniversary. As its only living founders, Yvonne and I were honored to reflect on those early years and speak into the future.

Occasionally I consider the disparate church paths my colleagues and friends—all leaders—have taken, wondering how diverse their ecclesial pilgrimage was. Was their story "steady as she goes," never changing, never departing from their church stream? Did they start similar churches with similar theologies and ecclesiologies? In essence, God's missional leaders must be committed not only to the universal church, but to the global church, and to the local community of believers. It is at this micro, grass-roots level that we grow, we experience *the body*, that we are known as simply human, are held accountable and experience community. This local community shapes us to better serve and lead in God's global church.

Why were five of those seven first-generation Revelation churches so judged by Jesus? How rapidly those communities deteriorated—by deception, division, ethnic rivalry, theological variance, heresy, immorality, apostasy! Why were those early chapters and stories not photoshopped or shaded with a dash of hagiography? Simply, because the Spirit is not in the business of hagiography. The biblical narrative reflects the reality of the embodied churches of Jesus Christ, whether in their first-generation realities or extended life and in their countless manifestations across history, geography, culture, and language. Leaders must acknowledge and face those challenges, all the while battling for integrity and orthodoxy, for justice and righteousness, compassion and love.

To Canterbury, Rome, or Byzantium? Somewhere in the early 90s, late at night, Yvonne and I were both reading in bed. I was probably reading a spy novel, and she was reading Frederica Mathewes-Green's book, *Facing East: A Pilgrim's Journey into the Mysteries of Orthodoxy*. At one point the bed shook with Yvonne's laughter, and I looked over asking, "What are you reading now?" She showed me the title and I asked, "What's so funny about her?" Following Yvonne's explanation (Mathewes-Green really was funny), a peculiar frisson stirred me; a deep disquiet surged within me. I did not know where my wife was going in her theological and ecclesial pilgrimage. I quietly probed, "Yvonne, are you crossing the Tiber (Roman Catholicism), headed into Byzantium (Eastern Orthodoxy), or walking towards Canterbury (Anglican)?" She looked up at me and simply said, "I don't know." I slept uneasily that night, knowing she was on a journey to a stream of the Christian faith that would nourish her roots. I was apprehensive. I thought, "Well, Billy boy, what happens to you if your wife heads into Rome or Byzantium? How will you explain a Catholic wife to our donors? Prepare to find a new job." I was honestly apprehensive. And then God led us both.

Today I want to remain open to the Spirit's leading. The path into our most recent ecclesial assignment led through Singapore, Santiago, Nairobi and Kampala, centers of vibrant evangelical Anglicanism today. Have all these factors shaped me into the global evangelical leader that I am today? Yes. Will I remain in this space? Only God knows.

Reflection Questions

1. Why should, must, a leader be committed to a local church?
2. People change, leaders grow, deep questions must be answered. Do ecclesial journeys reflect weak or robust leadership qualities?
3. What has been your experience with the church "gathered and scattered"?
4. In what ways does a leader's ecclesial journey shape our understanding of leadership?
5. Why is it important for a leader to understand evangelical global ecclesial diversity?
6. Describe your church journey? What shaped you in each stage?

7

The Spirit, a Mystery to Embrace Not a Certainty to Master

> And in the last days it shall be, God declares, that I will pour out my Spirit on all flesh, and your sons and your daughters shall prophesy, and your young men shall see visions, and your old men shall dream dreams; even on my male servants and female servants in those days I will pour out my Spirit, and they shall prophesy.
>
> (Acts 2:17–18)

"No Quiet Time, No Breakfast"

Where did this hard-ball slogan originate? Perhaps I heard it at age seventeen, striving to be a "Moody student on fire for Jesus," or from my InterVarsity years first at the University of Illinois and then North Texas State University. It was at the U of I that I first discovered the revolutionary IVP booklet, *Quiet Time*.[1] Its language captured me forever, and I always remember those introductory words: "The astonishing marvel is that the living God wants to have a personal relationship with you." That little book has traveled with me for sixty years, into all my dorm rooms, apartments, and then homes with Yvonne. I know exactly where it is right now—on the upstairs landing next to my collection of worn inductive Bible study guides.

My journey regarding the Spirit began my high school senior year. The Wheaton Bible Church youth held their 1957 winter retreat in a Wisconsin ski park (I had never skied in my life, so I well remember two memorable crashes). Our pastor was the speaker, Rev. Malcolm Cronk, a rather eccentric yet endearing man with a heart for youth. I was the immature MK, who three months before had eaten his very first pizza. During the question-and-answer time I asked, "Sir, what is the Holy Spirit?" I had no idea what "it" did nor what "it" meant. The Trinity I grew up with was the Father, the Son, and the Holy Scriptures. His answer was gentle; I don't remember the content. I do remember

---

[1] InterVarsity Christian Fellowship Staff, *Quiet Time*.

his heart. He, Spirit controlled, discerned my heart, saw me, and spoke wisdom. A first building block had been laid for a long journey.

But little did I know what awaited me.

In a recent conversation with Yvonne, I tried to recreate what my Moody theology classes taught me about the Spirit. He ("it" in the King James Bible) was a member of the Holy Trinity. That I remember. In my world the Spirit's primary work was conversion—"The Great Miracle." I understood so little about the Spirit's multifaceted work: wrapped up in salvation, sealed, baptized, empowered for sanctification, and endowed with gifts (natural and supernatural) imparted to each believer for character, service, and mission.

My InterVarsity years added little. My Dallas Theological Seminary years provided a greater emphasis on the person, work, and empowering ministry of the Spirit in our lives. The Spirit's gifts were important, but we argued from Scripture, history, and theology that the supernatural gifts were only for the first century. We had to be cessasionists to graduate at that time. Questions would surface later.

During my 1972–1974 PhD studies in Austin, I began questioning my stance on the Spirit's gifts when our church invited me to teach a series on "Discovering your spiritual gifts." I embraced a major season of biblical and theological study. By early 1974 I concluded there was no clear exegetical basis for the supernatural gifts to disappear. Our Guatemala field leader heard reports that I had "changed my theology of the Spirit," which led to a healthy conversation as to where I was headed. During those years my views remained discreet, but internally I had crossed a line. Later, when asked to teach at DTS and serve on the board, I stated my position. Surprisingly, it did not bar me from either opportunity. I was a subdued continuationist.

My theological-biblical-spiritual-experiential crockpot brewed over the following years. Late during our Guatemala season, I transitioned into an empowered evangelical. But early on I didn't have language for that category. I had asked God for new spiritual gifts but did not receive any. The Spirit's internal witness assured me I had enough gifts which I was to hone. I transitioned into a passive supernaturalist. I was still in process. In addition, we did not want to resign from SETECA or our agency. That freedom would come later.

But how and when would I reveal my practicing supernaturalism? That question swirled in my heart and spirit, with resolution coming during my early WEF years. In that global, safe community we encountered godly, gifted, engaging women and men who loved God and his Word deeply, serving in both the local and global church. They represented Pentecostal and charismatic, Methodist, Lutheran, independents, Anglican, Swedish Baptist Pentecostals, and more. The body of Christ expanded exponentially before our eyes. When colleagues discovered I was a Dallas graduate, good questions always emerged. Asked infrequently if I still sustained the full DTS statement, I affirmed my agreement with its core tenets but differed on some topics. The mutual respect was authentic. Later years in WEA we never had theological arguments and that was a gift. We had greater enemies to battle.

> But how and when would I reveal my practicing supernaturalism?

Encounters with the Spirit

Mulling over my pilgrimage with the Spirit, I have asked myself, "What does this have to do with leadership?" I'm convinced that a robust understanding of the person, presence and power of the Spirit today in our lives, church, and cultures is crucial as we are emerging, emerged, or former leaders. This dimension has little to do with personal charisma or amazing public leadership gifts, and everything to do with character, integrity, vulnerability to the Triune God, and finishing well. These realities are our companions on the downward way to the cross—Jesus our supreme example.

One evening during Lausanne II in Manila, July 1989, I experienced my first serious encounter with the Holy Spirit. J. I. Packer and Jack Hayford had shared the platform, each articulating his convictions on the Spirit. As I sat in the balcony with my friend and mentor, Dave Howard, the conference was invited into silence to listen to the voice of the Lord, and to enter a space for God to do true and deep work. The Lord was speaking to me. Again, I asked, "Do you want to give me something new?" I stood, waiting. Something unexplainable dislodged inside of me. There was no change, but God blessed another openness to himself, and Dave later helped me process that experience.

A second major Spirit encounter took place around 1994 at our then-home church, Hope Chapel. The visiting speaker was to teach on prayer; surprisingly, she changed topics at the last minute to teach on the gift of tongues. We transitioned into an extensive ministry time focused on that gift. Yvonne remained seated; I went forward. The speaker came to me and prayed extensively and earnestly for me, encouraging me to just utter syllables, like priming the pump. Nothing. She passed me over to her husband. After some forty-five minutes I returned to my seat and said, "Nothing new happened, but I made myself fully available to the Spirit and I discerned the Spirit's whisper: 'Bill, I am pleased with your heart, but I'll not give anything new. Hone the gifts you already have.'" Yvonne, our true family charismatic, said, "Bill, be at peace. The Lord has you where he wants you. Otherwise, it might have cut you off from the broader, global ministry God has for you." Mysterious quietness seeped in. From then on, I rested while continuing to live in openness and expectancy to God's Spirit.

During 1995 I visited the DTS campus four times. In January I spoke with Yvonne during four chapels at the annual Spiritual Formation Week; in May at a board meeting; in June in a summer school class; and in November at the Mission and Evangelism Lectureship for four plenary chapels.

For years, the DTS chaplain had invited both of us to speak at the January conference. Yvonne was reluctant, given where our journey had taken us. We had warned him of what the Lord might call us to share as we addressed the spiritual journey. Student leaders picked us up at the airport and that night we met with the full team for orientation and prayer. The Assemblies of God student intrigued me. Why had she selected DTS? She explained she wanted to study the Bible thoroughly and this was her top choice. When she interceded over me, she did so in English and a prayer language. I said to myself, "Well, Bill, that is a DTS first for you. A Pentecostal sister prayed for you in tongues."

Yvonne and I shared the Tuesday chapel; on Wednesday I introduced her to speak alone on *The Dark Night of the Soul*; I spoke on Thursday; and Friday we concluded together. We sensed the Spirit's strong presence that week, albeit with turbulence and spiritual warfare. On Tuesday we had invited students and faculty into a deeper spirituality with its disciplines. Apparently, we pushed the envelope. Was it because we had invited all to stand and open their hands, asking God to meet us? Or was the envelope pushed during Yvonne's chapel, a new concept to most? She was honest, biblical, and vulnerable as she opened her heart regarding her own faith struggles. She shared how God took her through darkness into a deeper relationship and understanding of himself and the spiritual journey. That topic stirred campus-wide conversations and late that night we met with the chaplain and student team to debrief and pray.

Anonymous letters accused us of being a front for the New Age, though Yvonne had spoken of "spiritual direction," *not* "spiritual guide." We sensed a deeper spiritual battle going on, and that Wednesday night my computer strangely crashed, causing us to lose all our notes. We worked late into the night from earlier paper drafts to recreate our talks. Thursday morning, we openly addressed the concerns that had been stirred up. During Friday's conclusion, we both again sensed the grace of God's Spirit. I will never forget seeing the then-dean, later-president, now-chancellor, taking Yvonne's hands in his own, and with tears in his eyes, saying, "I cannot thank you enough for speaking to us as well, the faculty." Other faculty, department chairs, and many students expressed appreciation, thanking us for a new perspective. However, some professors and friends strangely said nothing. Months later the angry letter-writer wrote asking for forgiveness. It was granted, but Humpty Dumpty had fallen off the wall.

To my astonishment and consternation, a week after the series, the then-president (absent that crucial week) wrote and charged us of inadequate biblical grounding; students had complained; we were accused of causing more turbulence than blessing. He questioned whether I could honestly continue serving on the DTS board if I was a *crypto-charismatic*. In my response I asked him if he had interacted personally with his vice president, his dean, and other faculty and administrators. He had not and immediately wrote asking forgiveness; it was granted. Humpty Dumpty again.

Other problems emerged. I wrote the DTS media department requesting a copy of those four chapels. I was told that "due to technical problems, those recordings were defective and useless." Why were we not surprised? A senior professor later told me that I had failed to stand alongside Yvonne when she spoke, thus leaving her vulnerable and causing uncertainty.

Yvonne had anticipated potential opposition and spiritual warfare, but we had chosen to speak out of obedience to the Spirit. Yet this bruising experience called us anew to continue our journey of discovery and to remember that his household is unimaginably more spacious and multifaceted. We were led to walk with the broader, yet biblically and historically grounded body of Christ. Over time we discerned that our words to students and faculty would be used perhaps ten or more years later when their journey would shift from intellectual certainty to a willingness to "go further in, higher up" into intimacy with the One "who dwells in mystery and inapproachable light." But the experience was another strange watershed time in our journey with the Holy Spirit.

Spring Harvest, UK

My third close encounter with the Spirit came one year later, in 1996, during four months in the UK fulfilling a spectrum of commitments. The director of Spring Harvest, Clive Calver, a good friend, had invited me as a mission speaker to share the platform with a gifted Englishwoman mission leader. Spring Harvest was an annual Festival of Discipleship held at a gigantic recreation-entertainment-vacation park with housing and entertainment for all ages. Families were registered during each of the four weeks of the conference. Children and youth were provided age-appropriate activities, while the adults engaged with friends and peers. Our week coincided with the Holy Trinity Brompton (HTB)/Alpha network churches, with close to 15,000 people in attendance. HTB church activities had been cancelled the entire week to provide incentive for all to attend Spring Harvest.

It was our first introduction to both Spring Harvest and HTB-Alpha. What a week! I had been assigned to the "gentle charismatic" auditorium without knowing what that meant. The "Big Tent" venue was where heavy-duty action took place, with HTB leading that "nitro-charismatic" program. While my speaking went well, I was humbled to discover that it really didn't matter what I said nor how relevant I thought it was. "The Spirit was present." Yvonne and I served on the post-service ministry team. We prayed for many and saw some gently slip to the floor in deep rest, nicknamed *carpet time*. We really didn't say much; these dear believers simply wanted more of the Lord. A gentle prayerful touch on the forehead and down they went.

One free night we attended the *Big Tent*. The worship was rich and heavy, the emotional service packed with new coded spirituality for us. One speaker gave an extended message in tongues. But that's when complications emerged, for two very different interpretations were given of the same "prophetic word." I thought of 1 Corinthians 12:7–11, wondering how Paul would have handled this case.

The speaker that night preached on the gift of tongues, inviting all to receive that gift, and ministry time followed suit. Again, I went forward, was prayed for, and waited in silent expectation. Nothing. The main meeting concluded. I stood to one side of the tent, observing the ongoing ministry, mulling things over. Then I heard, "Bill, have you ever received the gift of tongues?" I looked up, responding, "No, I have not." "Would you like to pray to receive the gift?" he asked. "If this is the Spirit's desire for me, yes, I am willing." Then Rev. Sandy Millar, senior priest at HTB, laid hands on me, praying for me, inviting me to speak out what I sensed the Lord was saying to me. Not sure what to say or expect, I knew I was in the right place and space. "Bill, open your heart and spirit to the Spirit." I did, and after about thirty minutes he paused and warmly said, "Bill, remain open, OK?" The invitation was to anticipate, not just wait passively. "Thank you, Sandy, I shall." We embraced as friends.

Nothing happened, but everything happened. I knew I was open to a new work of the Spirit. I also knew that the Lord was satisfied with my gift combination, and I was to sharpen what I already had. Both a grace and a relief, it settled the issue. We left Spring Harvest on Holy Saturday, driving through Salisbury to visit its exquisite cathedral. We had met another Anglican priest at Spring Harvest, Rupert Charkham and his wife Liz. Rupert, a convert from Judaism, was rector of St. Paul's Church and we wandered into the property. The church was closed, but we boldly knocked on the parish door. To our surprise they both welcomed us in for tea and scones. A unique friendship was sealed, beautiful to this day. Shortly afterwards we drove to Salisbury to preach at St. Paul's.

On Easter morning of 1996, we attended HTB, having been invited to lunch at the Millars' parish home. It was a posh culinary and social event with sherry and port at their appropriate times. That night we worshiped at All Souls, Langham Place; and though John Stott was not preaching, he was the after-service door greeter. Approaching him, he looked at us and said, "Well, Yvonne and Bill Taylor from Guatemala. Welcome!" We were astonished that he remembered that visit to Guatemala so many years before, and the dinner in our home during his Latin America expository teaching and preaching tour with René Padilla.

A few years later we spent some days with Rupert and Liz in Cambridge where Rupert was then vicar at Holy Trinity Cambridge. He honored me by opening his pulpit that Sunday. I felt unworthy to preach in the historic church which Charles Simeon (Eton and Cambridge graduate, where he came to faith his first year) shepherded from 1782 to his death in 1836. Simeon oversaw a powerful spiritual revival and over the years Holy Trinity sent out some 140 missionaries. One of the early ones was Henry Martyn (1782–1812), an Anglican priest who served in India and then Persia. Before his early death at age thirty-one, Martyn had translated the Bible into Urdu, Persian, and Arabic. Others included the famous Cambridge Seven who went to China with Hudson Taylor's new China Inland Mission. While overwhelmed with the honor of preaching in that sanctuary and weighted by holy history, I felt the presence of God's Spirit.

Other Pieces from the Journey with the Spirit

Little did I know what God had planned for this Spirit journey. Jesus's life and words continue to impact me deeply in this stage of my pilgrimage. During Holy Week 2020 (at the start of the global COVID-19 pandemic) while walking in real-time through the days of Jesus's passion, Yvonne and I watched several films, moved anew by *The Gospel of John*.

Yvonne's journey in the Spirit was unique to her and she was always a few years ahead of me. In our latter years in Guatemala, she was learning and growing in her understanding and experience of the Spirit in ways she could share with only one or two friends. Otherwise, our mission would have asked us to resign. Her Celtic pilgrimage started in 1990 with the haunting music of Irish singer-composer, Enya. The Logos Christian bookstore served as a resource treasury on Celtic spirituality and other streams of Christianity.

> In our latter years in Guatemala, she was learning and growing in her understanding and experience of the Spirit in ways she could share with only one or two friends. Otherwise, our mission would have asked us to resign.

Her journey of Celtic learning, growth, and spiritual practices stimulated repeated pilgrimages to Wales, Scotland, Northumbria, Cumbria, Cornwall, Devon, with memorable stays at Iona, and various ones on Holy Island. I became her squire, serving her as I accompanied her. But later I discovered that my mother's Britt family might have come from Brittany's Celtic stock. That familial link plus what God was doing in Yvonne drew me across a line; and the mystical became real. Two pilgrimage moments stand out in my memory: the "thin place" experience on the island of Iona, and the days with spiritual director Ray Simpson on Holy Island, Lindisfarne. God gave Yvonne a special relationship with Ray, the Celtic spirituality leader and author, as she sat under his teaching at his retreats. Today, almost anything Celtic moves us: St. Patrick's birthday on March 17; secular and Christian Celtic music—especially by our friend Jeff Johnson; local Celtic festivals; Irish dance; or our Warner grandchildren's Celtic names.

In 2007 SETECA invited me to give four lectures on spiritual formation. The literature on spiritual formation in Spanish was scant at that time with only one book by Dallas Willard. Teaching focused on the spirituality embedded in the Advent narratives: the pregnant teenage girl, Mary, with deep justice convictions who knew her Yahweh and Scripture; Joseph, the practicing supernaturalist who listened to God's voice in dreams and visions, a manly man who protected his beloved espoused young love; the older Elizabeth and Zechariah who heard and saw God both through Mary and in the temple; the elders, Simeon and Anna who waited for so long. It was an honor to speak to a new student and faculty generation of the seminary where I served those seminal years.

God was giving unique freedom to speak on the fullness of the missional Trinity, and especially an empowered theology of the Spirit and spirituality. Strong spirituality resources have shaped me: Eugene Peterson, Henri Nouwen, Elisabeth Elliot, A. W. Tozer, Gerald Sittser, Gordon Fee, Jack Deere, Rich Nathan and Ken Wilson, Rodney Stark, Andy Crouch, Augustine, my son's book on the Psalms, Celtic writers and prayers, vulnerable memoirs and biographies. Yvonne adds saints of yesteryear who walked her through darkness: Michael Molinos, Madam Guyon, Fenelon, John of the Cross. No evangelical writer approaches their depth. Others shaped her: Richard Foster, Wesley Duewel, Rees Howell, Tozer, Thomas Merton, Nouwen and Houston, Alexander Schmemann and Timothy Ware. Add in other Celtic writers and intercessory prayer resources. She lives in mystery but battles with God—theodicy is a tough nut to crack.

I grappled with three doubting periods that rocked me to my core. But I took my own three-fold counsel: doubt my doubts; I'm not the first one with hard questions; seek the resources out there. The first was as a senior in university, the second during PhD studies, the third one at age sixty, triggered by Stephanie's faith crisis. My son David encouraged me to focus again on the unique Jesus Christ, assuring me that no composite religious construct can match our Lord.

During that last trial, I developed five critical questions to ask all faith systems, whether Islam, Animism, Buddhism, Hinduism, Secularism or Christianity. 1) How do you explain the mystery of the created world? 2) How do you explain the mystery of the human person? 3) How do you explain the mystery of what's gone amok with humanity? 4) Which system has the best solutions to humanity gone rogue? 5) What's the future of creation and of humans? God's Spirit accompanied me in my battles, in the counsel I received, and in my response. And the faith walk continues, as do God's periodic silences. He is. He is good. He is present. He can be quiet.

Embracing Mystery

From mid-1990–1991 Yvonne, Stephanie and I lived in a rural area east of Austin, awaiting the construction of our home and recovering from the four Arkansas years. Yvonne entered her two-and-a-half-year "Dark Night of the Soul," and I found myself lost in a spiritual desert. Stephanie had her own struggles with schooling and life in Texas. Not understanding what was "wrong" with Yvonne, I tried to fix her. I am embarrassed by my foolish behavior one day when she picked me up at the airport after one of my "saving the world" trips. I was spiraling and I lost it. About a week later, from the depths of her darkness and struggle she spoke gracious truth: "Bill, you are gifted but you are too thin. If you are going to be the man God wants you to be, you must grow deeper spiritual roots." Her Spirit words penetrated like a stiletto. And I took her counsel. To remind myself of God's loving sovereignty during those hard transition years, I discerned that the Spirit left me walking with a kind of limp—not physical, but spiritual. It was not a punishment; it was a reminder.

> **Today I'm on a missional pilgrimage with the Triune God.**

Was it legitimate for an emerging global mission leader with WEA to have these battles? If so, why? And there was no rapid lane before me. My story is mine. My friends and colleagues have experienced their own journeys. Did any question their initial spirituality? What happened to their spirituality over time, having left their mother culture to serve in another, bearing and raising children in these challenging contexts, following their Savior on challenging mission?

Today I'm a leader embracing elusive mysteries and on a missional pilgrimage with the Triune God. Why did I keep faith and others did not?

Why did some of my closer TCK friends, even ministry colleagues, abandon faith, or why did their marriages fail? I cannot understand it. When, where and who was involved? I have discerned how my spiritual journey has converged with my ecclesial one. The liturgical-sacramental streams have expansive context, space, and place for mystery, as well as an ever-maturing spirituality.

Conclusion and Lessons

Mulling over this chapter, I realized how vital the Spirit's work is in leadership. It's a Genesis 1–3 gift; the Garden creation and cultural mandates are given to both Adam and Eve. Throughout Scripture the Spirit empowers for leadership and service. Bezalel is endowed with special wisdom and creativity gifts in the design and construction of the tabernacle, including the ability to equip others. The Spirit even comes upon people who end up disastrous leaders—like Saul. He visits those who will be quality leaders; think of Moses and Joshua. The prophets Isaiah and Ezekiel receive special visitations.

In the New Testament Jesus selects strategic groups, the three, the twelve (a unique mixture of personalities and backgrounds), but also the seventy, then the Upper Room community of men and women. Paul's most extensive teaching on the gifts is in 1 Corinthians 14–16. They are all for the body, serving the faith community. Studying the key passages, you discover that *each* member of the Trinity gives spiritual gifts. Ephesians 4 lists what some call the leadership gifts: "And he gave the apostles, the prophets, the evangelists, the shepherds and teachers, to equip the saints for the work of ministry, for building up the body of Christ ... " Their central function is to serve and strengthen the community of Jesus followers.

Questions emerge. Do the gifts—natural and spiritual—that we need all come at the same time, or do they emerge as we grow and change? Might the Spirit empower us when entering a new phase of life, ministry, or leadership. Does that unique combination of skillset and spiritual gifts unpack itself over time because they were present from the start? I think some of mine existed first in embryonic form but were birthed in the early WEA years.

Is it appropriate to desire new leadership gifts? Scripture describes the Spirit coming upon Old Testament saints, kings, and prophets in the hinge moments of their lives. When appointed to leadership of the

Mission Commission in 1987, I had no idea what was before me, but I asked God to help me. Significantly, that assignment came in the same season of my self-recognition as an empowered evangelical.

Enter the psalmist,

> O God, from my youth you have taught me, and I still proclaim your wondrous deeds. So even to old age and gray hairs, O God, do not forsake me, until I proclaim your might to another generation, your power to all those to come.
> (Ps 71:17–18)

Come, Holy Spirit. Empower me to serve-lead with integrity, to finish well, to follow Jesus.

Reflection Questions

1. What is the relationship between robust spirituality and gifted yet humble leadership? Describe the case of a Christian leader with questionable spirituality?
2. What has your journey with the Spirit been over the course of your life?
3. In what ways has your spirituality changed, and in what ways has it changed you?
4. Do you know of emerging leaders who received new gifts for a new season of their lives? Describe one.
5. In this chapter, what caught your attention the most?

8
Letting Go—The Foothills Vision

> True leadership must be based in the security of God's love. It establishes different marks of success than leadership based on fear. You then lead to please God and to bring him joy. Everything is viewed through the perspective of God's kingdom values, and therefore it does not quite fit the perspective of this world.[1]

The Gwandará

Stories breathed flesh and blood life, space, and place during my global decades. They galvanize me today, deepening my respect for God's power to transform individuals, families, communities, and peoples. My Nigerian friend and fellow-colleague, Panya Baba (former distinguished leader of the Evangelical Missionary Society [EMS] and the ECWA church, now "Home"), first told me the story of the Gwandará people of northern Nigeria. This agricultural people group, numbering close to 10,000 in the early 1980s, had existed for most of its history untouched by the gospel. Western missionaries had twice attempted, and failed, to reach this animistic *ethné* with the gospel.

In the early 1980s a third team of long-term cross-cultural servants moved into the territory with their families, chickens, and goats, having garnered permission from the local elders to build homes and cultivate the land. They already spoke Hausa, so the main barriers were not linguistic but relational, cultural, and spiritual. Trust developed incrementally as they discovered that in "deep Hausa" this ethnic group were not the "Gwandará" but the "Gwandará-wa." The difference? "Gwandará-wa" literally refers to "a people who prefer to dance over religion." Dialoguing with the elderly storytellers, they learned that early in the nineteenth century Muslim armies of Hausa/Fulani Jihadists had swarmed Nigeria from the north, forcing conversions at sword point.

The Gwandará-wa rejected the legalistic invaders, preferring their spirit-worship and dances over Islam's legalism. The missionaries

---
1 Overstreet, *Unleader*, 108.

convened, asking, "How does this new information shape our communication? What might be the cultural bridge that enables the gospel of Jesus to flow to these peoples who so love to dance." Purposing to speak stories of grace and liberty, they determined to dance the biblical narrative to the people! Creativity was unleashed as appropriate rhythms, words, and songs began to unveil the true Creator, his cosmological story of redemption through the narratives of the nation Israel and into the life, ministry, death, resurrection, and ascension of our Lord Christ. Panya told me that as they danced into the beginning of Acts, the Holy Spirit broke through among the Gwandará-wa with supernatural power. The first believers emerged, and the church was birthed.

Who were these creative missionaries, selected and equipped in their prefield service training program then sent into pioneer mission, who discovered that artistic cultural bridge to human hearts? They belonged to the African cross-cultural mission force from the EMS. EMS, founded in 1949, is the mission agency of the Evangelical Church Winning All (ECWA), one of the largest Christian denominations in all of Africa. The ECWA currently encompasses 6,000 churches and congregations, an adult membership of 2.5 million people, thirteen vernacular Bible schools, five Bible colleges and seminaries, over 1,600 missionaries within Nigeria and seventeen other nations, a publications program, a powerful rural, educational, and medical ministry, and with scores of highly trained and gifted Nigerian leaders. And where did the ECWA church come from? God chose to bless what was originally a Western mission agency to establish this church in Nigeria.

By God's grace, ECWA and EMS exist because of SIM, an agency birthed in North America through prayer and sacrifice. Persevering pioneers from the Global North traveled by boat and overland to reach Africa's interior, many packing their belongings in large, long rectangular boxes—coffins.

Who were the backstory players? Canadian Margaret Craig Gowans, a Scottish immigrant was one, a vital contributor to the future SIM and ECWA. In the late nineteenth century, she captured a vision for international missions. She encouraged and released her son, Walter, to go to Africa, and her daughter, Annie to China.

Why single out these agencies—one Western in origin (SIM) but now truly internationalized, and the other African (ECWA)? They represent how the Spirit links intercession movements with families, perhaps with newly established agencies based in a home or a street address. But on the "field" they become networks of living congregations and churches, emerging as unique missional denominations. Always there is sacrifice, perhaps martyrdom. Worldwide, indigenous church movements then capture a mission vision for their own peoples and beyond while generating new sending agencies. Thus, the creative Spirit of God advances on mission. And in all cases, mission advance requires a combination of bold prayer, visionary leaders, persistence, and even a willingness to die in the process of obedience.

I am both a product and a lifelong participant witness of this global divine mission. Because that is also the account of our own mission agency. CAM was established in 1890, my parents joined in 1937, and Yvonne and I in 1967. Around the globe during my tenure with the MC I have seen this model reproduced repeatedly, each a new chapter of God's Epic.

And these were the stories I was introduced to, entering those narratives, rejoicing in God, seeing his Spirit at work through our majestic Christ in all cultures and languages. God uses many transitions to create the tapestry of his story.

The Foothills Vision Slowly Emerges

In the midst of those global experiences, I rejoiced in stories such as the Gwandará as I pondered my development as the MC leader. However, unexpected thoughts began to seep into my mind and heart as slow-motion revelations. Somewhere around 2002 I realized that my leadership term as head of the WEA-MC was coming to an end. I honestly had concluded that I did not have the knowledge, nor the gifting, nor the physical capacity to take this unusual ministry alliance-network into its preferred future. I was sixty-two years old when I informed the MC Executive Board of my decision and asked them to lead the process of leadership succession and continuity. In God's providence, Dr. Bertil Ekström, another TCK (Sweden and Brazil) was appointed—from within the MC ethos—to succeed me. He graciously asked me to continue in new roles, which I did for another decade. Then it became time to step down totally from all WEA platforms and positions, to embrace the next, and unknown season of my life. I was radically different—inside and out—from the Bill that began with the MC in mid-1986. But who would I become?

> **I was radically different—inside and out ...
> But who would I become?**

I remembered Sonnenfeld's thought-provoking book on the retirement of fifty well-known leaders.[2] He named four prime *departing* categories: the Monarch, the General, the Ambassador, the Governor. He also discussed the reluctant farewell, the family patriarch, and other examples of leaders that shaped my own journey. Of these four leadership models, I longed to be the ambassador, one who continues to champion his former organization.

On December 31, 2016, I completed thirty years in MC and WEA leadership. On January 1, 2017, I awoke to a strange new reality and existence with an uncertain future. Who was I now? Were my strong years over? Was leadership over for me? What would I do? How long would my transition take? How would I embrace the holiness of the ordinary, the spirituality of the quotidian? How strange to meet a "new stranger" called Solitude. I was forced to sift and sort "stuff" through in a process lasting some two years.

As I sifted, I discerned both good and disconcerting news. Good: The Spirit had released me into a new life of continuity plus discontinuity. Disconcerting: the Spirit had released me into a new life of continuity plus discontinuity. And amid those uncertainties, a vision emerged that allowed me to understand my entire life trajectory in the imagery of a topography of foothills, mountain ranges, and valleys. On the cusp of our departure to Latin America in late 1968, the first mountain range had emerged. I said, "This range I am to cross and then serve in the next valley." My previous life, camp, church, and IVCF ministries were introductory foothills to the range that had been set before me. The seventeen years assigned to SETECA allowed me to embrace the challenge of early cross-cultural ministry, service, and initial leadership. The lessons I had learned were permanent. The mistakes were all too real. The unexpected invitation to leave Latin America, which conferred on me three deaths, led me to a new steep, cliff-filled range, descending into the valley of shadows, sadness, brokenness, loss, and desert. My resurrection into WEA opened the pass through that massive range to serve the thirty years which radically transformed me. It was also a new crucible that burned the dross of my essence as a person and leader. And then it concluded. The vision was poignant, bittersweet, and long term.

That's when my future landscape strangely changed. I did envisage another massive range, preceded by a series of foothills. But the inner locution spoke, "Bill, you will not cross that range. I will walk with you

---

2 Sonnenfeld, *The Hero's Farewell*.

to the foothills, and in my time, I will lay you to rest with your fathers and your people."

Solemn, serious, bittersweet, poignant, yet clarifying words.

Who Am I Now?

As I reflected on that season of new aloneness and began to know the new friend, Solitude, the first truth God drilled into me was, "Bill, you are my son, a beloved one." The Voice didn't focus on my job, my CV, my publications, my speaking or teaching. It wasn't about accolades for distinguished leadership. Rather, my essential identity was affirmed and confirmed. I was to walk in that God-endorsed self-realization. This Voice gently spoke into my life, centered me, and gave me focus for my next stage and assignment. "Bill, you now know who you are. I will show you what is to come." The language of trust gave peace.

I was loved, unconditionally, and I would walk in that reality. It was enough.

Gradually things began to make sense and reveal perspective. My public life had given me just under twenty years in Latin America; two years for the death-pivot-resurrection, and thirty years in the global arena. These decades had permanently transformed me. As 2017 flowed past, I valued these truths: I was a Jesus-lover, committed to orthodox Christianity; I was an internationalized evangelical. Surprisingly I was now an Anglican. I was a leader. I had countless acquaintances and colleagues in other cultures and nations. My phone directory had information on 3,351 people. My trusted friends were few, select, special, battle tested.

I was also exhausted; weary from spiritual warfare and ministry, my body having paid the price of so much travel and diverse diets. I was also now father-in-law to three adults and the Papa of eight grandchildren. I was now seventy-five years old, an elder, a veteran, with ministry victories and also wounds and scars.

During those reflective years I studied Scripture I was intrigued by the Hebrew terms for *zaqen*: elder; *chozeh*: seer, and *chakam*: to be wise, wise-hearted, skilled. These reflections led me to ask, "I wonder if the Spirit of God would want me to become a sage, a seer? What does that mean?" I knew God had recommissioned me to life-shaping, intentional mentoring. I was also released to write from my own heart and experience. I was reticent to call myself a "sage"; so, I waited. The confirmation would come through a small mentee community.

These words led to yet another renaming of Bill Taylor, and it revealed itself as in a time-release message from the Spirit: "You are in a new season, and I shall guide you accordingly. Prepare to step down from offices and influence. Pour your life into others—especially emerging and younger leaders." The vision and the renaming converged to shape me into who I am today. These words did not create uncertainty, for I knew I was in the hands of the living God with another application (totally out of context) of Genesis 24:27 (KJV), that I, being in the way, would be led by the Lord. Concurrently, this season invited me to examine the three dimensions, or realms, of my life: the public, the private, the secret. Did my life speak internal and external consistency? What more did God ask of me?

Little could I have even dreamed what my life would become in my late seventies after decades in service of the global church on mission. When I started mid-1986 with the MC, did I know what I was doing. No. Was I waiting on the Spirit and colleagues to guide me in those first years? Yes. Little did I realize how God would shape my leadership and style. But I was absolutely convinced of the rightness of that scary Singapore decision in late June 1986. It became a matter of living it out, walking in faith with sufficient light just in front to slowly dispel the darkness.

Organizational Reflections

Over those three decades I had become a player-coach-leader within WEA's global network-movement. I flowed in the streaming heritage of Christian leaders fulfilling its history, its values, and its vision. The same with the Mission Commission. I worked with WEA top leadership, other visionaries and organizers, and some historians and writers. I counted W. Harold Fuller, the Canadian SIM veteran and author of *People of the Mandate: The Story of the World Evangelical Fellowship*,[3] a friend. I was a servant and colleague of my lifelong mentor, David M. Howard, author of *The Dream that Would Not Die: The Birth and Growth of the World Evangelical Fellowship 1846–1986*.[4] I started in 1986 with no knowledge of WEA nor the MC's history. My veteran mentors and coleaders were my faculty.

> It became a matter of living it out, walking in faith with sufficient light just in front to slowly dispel the darkness.

---

3 Fuller, *People of the Mandate*.
4 Howard, *The Dream That Would Not Die*.

As the MC leader, an intriguing question niggled at me: How and why do people come together in common cause, whether it be in secular, religious, marketplace, global entities, or NGOs? Are these groups the result of changing sociological realities, the ebb and flow of peoples, the role of information and technology or historical periods? Are they built into the God-designed DNA of human society? Do we Christians just adopt and adapt "secular" concepts and structures, shaping and reshaping them into what's needed for their God-calling? Probing deeper, does God have anything to do with these human organizational dimensions that so shape our world? Is this common grace? Christian organizations reveal a diversity of structures, and most are conceived with pure motives, led by gifted and godly (we hope) people with the charisms to carry forward a group, or agency, or movement, or fellowship, or alliance, or network.

Going further, what is God's design for the lifecycle of an organization? Too many times entities run their course, some becoming dead trees, dry streams. Perhaps we should create honorable "burial (memory) ceremonies" that celebrate the now-defunct status of a Christian entity. Jon Lewis's dry humor led him to say, as we discussed how to renew WEA and the MC, "Howard wrote about 'the dream that would not die,' but what if it's 'the nightmare that won't go away'"?

Few leaders courageously ask, "What would happen if we dissolved our organization?" Some of us in the MC asked this very question about ourselves and WEA—especially during the cyclical seasons when the Lausanne Movement seemed to ascend, and WEA descend. I knew of the confidential conversations that occasionally took place regarding the possible merger of WEA and Lausanne. It never happened. Why? Because the DNA, ethos, and leadership of each entity was genetically different, and the merger would not have birthed a healthy organization. I am convinced that God did not allow that to take place. Had WEA died, within short years a creative group of people would create an entity with a new name but with similar vision, leadership structures, functions, and values.

For the MC, what terminology best described our preferred structure? As the MC's leader it was an honor to grapple with these issues in strategic collegial conversations held in Canada, England, Holland, Sweden, and South Africa during the early 1990s into 2004. We collegially sought renewal, a re-envisioning of our global ship to navigate the world's human oceans. Were we a federation? No. Were we an association? Not really. Were we then a fellowship, as fuzzy as it sounds? No, we were more than that. Were we an alliance? Probably, but was that all? Were we a network, a flexible structure functioning with minimal structure and systems, convening in a common cause and crucial times for shared purpose, guided by revolving leadership? Yes, perhaps. But networks have their own weaknesses. In network flux, life depends on the key convener and critical issues. People roll on and off as they desire and change. Too many times the champion is left with only a mailing list, a handful of concerns, a fuzzy legacy, and a financial deficit.

And hovering over all our re-envisioning was the challenge of fundraising to support the MC's team, projects, publications, programs. While we served WEA, truth be told, we were not necessarily supported financially by headquarters. Staff raised our own support, a heavy challenge, especially when wanting to bring on key players from the Global South. We raised our own funds even to attend key WEA events and leadership forums. This reality, however, also reflected leadership from below.

At the end of that season, to me the best language and most viable MC definition called us a hybrid, a "network with the leadership and services of an alliance" that focused on building, sustaining, and serving a global missional community. We were not information driven but relationship driven, thus birthing a singular alliance of colleagues and reflective practitioners with shared mission passions. I had no hierarchical authority over my colleagues; we were all volunteers in a common cause. A "network with the leadership and services of an alliance." This language best described what the MC became over the years.

Reflecting on the MC years has led me to ponder these personal questions. What might I have done differently? What mistakes did I make? Were some of them redeemable? Did I have enough faith in the Spirit's capacity to guide and empower us? Did I centralize too much in my hands? Was I an effective delegator, releasing others into their fullest gifting and spheres of influence? Did I mentor younger and emerging leaders well?

Other disturbing queries emerged: Did I make adversaries during those years? Possibly, yes. Another chapter tackles that topic. Did I have the courage to dismiss MC associates who had violated our unspoken communal covenants? Yes, but this was so difficult. Should I have totally left WEA in 2006? No, but I never regretted turning over leadership to Bertil and his team.

A highlight period within the broader WEA came during 2001–2002 when I was invited into its Interim Leadership Team, led by Dave Detert, WEA's then International Council chair. Honored to serve our broader global community, I gladly joined this international diverse and gifted team of women and men. We received, studied, and welcomed the groundbreaking 2002 *Interdev Study* with its comprehensive evaluation of WEA, its outcomes, and clear recommendations for our preferred future.[5] But we learned a painful lesson on leadership. Consultancy gifts don't necessarily convert into the competencies needed to lead an entity like WEA. Regretfully and mysteriously, within a year of its approval, the report disappeared, was never discussed, and thus never implemented. It became one of my greatest disappointments. I felt at the time it had the potential to revitalize our struggling WEA community. My computer guards those files, worthy of a doctoral dissertation on flawed institutional decisions.

I learned much about leadership selection and especially leadership succession. Scripture reveals different kinds of leadership categories, arenas, positions, qualifications, and expectations. Jesus had the twelve, the seventy-two, and larger groups of disciples (in the broadest use of the term). But he personally selected and invested in life-on-life training for the twelve. His tightest group was Peter, James, and John. Our Lord honored and was served by a band of gifted, financially resourced, dedicated women. He delegated authority to the apostles and gave them his promised Spirit to empower them. The Spirit fell upon women and men. The Acts narratives reveal the diverse handling of emerging and recognized leadership, of intentional and relational equipping, of spontaneous leadership emerging in both women and men. We also read the disturbing stories of sin, deception, ego, and apostasy—in a first-generation church! When Paul and Peter write about church leadership qualifications, they focus on spirituality and character and less on skills, gifts, and structures. These values shaped their core training curriculum.

I witnessed leadership transitions numerous times in WEA and the MC. In 1986 I was appointed unilaterally by two WEF leaders with only Theo Williams guiding me. Other veterans mentored me, and our team grew little by little. The MC Executive Council (ExCo) became our board. But we essentially "assembled the plane in the air." The first bylaws clarified issues and provided answers to emerging structural

---
5 *The Interdev Study*, unpublished WEA document, 2002.

and governance questions. Candidly, the best leadership transition I saw was the 2006 one from me to Bertil. I was keenly disappointed with the transition from Bertil to David Ruíz, a process marred by the isolation of the staff team, disregarding historical documents that had guided us from 2003–2006, and grave misunderstanding due to culture and language. Our MC strength—diversity—might have become our weakness. A healthier process took place later when New Zealander Jay Mātenga was named executive director.

On Legacies: A Dicey Topic

Thankfully, those three MC decades were not about my legacy That perspective made me uneasy. Yet, upon reflection, several conclusions emerged. First, as my core instincts were released along with my deepest values, gift mix, and skill set, I am most thankful for the worldwide relationships and friendships that God birthed. This in turn led to the creation of a singular missional community of reflective practitioners, colleagues, and friends.

Second, God provided wisdom and mentors during my early years. I was "soft-mentored" to lead, not intentionally nor though books, nor formal study. It just happened by God's mercy and the Barnabas model. Thank you, Dave, Theo, Ray, Stanley, Panya, Barbara, Wade. Progressively, God grew our scattered band of gifted and godly men and women to become a global community of reflective practitioners.

Third, no national, regional, or global evangelical body represents everybody. As a Nigerian colleague once said, "There are too many contrasting streams in Africa for us to flow down one channel." So, all praise to Lausanne and WEA, to the Association of Evangelicals of Africa and MANI (the Movement of African National Initiatives), and other free-flowing networks. I knew some people maneuvered to play a primary MC leadership role, but with impure motives. Their intentions were ulterior, desiring power and influence. God delivered us from most.

Fourth, due to our creative and global MC team, several structural changes of our "alliance" lasted longer. We created a singular system of "docking to the MC Mother Ship." This brought in a group of parallel networks and other mission structures, providing all players with clear value-added benefit. These independent entities could undock as desired. At one point we had at least ten of these along with another set of "MC" units. The MC launched a few long-lasting task forces that continue today as vital, working expressions of our vision: the International Missionary Training Network, and the Global Member Care Network. Some of our MC-founded entities spun off into their own independent orbit. Some temporary study units were created, such as the one on globalization, which led to a publication and a Global Consultation. Others had a shorter shelf life and were laid to rest.

I am grateful for the MC consultations convened and publications released during those years. These substantive and valuable resources reflected my commitment to release global voices to speak into global issues—by women and men, younger and older, from Global South and North, representing diverse missional-minded structures. Topics included missionary training, strategic alliances, missionary attrition and retention, global missiology, the church in mission, contextualization, mission mobilization, persecution and martyrdom, spirituality and mission, and others. When I gaze at my robust MC bookshelf, I thank God.

Finally, the human legacy. Intentional, relationship-focused mentoring has been a gift and lifelong passion of mine. I can trace some younger friends all the way back to my IVCF staff years, to the years in Guatemala, the WEA decades, and today. In God's peculiar providence, it came to me yesterday that five mentees have played significant roles within WEA, and not all because of my connection with them. It just happened.

The Vision and Life's Tapestry

Perhaps seven years ago another word from the Lord came as I evaluated three decades of MC publications. "Bill, you dedicated yourself to publish the voices of your global colleagues. Now you must write and speak from your own experience, wisdom, and heart. Be released." In January 2020, I spent some days with a small group of treasured Latin American mentees. As I shared my musing on this word from God, my tested friend, David Ruíz, spoke prophetically, "Guillermo, you must exchange your tongue (your teaching and preaching voice) for your pen (your writing in Spanish and English)." I took that word to heart.

> Intentional, relationship-focused mentoring has been a gift and lifelong passion of mine.

Now eighty-four, may God help me understand in what ways my entire life was a prelude to this season. I am because of what I was, have been and done, and grown into. I am because of others. I am because of my family. But I have also been recommissioned and gifted for the next assignment, the last lap of the marathon.

In 2017, Ted Esler, President of Missio Nexus, astounded me when informing me that his executive team had voted to give me the "Lifetime of Service" award at their annual gathering in September 2018. Never had I imagined that anything like this would happen to me. It was such an unexpected gift. I was deeply humbled to be chosen for this honor. I was delighted that Yvonne, Christine, David, and Stephanie accompanied me to celebrate that moment. During that ceremony I opened my heart to tell that audience of church and mission leaders, "You, Missio Nexus community, with so many acquaintances, colleagues, and friends, are My Tribe." I was a lifelong, cross-cultural servant out of that North American movement. I belonged to them and they to me. All associated with the movement had responded to that global "call," had invested lives in other cultures, paid a heavy price; and (thankfully most) remained as followers of Jesus.

At times I ask myself if I am retired, or retreaded, or reassigned? I trust the latter, even as I downshift and acknowledge limitations, and as I come to grips with my inevitably aging body. I am invited to embrace the ordinary and to experience another dimension of the downward path of the cross. It's the Jesus way. Stuff happens: including my perennially problematic digestive system (thanks to eighty-four years in too many places, where my only choice is to eat what is set before me). I appreciate what Ted Esler said in a recent email, "I am on a global walkabout. I will have email access on and off, mostly off, so please be patient with me. I will be back in the office July 31st, hopefully having avoided becoming a playground for some new kind of parasite." Other challenges include sleep issues, with circadian rhythms permanently disoriented, and neck bone spurs and degenerative arthritis. I thought I had already paid health dues, but on Thursday, September 13, 2018, I sat in the clinic of a new physician, evaluating whether he might become our primary doctor. As he moved through the standard procedures, thumping, probing, and testing this and that with hands and stethoscope, he paused. "Hmmm. Let's do that again." He stopped, looked at me and said, "Mr. Taylor, I know you did not come in to see me for this reason; but you have a serious case of Afib—Atrial fibrillation, abnormal heartbeat. You need to find a cardiologist right away to get tested, and you must start now on a blood thinner. I have free samples."

Suddenly. Everything. Stops. I called Yvonne, who immediately started praying for healing and wisdom. Within days I met my new cardiology team. New procedures, echocardiograms, cardioversions, an ablation. Medications, some with negative side effects. Apparently, my heart had Afib symptoms for years, but I was unaware of it. I remembered that during the violent Guatemala guerilla war I experienced tachycardia—racing heartbeat—but not Afib.

I saw with crystal clarity that my life would no longer be the same. I was invited into more quietness, and I cancelled "excellent" speaking engagements, retreated to quiet writing, into an undefined process with an unclear ending. Thanksgiving week, 2021, found me in the hospital with another heart crisis, this one leading to the insertion of a pacemaker. A more recent bout with Afib plus a six-day stay in the hospital cardiac ward in October 2024 underscored the need to trust God with my life. It was another reminder of the foothills.

Conclusion and Lessons

A unique providence took place during the 2010 Cape Town Lausanne Congress after I found my seat at my designated roundtable. A young African sat also. When introducing ourselves, I noted his name tag and gasped. He was Rev. Stephen Panya Baba, the son of my dear friend, Panya—now with the Lord. Stephen, a chartered accountant by training, was now the head of EMS (later to become ECWA's president). He updated me on the Gwandará church. In a later email he reported. "No real survey has ever been done on the number of Gwandaras that are Christians but considering that Plateau State alone was reported to have had at a time 12,000 Gwandará believers, the total figure will definitely be over a hundred thousand, and that is being very, very prudent." They are now a sending base, generating a steady stream of pastors, missionaries, and committed believers into all of Nigeria.

I wish I could update our patriarch Abraham, reviewing Genesis 12, that through his seed all nations would be blessed. I wondered whether he had an honored seat to watch that promise become fulfilled over the years. Then I realized that Gwandará-wa people were already with him, perhaps including some martyrs. But over one hundred thousand headed Abraham's way?

Little could I have even dreamed what my life would become after those three decades in service of the global church on mission. There is no way to compress the narratives, lessons, or engagement with such a global diversity of mission leaders and structures. Today I'm an older veteran leader, an empowered evangelical, a man scarred by life's blows, a man wisely deconstructed and released to walk into my new assignments. I am an indebted servant who reflects on these decades, their impact on me, and any legacy. I am a resident alien in this human journey in the kingdom of God. I am a husband, a father, and a grandfather.

However, I'm not to withdraw from life and ministry. While I shall not cross the range ahead, I can engage the foothills. I'm not to brood over mistakes, disappointments, and unanswered prayer. My challenge is now to walk with courage into this final life season, to press in, deeper, tougher, and higher. I am to invest in the less-visible dimensions of global mission. I am a grateful participant and witness of the global evangelical movement and its missional dimensions. This marker is critical to leading from below: having a heart focused on the Son, the Servant King.

And now I walk into the foothills, an elder loved by the Father, redeemed by the Son, enabled by the Spirit. Little did I know how God's loving and sovereign plan would knead me at my core. This all pours into finishing well.

Reflection Questions

1. What impressions strike you about the Gwandará-wa story and mission agencies?
2. What does "to walk towards the foothills" evoke in your mind and heart?
3. What does it mean to open space for "global voices to address global issues"?
4. Is it legitimate to wonder about one's legacy in life? What are the dangers?
5. What might "walking to the foothills" mean to you?

From TEDS back to Guatemala, 1983

Three Young TCK's

Historic and Global Transitions

Dr. Max Pérez, Dr. Emilio Antonio Núñez

Russellville, AR, USA, 1990

Family Book

World Missions for the Local Church, 2014

The Watershed Venue

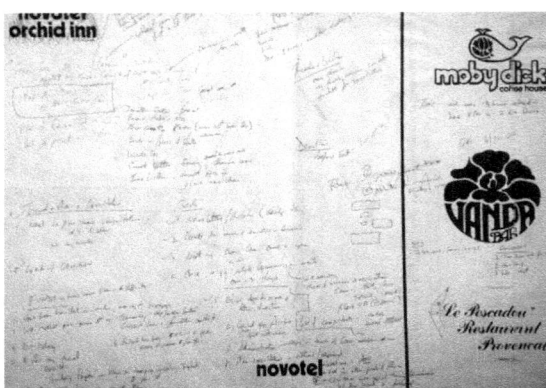
The First MC Job Description

David Howard, mentor since Urbana, 1967

Esther and Theo Williams, Bangalore, 1988

WEA International Council, 1986

Mission Commission Exec. Council, 1992

Leadership to Bertil, South Africa, 2006

MC Staff Team, Pattaya, 2008

WEA General Assembly, Singapore, 1986

Latins at MC Global Consultation on Missionary Attrition, All Nations College, UK, 1996

MC Global Consultation on Missionary Attrition, All Nations College, UK, 1996

MC Global Roundtable, South Africa, 2015

Pattaya, Thailand, 2008

Connections: A Dream that Died

MC Global Consultation on Missionary Attrition, All Nations College, UK, 1996

9
Honest to God About One's Blindness

As recently as the end of 2019 I was present at a dinner in Kuala Lumpur where a representative from a megachurch in the USA was introduced as having come to promote the leadership program that his church has been running globally for some years. I was rather surprised, to say the least. Did not his church make headlines in the USA and elsewhere earlier in the year because the senior pastor had to resign over sexual abuse charges? And did not the whole eldership board resign subsequently in admission of their failure to deal adequately with the complaints that had come much earlier? And was there no recognition of the fact that there may just have been some connections between the leadership program that his church was running globally and the leadership implosion in his church? Clearly not! In any case, as they say, the show must go on![1]

Michelangelo's affirmation at age eighty-seven, *ancora imparo*, "I am still learning," encourages me. My mind still functions, embraces the new, expands, and changes, hopefully with thoughtfulness. I have not arrived. I am a man *on the way* with Jesus. I am a servant who has asked forgiveness for my shortcomings and mistakes. God delivered me from blindness in five specific areas. I receive these delayed gifts to this pilgrim on a journey into the eternal mission of the Triune God.

> I have not arrived. I am a man *on the way* with Jesus.

However, I wish I had been able to identify my myopia in order to correct course earlier in my life and ministry. Doing so would have impacted my service in cross-cultural mission. I would have been a better and wiser parent and leader had I known these realities earlier than later. The leader from below must be honest regarding shortcomings for it

---
1 Yung, *Leadership or Servanthood?*, 17.

reveals development in character and wisdom, welcoming new insights and new gifts-skills for the task ahead. God in his gracious timing brought me revelation and transformation.

The Theoretical Supernaturalist

Evil supernaturalism gobsmacked me in Guatemala. Some colleagues had called these malignant manifestations mere "superstitions," and for too long I left it there. During our first term of service, David Howard's life, stories, messages, and books on the supernatural—evil and good—during his years in Colombia destabilized my then-settled beliefs. I possessed neither a theology nor pastoral skills to confront evil supernaturalism. Deeper than that, I had relegated the miraculous—both evil and good realities—to phenomena belonging to the church's first century. But had they ceased, really? Life experience came first, as I encountered realities I could not handle. Dave's powerful stories drove me to reread Scripture and revisit church history. Finally, that revised understanding affected my theology and pastoral practice. I do remember reading for a Moody missions class a little book called *Demon Experiences in Many Lands*.[2] Of course, the book did not include cases from USA or Europe. Ironically, some of the chapters were written by veteran colleagues I would meet in Guatemala. But I could not grasp the reality of those narratives.

Two cases illustrate my conundrum. Once in Guatemala, out of curiosity, I entered a peculiar-looking religious building similar to other traditional Catholic churches. But inside, my nascent discernment instantly went on high alert; I felt a very deep unease, a discernment of evil that was new to me. What was it about this church structure close to our home during those years? I discovered it was the central worship sanctuary of organized Guatemalan spiritism—open demon worship.

Then, the poltergeist experience in the home of a new believer of our Guatemalan church shook me. She had come to her young pastor seeking help, but I was clueless. Oh, I suggested the displaced furniture and noises were caused by her dog shifting the furniture around at night. How ludicrous I must have appeared, especially when she told me they had no dog. My inadequacy as a lead elder made me pass that case to our trusted friend and Yvonne's prayer-fasting partner, Lois Morales. Later I sheepishly asked what she had done, "Oh, it was obviously demonic. I went to her home, listened to her stories, then we prayed and anointed

---

2 Moody Bible Institute, *Demon Experiences in Many Lands*.

the doors and windows with oil. I rebuked Satan and banished the demons from the house, we read Scripture, prayed again, and I left." I said nothing, but I pondered her words in my heart.

My next challenging step required me to reread Scripture with a different kind of Spirit-directed perspective. My modernity-shaped worldview and theological presuppositions had controlled my understanding of Scripture, my spiritual categories, and my pastoral practices. I wondered what would happen if, well, I had been wrong? Yvonne, my crypto-charismatic, had already embarked on the journey as a practicing supernaturalist, not tied to my bounded theological constructs. Returning to Scripture anew, I imagined myself as one of the original hearers or readers, attempting to free myself from the evangelical rationalism that had misshaped me. I again studied the cessasionist arguments on the sign gifts, concluding that they were inadequate. This internal conversation lasted for years, until I openly transitioned into the empowered evangelical framework. It was a change, but within the broad orthodox WEA world, we were on safe ground.

That transition released me into a full spectrum understanding of evil supernaturalism and how to grapple with it. Perhaps more importantly, it guided me into an expectation of God's good supernatural power released through the empowering presence of the Spirit. Additionally, I began to read Scripture more from a Hebraic perspective, where supernaturalism, as well as the reality of animistic cultures around Israel (i.e., the entire Bible), were presuppositions and natural realities. Our decade at Hope Chapel provided an ecclesial community that lived in these realities. Our most recent transition into the three-stranded Anglicanism—Scripture, Spirit, Sacraments—provided organic and global continuity. Friends have asked me, "Have you received any new gifts or manifestations?" My answer is "No, though Yvonne has." In my case it's more of an affirmation of the Spirit's internal witness, "Bill, you are where I want you to be, now. Sharpen your gifts."

I wondered. What if I had made this paradigm shift earlier, while in Guatemala? Possibly we would have had to resign from the mission. So, was the Father waiting until his time for me to transition at the right time, later? Perhaps. But I wish I'd had the theological and pastoral template to deal with both evil and good supernaturalism. Jesus certainly was a practicing supernaturalist.

No Theology of Social Justice

I grew up *around* poverty in Costa Rica but never asked why the majority were poor and so few better off, including my family. The question didn't exist in my child's understanding of the universe. When I returned as an adult in 1968 to Latin America with my wife and later with children, we committed to micro economic development projects, primarily on behalf of some families and single mothers who had worked in our home.

They, by extension, blessed their broader family network. We demonstrated organic compassion at the personal level. But was that enough?

Over my years I also observed religious and political hypocrisy. Liberation Theology defended the "preferential option for the poor." However, I knew no evangelical advocate of Liberation Theology who lived poor, with, or among the poor. They preferred the preferential option for the poor but not the poverty.

One memorable exchange took place in 1970 at InterVarsity's Costa Rica Overseas Training Camp program under David Howard's leadership. The speaker that day was chairman of the national Communist Party. Delighted to lecture these young, American students, he eloquently argued for Costa Rica's downtrodden and how the entire system itself had to be radically transformed. However, I knew something about him: his wife was a wealthy landowner, a member of Costa Rica's historic oligarchy. So, in the Q&A time I innocently asked, "Don Francisco [pseudonym], thank you for your informative talk. Should not wealthy landowners set an example in giving up their riches to help the poor?" He said, "But of course they must and can lead." Again: "Does that mean that your wife and you would model land reform by distributing your own coffee plantations?" He stuttered, "Well, it's a complicated situation and must be done appropriately."

Social justice never appeared during my seminary studies. Even during our early years in Latin America, my mission colleagues never addressed justice and transformation issues. The exception was the tangible proof of the gospel transforming individuals and families. I had no biblical nor theological foundation even for micro-justice projects. One colleague argued that to get involved in social action was anti-gospel, delaying our Lord's return. He vehemently told a Salvadoran medical doctor that his orphanage was not blessed by God. I thank God for that courageous believer for openly and rightly rebuking the American missionary.

What would I have done in Guatemala had I made the paradigm shift into a robust theology of compassion and justice, denunciation, and transformation? I would have faced pressures from mission leadership, though probably not be required to resign. Within our agency I found myself more on the social justice side than my other North American colleagues. René Padilla, Samuel Escobar, Emilio Antonio Núñez, Pedro Arana Quiróz, Orlando Costas, Valdir Steuernagel and others shaped my perspective through their speaking and writing, reorienting a generation of evangelicals.

Yes, God was patient with me, but I wish I had had a stronger biblical and practical approach to injustice—personal and structural. I did not fully understand the impact of Leviticus 19, Psalms 82 and 146, Mary's Magnificat, Luke 4, and Matthew 25. As I write this line, I gaze at my recently purchased copy of the *Poverty and Justice Bible*.[3] I continue to grow.

During the recent 500th celebration of the Protestant Reformation and its Latin American iteration, my younger Latin colleagues taught me something totally new. That epiphany led me to understand a critical historical factor. The Protestant Reformation values coming to Latin America were mediated by the European and North American church and mission movement, and its strong pietistic, individualist spirituality. But those importations were bereft of the biblical social implications of the gospel and the power to transform the larger society, with no theology of work, also central themes for the Reformation. Neither did we understand the Reformation's position on the dignity of vocation, justice, and law. The results are all too evident today, factors that alone demarcate nations and cultures, especially the failed ones in Latin America.

No Vision of Missions from Latin America

Ana Eloisa, a SETECA student, jarred me around 1980. "Don Guillermo," she said, "God has called me as a missionary to the Maya Ixil people of Guatemala. How should I prepare and what mission society can I work with?" I silently said to myself, "Nope. No way sister. What's more, your vocational certification is automobile electric technician, and your academic track record here is spotty at best." I was speechless, and simply listened and tried to encourage her, then prayed with her. I was unable to guide her. Worse, I was faithless. I saw no place for her dream, or her

---

3 *Poverty and Justice Bible*, American Bible Society.

word from God. She proved me totally wrong. Against all odds she served for many years in the Ixil Triangle, an exceedingly dangerous region of Guatemala during its latest civil war. Then, to my surprise, years later Ana Eloisa transferred to another ministry, this one based in Albania. My sadness is compounded when I realize that neither missionary nor national faculty shared her vision in those years. It was a non-starter.

Missions then was "far away, over there," international, to the ends of the earth, cross-cultural and long term. Binary. It belonged primarily to Europeans and North Americans, *from the West to the Rest*. Latin America was the mission field, not a mission force. That category did not significantly change until the early 1980s, pioneered by colleagues who reshaped me; Luis Bush was one of those creative pastor-mission leaders for Latin America, later the world.

But it was the TEDS missions class (November 8, 1982) where my own teaching convicted, converted, and redirected my life. In the very middle of my class, having researched Third World Missions to teach that day, I realized I had done nothing in my own arena of influence—SETECA and our local church—much less a broader context. I returned to Latin America with a new vision and a sense of holy anticipation. This conversion was imperative if God were to invite me to serve the global church for the rest of my life. Little could I have dreamed that for twenty years I would lead a global ministry focused from everywhere to everywhere.

Over my stronger years, twelve American churches have invited me as consultant to their process to start or revitalize their missionary vision and program. However, most focused on "missions out there," far away, distant, overseas, cross-cultural, the broader world; and in one it was only for the 10–40 Window. Around 2006, Cliff Warner (my son-in-law), in his first year as priest at our church, asked me to articulate a church vision for mission from an Acts 1:8 perspective, starting with the city of Austin. That experience was important for me, because it was the first time that I specifically rooted the church's outreach vision in its own "Jerusalem"; then to its Judea (geographically and culturally close); then its Samaria (geographically close but culturally different), and from there to the ends of the earth (geographically and culturally distant). Why had I missed that before? Even here I had lived a false binary. I was awakening and growing.

Americans divided the world into "home missions" and "overseas missions." American Southern Baptists are familiar with their two annual mission offerings named after remarkable women—Annie Armstrong home, and Lottie Moon international.

I returned to both Testaments, reading God's heart for the nations (political, geographic and ethnic), examining the early church's own obedience to the flow of Acts 1:8. Other crucial passages from both Old and New Testaments revealed the missional heart of God. Some thirty years ago, my preaching and teaching changed to teach a wholistic integration of five elements: Good News, church/community, compassion, justice, and all within the context of persecution. This emerged from my understanding of the Luke 4 Nazareth Manifesto, now integrated for me with other Great Commission passages.

Nevertheless, in the middle of these slow-motion reflections some two decades ago, I noticed an emerging danger in the USA. When a church focuses primarily on the local arena (their Jerusalem and perhaps a symbolic Samaria), but excludes the outward spirals, it runs the risk of a truncated local program focused on the local, and many times only on compassion and justice ministries. Is it a flaw seen also in some seminaries? Already we have documented case studies of terminated cross-cultural ministries focus only on compassion and justice.

No Theology of the Arts—in Mission or Vocation

"What do we do with Mildred and Manolo?" This musically gifted couple had been one of Guatemala's most popular singers in night clubs and music festivals. When they came to faith and our relationship began, the question arose, "What now for them?" Well, that was relatively easy (to me): they should sing Christian songs. But must they totally leave their former world and friends? In their case the journey led more into Christian music and a creative evangelistic ministry.

What about Elías and Ana Elsy, professional ballet dancers and stars in Guatemala's National Ballet Company? Yvonne had led Ana Elsy to Christ, and Elías committed his life a few months later. Were they to leave that world and try to make another living? I assumed that they would have to find a totally new career. Ha! Ana Elsy transformed my mind and heart. Her ballet career concluded with the starring role in Coppélia, and we were her special guests that night. It was magnificent and beautiful, stirring something deeply in me. After the finale, we met her in her dressing room where, with radiant face she exclaimed, "Yvonne and Guillermo, as I listened to the orchestra's overture, waiting for the curtain to open, I dedicated Coppélia to Jesus Christ!" They became Stephanie's ballet instructors. They also became lifelong friends. They came to our fiftieth wedding celebration in June 2018 in Antigua, Guatemala, and I'll never forget the embrace between them and Stephanie that afternoon. There they told us of the series of Bible studies and conversions of fellow ballet dancers in the succeeding years. In their upper 60s, they still teach classical ballet.

But all this still did not prepare me for what would later unfold. In 2008 I participated in an event that would ground my incipient theology of the arts and its place in the global mission of the church. The Austin symposium, "Transforming Culture: A Vision for the Church and the Arts," had been conceived, convened, and directed by our son David, cosponsored by The Hill Country Institute for Contemporary Christianity.[4] Some 500 pastors, artists, theologians, educators, ministry leaders, and ethnomusicologists attended the local church venue. The speaker lineup was unique, drawing on David's personal relationships: Eugene Peterson, Andy Crouch, Jeremy Begbie, Barbara Nicolosi, John Witvliet. Some twenty-seven breakout sessions complemented the plenaries. The nonstop discussions were rich. Reading my copy of the program I see that I was listed as a Senior Advisor since I was then WEA's Global Ambassador. What did I know about this topic?

At this event, I encountered a company of extremely gifted women and men with a passion for the arts in the global mission of God. Some were professional artists, others were teachers and trainers, yet others were ethnomusicologists. All affirmed the arts as expressions of God's character. Their passion was arts in and for mission. They all knew each other; I was the newbie. Yet they invited me, because I represented the WEA-Mission Commission, to gather with them after the symposium. Thank you, Robin Harris, John Franklin, Colin Harbinson, Jill Ford, Frank Fortunato, Brian Schrag and James Kraybill; you changed my life. I had simply never understood this artistic tapestry of God's character, his community and artistic proclamation. Soon after, Bertil Ekström asked David, accompanied by other key advocates for the arts in global contexts, to speak on the arts at the Pattaya, Thailand, consultation in November 2008. There the MC established a new task force on mission and the arts, affirming its commitment to the arts, culture, and the church's mission. We soon dedicated a double issue of our MC journal, *Connections*, to this topic. This event led to David's edited publication on the arts and the church, his first on that theme.

This awakening was not only in relation to arts in, or for, mission, but also the calling and vocation of the Christian artist. Those of us in the mission world might unfortunately fall into the trap of seeing arts only

---

4 Taylor, *For the Beauty of the Church*.

for mission, regardless of the medium. We are familiar with YWAM's pioneering work and its creative production in public street drama, which opens conversations that point to Jesus. But it's different when we think of the artist themselves, how best to disciple them, how to welcome them into the Christian community, and how to affirm their vocation and calling. The goal here was to invite artists into a lifelong occupation to do good art for the glory of God and to reflect his character in all we do.

A personal coda. A further chapter of my pilgrimage in this realm came when David married Phaedra, an artist with a profound theology of art and beauty, generating art with subtle, deep and poignant meaning.

No Theology of Creation Care

The first time I heard colleagues advocate for creation care as central to God's mission they unsettled me. At best they seemed to divert attention from the essentials to this tertiary topic. In 1996 Yvonne and I served for a short time as visiting tutors at All Nations Christian College (ANCC), with Chris Wright as principal. The other visiting tutors included Miranda and Peter Harris, founders of the conservancy program, A Rocha International—an organization that today has a tangible presence in twenty-one nations. During our shared weeks at ANCC, they graciously and articulately advocated for a broader concept of mission, with nature conservation at the center of God's heart for his creation.

Initially, their promotion disturbed me. I asked questions, for I respected them. Later I discovered another trusted WEA colleague from India with the same passions. But it was at our MC consultation in Iguassu, November 1999 where the issue emerged (thanks to Chris Wright's presence with us), and we all were challenged. A team of seven women and men from six nations produced *The Iguassu Affirmation*, which was debated among the 160 participants from 53 nations. We signed its formal draft that final night. Chris served on that team. The twelfth declaration reads:

> The earth is the LORD's and the gospel is good news for all creation. Christians share in the responsibility God gave to all humanity to care for the earth. We call on all Christians to commit themselves to ecological integrity in practicing responsible stewardship of creation, and we encourage Christians in environmental care and protection initiatives.[5]

---
5 Taylor, *Global Missiology*, 20.

Following Iguassu, Chris continued to reshape my understanding of this wholistic nature of God's mission and creation care, which are central to God's mission and hence ours.

Truth be told, our roots in Guatemala were green long before green was a thing. We repaired and recycled everything possible, and we were within a Guatemalan society that repaired things, reutilizing much trash. Over the years we committed to living frugally, resisting American consumerism and waste. Yet, the fact is that back then our commitment to creation care and concern to preserve Guatemala's natural resources and environment were not guided by an articulated theology of creation care.

Conclusion and Lessons

They ate the chicken bones!

I vividly recall the short-term vision trip we led from Arkansas to Guatemala in mid-1988. Under the leadership of a dear family friend, Lisbeth Piedrasanta (SETECA grad with an MA in Christian Counseling from TEDS, also cofounder of The Potters House ministry at the Guatemala City dump), we visited a rural Christian school where the children came from absolute poverty. I've forgotten our tasks for the last day, because what was *done to me* undid me when we brought in buckets of the Guatemalan chicken specialty, *Pollo Campero*, to share with the kids who excelled in their studies. Sitting at a large communal table, we prayed and began lunch. I consumed my salad, fries, and meat, naturally leaving the bones to one side. But not the kids to my left or right. Glancing at their empty plate, I wondered where the bones had gone. They were eating them! What? Didn't they know you don't eat the bones? Or had they never eaten chicken before? Or were their calcium-depleted bodies demanding bone nutrients? I have never forgotten that meal. I still see those bones disappearing.

After lunch the godly school director and his wife related the story of a pestilential odor that had oozed from one section of the wall of their main hall shortly after renting the space. It was mysterious; it was evil. Nothing in the natural realm caused the stench. He continued his story. While praying, they discerned in the Spirit that the previous owners of the building had cursed the Christian school and had buried something in the walls. They broke into the concrete block walls where the putrid odor was strongest, and to their astonishment discovered a pouch of demon-saturated bones and other objects and artifacts, the source of the reeking smell. They destroyed the pouch by fire and strong prayers of deliverance from demonic forces and the malignant emissaries sent to oppose the school. Satanic powers were broken. Natural breezes refreshed the room; the enemy was banished. But we Americans, me included, were silent, speechless, pondering. Many had absolutely no category to understand what we had just heard.

Why did this happen to us, our small team from a small church in a small Arkansas town? And why do I still remember it so intensely? Partly, because it illustrates two of my blind spots during that first major season of my life and ministry—poverty and injustice, and evil supernaturalism destroyed by God's power. I wish my background had better prepared me earlier, but by God's grace I was growing and changing.

> I learned from my own blindness. All this was part of the Father's retraining me for the rest of my leadership.

I learned from my own blindness, and I thank God for new eyes to see and discern. All this was part of the Father's retraining me for the rest of my leadership.

Reflective Questions

1. Why is it appropriate for a leader to confess failures or "blindnesses"?

2. In what way is a blindness a gift? What does it have to do with forgiveness?

3. Which of the five themes caught your attention the most? Why so?

4. What do these "confessions" have to do with leadership?

10
Blessed Are They Who Do Not Take Themselves Too Seriously

Old Rabbi Moishe and the Pope

Many centuries ago, the Pope decided (again) that all Jews had to leave Rome. Naturally, there was a big uproar from the Jewish community. So, the Pope made a deal. He would debate a rabbi from the Jewish community. If he won, the Jews could stay. If the Pope won, the Jews would abandon Rome.

The Jews, realizing that they had no choice, picked the wise, old Rabbi Moishe to represent them. Moishe asked for one condition to the debate. To make it more interesting, neither side would be allowed to talk. The Pope agreed.

The day of the great debate came. Moishe and the Pope sat opposite each other in the Sistine Chapel for a long five minutes before the Pope raised his hand, showing three fingers. Moishe looked back at him, paused, and raised one finger in a side-to-side motion. The Pope paused, then countered by waving his fingers in a circle around his head. Moishe immediately pointed to the ground where he sat. Silence. The Pope then pulled out a wafer and a glass of wine. To which Moishe pulled out an apple. Astonished, the Pope stood, broke the silence, declaring: "I give up. This Rabbi is too good. The Jews stay."

Shortly afterwards in the Sistine Chapel, the Cardinals surrounded the Pope asking him what happened. His Holiness said, "First I held up three fingers to represent the Trinity. He responded by holding up one finger to remind me that there was still one God common to both our religions. I waved my fingers around me to show him that God was all around us. He simply pointed to the ground showing that God was also right here with us. I then pulled out the wine and wafer to show that God absolved us of our sins. He pulled out an apple reminding me of original sin. He had an answer for everything. What could I do?"

Meanwhile, the Jewish community crowded around Moishe the Rabbi. "What happened?" they asked. "Well," said Moishe, "First he said to me that the Jews had three days to get out of here. I told him that not one of us was leaving. Then he told me that this whole city would be cleared of Jews. I let him know we were staying right here." Asked a woman, "And then?" "I don't know," said Moishe the Rabbi, "He took out his lunch and I took out mine. Then he gave up, and we won. We stay."[1]

This is a favorite noncanonical example of human miscommunication, illustrating the challenge we face in cross-cultural interactions. I laugh whenever I relate it, whether in missiological lectures or other contexts around the world. Over my sixty years in cross-cultural ministry, I have made mistakes, some innocent or naïve, others dumb, yet others, stupid and perhaps serious. I could have entitled this chapter, "Mistakes I made, some funny, some dumb, some serious," but we left it more ambiguous, and intriguing—I hope. My *faux pas* shaped me as a leader, and I hoped I would not repeat them but learn from them and let them change me.

> I have made mistakes, some innocent or naïve, others dumb, yet others, stupid and perhaps serious.

Guatemala, Our Classroom

Our early lessons in cross-cultural life came while Yvonne and I were learning cultural features of our new shared world—gaining *cultural intelligence*. Culture certainly shapes time, as we soon discovered. We had been invited to dinner at the home of friends from my high school years in Guatemala, set for 7:30 p.m. (Perhaps I had not heard the nuance, "Let's aim for some time around 7:30 p.m. or so ... "). We showed up five minutes (American time) early to a dark house; we drove around

---

1 This story has been passed on by oral storytelling. This is a version retold by the author, with his own notes added in.

the neighborhood for over an hour, circling back periodically. On our last swing we saw a light, parked, rang the doorbell, "Oh, you came early. Welcome! Mario hasn't returned from the medical clinic but come in!" Mario arrived an hour later. In later years I conversely tried using Latin time with precise, visiting Americans. Bad mistake. Culture trumps all.

Another serious blunder came early in my SETECA teaching. As an egalitarian North American, with incomplete insight into the difference between the Spanish more formal, *usted* and the more intimate personal pronoun, *tú*, I wanted to build relational bridges to my students. I announced on the first day in class that we would use the *tú* pronoun. The outcome was negative and unexpected. I had broken a serious norm that protected the *tú* for trusted relational intimacy, close friendships, and respect. The *usted* preserved appropriate boundaries in formal relationships and social-class differences—as between faculty and students. There was no easy way to repair the damage or save face when I cancelled the failed experiment.

There were other gaffes. During our first term, I bought a motor scooter to save gas and have fun. Later I acquired a larger motorcycle. But after one major accident and two wipeouts, I said, "Bill, good man, sell this thing before it kills you." Later I discovered an old, very used Mercedes Benz needing repair, purchased it, repainted it, and felt rather stylish. I justified it because of its age. However, it was a dumb decision. It was imprudent for me, a missionary, to drive even an old Benz in Guatemala. I think the Spirit convicted me. I sold it. I should have never bought it in the first place.

Global Spaces and Times

Mid-1986, *en route* to Singapore, where surprisingly I would become the new MC leader, I stopped off in Tokyo and then Hong Kong to visit TEDS students. My gracious Japanese former student, Reiko, had asked me if I wanted to stay in a Japanese or American hotel. Not knowing what that really meant and wanting to "identify fully" with Japanese culture, I said, "Oh, of course, Japanese, all the way." Ah, what was I thinking? From the airport via bullet train to the city, an early dinner and later to the hotel, I was overwhelmed with the newness. It was my first trip to Asia. "Teeming millions" language from my missionary heritage was literally true.

Reiko checked me into the hotel—nobody at the desk spoke English—and they looked at me rather oddly (perhaps with amusement?). She instructed me all the way to my room. "Leave your shoes outside the door; no, nobody will steal them. Lower head as you enter. Luggage goes there. Let me check about the bathrooms." Hmmm. I reconnoitered my small room. No bathroom. No bed. A television. No phone. A very small window looking out to a small garden. She returned, "Oh I am so glad. The toilet down the hall is for men. The bathroom is next to it. The 'family toilet' is one floor up." Hmmm, "toilet and bathroom" are not synonymous? "Family toilet"?

Closing the door Reiko said, "We shall now have a tea ceremony. Sit there on the floor." Immediate anxiety hit me. I had never been in a bedroom alone with another woman other than Yvonne. To myself "Bill, breathe deeply, exhale, this is Japan; you asked for this." I experienced my first tea ceremony, an elegant affair that she prepared and served while explaining the elements, process, and meaning. Standing to leave, she gave me the final instructions. "Your mattress is behind those doors. The pillow is different; I hope all is OK. I shall see you tomorrow after breakfast at 9 a.m. for our city tour. Welcome to Japan, and goodnight." I was on my own.

Exhausted and sweaty from the long flights, I made my way to the "bathroom," discovering a very large tub structure with dark water. Curious but courageous, I stripped my clothes off and climbed into the pool and soaped up, fully relaxed. Glancing around I wondered what those small pans were on the wall, and then suddenly I realized, "Stupid! You aren't to get into the tub! You stand by the side using the pans to dip and pour." I levitated out of the tub, thank God before anybody else entered. I dried off with the very, very small towel, dressed and hustled back to my room. "Ah, dumb, ugly American." Curious about Japanese TV, I discovered to my distress that many channels showed only porn. Toxic. Not good. Off it went. The mattress was a thin pad, the pillow a rock. I did not sleep well.

The next morning, I wandered down to the lobby, searching for the restaurant. The clerks silently gazed at me with amusement, again. I found it across the courtyard, sat down but nobody served me. Nobody. Then a lobby clerk came to me and in broken English with hand directions led me to the small adjacent room where guests were served breakfast. Breakfast? The food served was very similar to what I had last night. But food is food. "Be thankful, Bill. Watch and pray. Remember, you asked for the full Japanese experience."

Reiko met me and inquired how things had gone. I answered with smiles and few details. But the night before I had overdosed on sushi and other delicacies; my stomach was now very queasy, worsening through the day. I was not in good shape to travel to Hong Kong that night. The gracious and delicate Reiko delivered me to the airport and off I flew. To this day I simply cannot eat sushi.

At that WEF General Assembly, I met pastors and leaders from Hong Kong and Japan. A lead Japanese pastor invited me to speak at his Wednesday night service during my route back home, with another layover in Tokyo. Entering the church, I embraced him with a hearty Latin *abrazo*—and immediately realized my mistake in the faces of the church members who had never witnessed such a physical invasion. I broke the abrazo, apologized profusely and bowed, and bowed low.

I scored zero on both Japan visits that year. Can I laugh as I write these stories?

Hong Kong: Goof, Gift, or Both?

My tenure at TEDS introduced me to remarkable students, women and men from many nations. Some became friends and others would become Mission Commission colleagues. In 2009, a Chinese grad invited me to speak at a Hong Kong seminary. I accepted with gladness because Yvonne and I knew and respected her, having visited her previously. The seminary covered travel and lodging plus a "modest honorarium." Simultaneous translation would be made from English into Cantonese or Mandarin. The themes were close to my heart: missionary attrition, partnership, holistic mission, the challenge of unreached peoples, the role of the Chinese church in missions, and persecution and martyrdom. While students were my core day audience, the evenings and weekend series were open to the public as a "Special symposium for pastoral staff, mission organization personnel, missionaries and missionary candidates, seminary faculty and students, church leaders and those interested to serve in mission in the future." I prepared with prayer and care. I was ready. So I thought.

After too many sleepless travel hours, my long-standing friend, Samuel Chiang met me at the new airport. We took the train into Hong Kong, lunched, and walked to the ferry station where the seminary's mission's professor would meet me for the final leg. Boarding the ferry (including one heavy bag packed with MC books) to a more distant island, I suddenly felt uneasy. Something was wrong with this picture. Was it ever! Assuming that I would speak at *Evangel Theological College* (historically related to the Evangelical Free Church of China and America), I discovered we were in route to the *Alliance Bible Seminary* (Christian and Missionary Alliance) on Cheung Chau Island where another former student served. I didn't know what to think. I kept quiet, wondering how I made this caliber of a mistake. OK, I can flex; but do I say anything?

The guest room was lovely, and the shower needed. An hour later the mission professor collected me, and we walked down near the ferry for dinner with the student mission team. It was a beautiful walking island; more surprises were yet to come. We sat at an open-air restaurant, with no menu. Still figuring things out, I asked about the students. "Oh, they are getting the food and will be here shortly." They soon arrived with three large plastic bags filled with our dinner—a variety of sea creatures, only three or four which I could identify, all of which were flapping furiously to escape their destiny. By then I could only laugh quietly at my predicament and settled into my serendipitous adventure. The cook took the bags, dumped the creatures into boiling water, and within minutes our steaming hot, very spicy, fresh seafood meal sat on the table. Some of those creatures were peculiar; I ate some of almost all. The conversation was delightful as we got to know each other, and the Spirit took over the space and place.

The revelations continued. I had misunderstood the complex layers of the commitment, with a very different audience at the Hong Kong city campus. My preparation had not included those variables but thank God I had anticipated some things rather well as I tried to repackage the eight plenary island talks for the city assembly. The side-by-side translation also reduced time for my content. Never in my life had I been so stretched with such a variety of topics and contexts, ferry trips back and forth, and of course, all at the *wrong* seminary.

What a crazy situation, but also a lavish gift from God. I spoke to exhaustion but departed enriched and changed. I discovered the exquisite *Songs of Canaan*, lyrics and music composed by a young mainland Chinese woman who had never studied music. My former student, Mrs. Mary (the older) Cheung had graciously welcomed me and by then I had solved my conundrum. Both shared the same last name. Before leaving Hong Kong, I lunched with Oi-Ling (the younger) Cheung and told her my story. We had a long laugh. But I never revealed anything to my gracious seminary hosts. It was my mistake—but God's sovereignty trumped it all. Uncontrollable stuff happens even to tested leaders.

Certainly, I am not alone in this category of mistakes am I?

A Potpourri of Lessons

Learning also took place in the USA—reverse culture shock. One Sunday a few months after our move to Arkansas, Yvonne related to me that some people felt that my sermons communicated uncertain convictions. A bit offended, I asked why, and she explained: "Bill, this is what I think is happening. Mentally you are translating from Spanish to English and using too many subjunctive phrases like, 'perhaps ... under these circumstances ... it may be that ... you may want to consider ... at times I wonder whether ... ' and more. It works in Spanish, but English uses the indicative tense more." While glad that my Spanish roots were still alive, I was confusing people with my language. My worst mistake came on our first Easter Sunday. I preached with passion, but also criticized those who attended church only that Sunday. Reprimanded, I upset some and alienated others. I was learning to preach and shepherd in the USA, and in English—an uphill trajectory.

In 1987 Yvonne and I fulfilled a series of commitments in England, then India, and finally Singapore, where we would visit David and Phyllis Howard and the WEF International headquarters. In Bangalore, India we were hosted by our friend and MC chairman, Dr. Theodore Williams and his wife, Esther. We stayed in a modest but comfortable hotel—the room fan worked—and I spoke at the triennial conference of the pioneer agency, India Evangelical Mission. Unforgettable stories stirred us. The gospel was penetrating cultures and peoples for the first time, and the growth was marked with signs and wonders in the first years of the churches. Men held my hand as we walked across that large venue. Relax, Bill! Our sisters and brothers loved us without measure, and our memories are indelible.

We were charmed by the variants of Indian-English language sayings and statements, a product of imported British English modified by Indian culture. An ad: "Family-bachelor room available. Fully furnished with wife." We read adverts in Christian magazines where parents were arranging marriages for their son or daughter. Many described a prospective wife as "homely," i.e., dedicated to the house and family. Other sayings included, "Liquid tea available here," "Out of station,"

"Beware, ferocious dogs and ghosts," "Prepone" [sic], "Do the needful," "Kindly adjust," "What is your good name?" And my favorite, "I passed out of college."

We flew Air India from Bengaluru to Chennai, rechecking our bags on Singapore Airlines. In Chennai, we sat in the hot humid lounge with about 150 others, I saw window air conditioning units, but they were turned off, cords simply unplugged. Surreptitiously I circled the lounge, connecting power. Nobody noticed. Later, I watched the security guard scrutinize hand luggage behind a compartment. I slowly drifted behind him to discover there was no X-ray machine there. But he was working. In that airport I encountered Asian squat-toilets. Then, Singapore Airlines rocketed us into the twenty-first century, and the modern city of Singapore gave us a look into the future of modernity.

During my first MC years, I served TEDS as an adjunct professor. I taught one 1988 class in Spanish on Liberation Theology near Barcelona. I flew to Barcelona by way of a connection through Brussels to visit TEDS friends. As I walked across the tarmac from the plane to the terminal, I realized my wallet was gone. I spun around and sprinted to the plane before the doors closed and it left for Morocco. Before I knew it, police officers in two jeeps roared up, stopping me in my tracks. I explained my crisis and to my surprise they said, "Go on board. We will wait here and take you to the terminal." The wallet, however, was gone, stolen at the Brussels airport newsstand. I called Yvonne to cancel the credit cards and began replacing crucial documents.

> Early in my MC tenure, I was invited to speak at a conference of wealthy American donors. I was "too intellectual." It was a costly mistake, generating zero funds, and I was not invited back.

That mistake triggered a set of safeguards to protect my travel valuables. I have a printed list I check off before leaving home now: wallet (front pocket), money belt (under shirt in earlier days), iPhone (cargo pants front pocket), passport (left side cargo pant pocket); color photocopies of all crucial documents; Swiss army knife packed in checked luggage. Recently I bought expensive picket-pocket-proof trousers with fifteen pockets.

Early in my MC tenure, I was invited to speak at a conference of wealthy American donors to Christian ministries, with potential new income sources. I seriously misjudged my audience, spoke too trends-oriented, too long, without practical applications, and with little time for questions. I was "too intellectual." It was a costly mistake, generating zero funds, and I was not invited back. That seemed to happen to me too many times in that earlier season as I learned how to communicate with drastically different audiences.

In those initial years my vocabulary grew. What did "networking," "networks," "synergy," and other terms really mean? One colleague told me that at a major conference he chose to attend no plenaries, but instead networked the entire time, making excellent WEA contacts. I asked him to tutor me.

Misreading audiences has popped up a couple of times. I don't like to speak at men's retreats in any culture or language. Yet around 2010 I accepted an invitation to speak to the men of a reformed Baptist church in Florida (Truly Reformed Five-Point Calvinist). I should have declined, but a financial partner urged me to come. Many of the men were military, current or former, serving US bases in the area. I was honest with faith struggles, realistic, accurately quoting my former son-in-law's pungent language. It was too much for men trying to overcome bad habits, military men who also wanted things orderly, with clear requirements, including God and the Christian life. Some of the men who came on Friday didn't return. I totally misread the situation. I had made too many assumptions and alienated the pastor. It blew up in my face. My conclusion: never speak at a men's retreat for the rest of my life, especially if they are Truly Reformed. I haven't. We also lost that support partner.

Finally, I regret the many times I over-prepared for my talks, lectures, or sermons. I ended up with twice as much content as I needed and then abused the time limitations set on me by the pastor or person in charge. To this day this problem dogs me. I have paid a price, particularly in American churches, though not so much in Latin nor African ones. Perhaps that was one reason why I was invited to speak once, but not necessarily twice at some American churches?

In August 2004 I spoke at Mission Korea, an annual student mission conference (analogous to Urbana). They had recently translated and contextualized the IVP book that Steve Hoke and I had written, *Global Mission Handbook: A Guide for Cross-Cultural Service*.[2] I was introduced as a coauthor. My dear friend and colleague, Dr. David Tai-Woong Lee, a visionary Korean mission pioneer, hosted me, drove me to the city where the conference was to be held, and translated for me. The hotels were booked solid, so he reserved two rooms for us in a strange place, a Love

---

2 Hoke and Taylor, *Global Mission Handbook*.

Hotel. David said we had to pray the cleansing power of the Spirit of God over the entire hotel, and particularly our rooms, and to address different levels of demonic presence. What? That hotel market is primarily for extramarital affairs or rented on an hourly basis for prostitution. Many rooms have hidden cameras, and all the rooms have garish decoration and lighting. Their second market apparently was low-budget tourists like us. Did the clerks think we were two older gay men? I have no idea and don't care. Neither of us slept well. After two nights David said, "Let's get out of here." It cut Mission Korea short, but that hotel was evil.

Towards the middle of my MC years, I had a commitment in Malaysia. My good friend and colleague, Philip Chang, met me at the sprawling ultra-modern Kuala Lumpur airport with his driver, an Iraqi Muslim background believer with riveting dreams of Jesus. Philip, a banker, invests his free time in national and regional mission activities. He has long modeled the bivocational Christian servant, and his singlehood provided flexibility and resources. The primary motive for my trip was to speak at the launch of the new National Mission Movement (NMM). I asked Philip and the event coordinator, Beram Kumar, to brief me on the new alliance and the role of the Malaysian National Evangelical Association in it. I was unexpectedly surprised to learn that the two organizations were not connected. While the Malaysian NEA *did* have a mission's commission, it was nonfunctional, and the vacuum led to the new NMM.

This put me into a predicament. "Beram, you mean this new group has no relationship to the Malaysian NEA? Do they even know about it?" He wasn't sure. I was in trouble, caught in an institutional, generational and cross-cultural pot of hot water. I, the head of the WEA-Mission Commission, dedicated to strengthening NEA mission commissions, was now backing the putative "opposition"? I immediately called the NEA head of Malaysia and explained my presence in his country. He was not happy, but I probed into the existence, viability, visibility, and vitality of their own mission commission. When he said it did exist, I asked under whom. Another surprise! The appointed head of this nonfunctioning entity was none other than Philip.

Somehow, I extracted myself from that embarrassing situation, blessing the new network in spite of the potential institutional duplication. But this case illustrated a worldwide problem for all MC leadership. Most of the strongest and most representative national mission movements around the world were not organically linked to their national NEA's. Why? NEA structures tended to build bureaucracy rather than flexible, entrepreneurial entities. We discovered too many national alliances whose mission commissions were nonfunctional, inadequately resourced, and without creative or competent leadership. Yet they *existed*, if anybody asked.

However, the weakness of the entrepreneurial network leader (wired differently from the alliance one) shows up when based primarily on strong, innovative visionaries. Some of them are great starters yet unable to sustain new movements. And too few commit to mentor new leadership that ensures continuity and effectiveness. We saw these problems in NMMs who favored the looser network structure. While gifted leaders initiated the network, too many soon moved to other challenges. Relatively few long-lasting NMMs were directed by people committed to stay long term and to be open to ongoing revitalization and change. That Malaysia trip alone challenged me to utilize all my understanding of human nature, cultural intelligence, gifts of the Spirit, wisdom and courage, and long-term commitment to long-term missional structures that would further the gospel from everywhere to everywhere.

And all of these experiences took place on the leadership journey. What a ride!

Conclusion and Lessons

A personal story: Proverbs speaks stringent realism into the concept of friendship: "Better is open rebuke than hidden love. Faithful are the wounds of a friend; profuse are the kisses of an enemy" (27:5–6). In the summer of 1967, shortly before Yvonne and I were married, I served on the staff of InterVarsity Christian Fellowship's student leadership training program at Bear Trap Ranch in Colorado. Jim Carlson, camp director, asked me to promote *His*, the IVCF student magazine of those years. I did. The audience and I rocked with laughter. It was fantastic. I was good. I had knocked the ball out of the park. Walking out, Jim asked, "Bill, how do you think your promo went tonight?" I said, "Great ... uh, why do you ask?" His words stung, "Well, I think you were a failure. What you did was draw attention to Bill Taylor, the laugh-maker. You have a gift I wish I had, that unique public sense of humor. But, Bill, you must learn to control it, not it you." Ah, the "wounds from a sincere friend." Or (from verse 17): "As iron sharpens iron, so a friend sharpens a friend." To this day I thank Jim for his courage. I have not forgotten that experience.

This very early lesson shaped and reshaped both my self-understanding and my sensitivity to the Spirit in all leadership opportunities. However, back then I had no idea what kind of leadership gifts would enable me to serve with grace, effectiveness, and wisdom. Each challenge was unique, and I learned each time. The movie series, *The Chosen*, has profoundly touched me. I have fallen in love again with our Lord, appreciating—especially as depicted in the early episodes—his sense of humor, his humanity, and the fact that he learned obedience through suffering and was tested in all ways as we—yet he was without sin. Jesus, my leader, was accessible, vulnerable, patient but firm as he shaped his apostles over the course of three years. This Jesus encourages me to finish well, despite my gaffes and serious mistakes.

Reflection Questions

1. Should leaders reveal their mistakes? Explain.
2. Can you recount any "Rabbi and the Pope" kind of cultural communication experiences?
3. What mistakes have you already made?
4. In what ways must we be prepared to make mistakes and learn from them?
5. Why is it important to laugh at yourself?
6. In what ways have you been rebuked in your leadership journey?

11
Difficult People I Met Along the Journey

And
that's
all
I'm
going
to
say
about
this
topic,
truly.

See the next chapter for the lessons I learned.

12
Never Too Proud to Learn from Such People

While we like to think that as leaders we would never succumb to the corruptive evils of power, the truth is, church history is littered with the names of those who have. So, the question is, what kind of leader would you be if you were suddenly handed more power, received that promotion you wanted, or were offered your dream job? Would your leadership be an example of servanthood and justice, or would you give in to the temptations that power so seductively offers? Would God be thrilled, or would he regret that he put you in the position he did?[1]

Painful Stuff

While this first story isn't directly related to leadership, it taught me some early lessons about friendship and interpersonal relationships. During my seminary years, one close friend was the son of a prominent American evangelical leader. He was brilliant. When we studied together for finals, he would knock off early while I kept at it for hours. He always asked me about my grades—I never bested him, not once. He was even in our wedding. However, right after we left Dallas for Costa Rica as newly appointed missionaries, he told our small group, "They'll return in six months because Yvonne won't be able to cut it." Unwisely, one of those friends related these comments to us. Well, he was wrong. Seriously wrong. Yvonne and I served in Latin America for seventeen years, not six months. She both survived and thrived, becoming a thoroughly multicultural person with a global heart. As it turned out, we never saw him again. Trust had been broken and our spiritual paths diverged significantly. We no longer moved in the same circles and our life was now far away in Central America.

---

1 Overstreet, *Unleader*, back cover.

But lessons I learned from that experience taught me that even what one thinks is a strong and enduring friendship or working relationship can take a different and unexpected turn, that the *heart* work of forgiveness is important, and that it is important to gain wisdom from the experience.

When it comes to working in the world of cross-cultural mission we rarely, if ever, get to choose our fellow workers "on the field." Our challenge is to play the hand dealt to us. We can't say, "Hey, God, shuffle the people deck and give me better cards." Consequently, we will have difficult colleagues and, in some cases, people with whom we just cannot work easily. Throughout my life these situations taught me about myself, about relationships, about friendship, even betrayal, and much about the relational values I sustain in this latter stage of my journey. An important caveat on this chapter: each person I reference (some with pseudonyms) has their own version of our interpersonal history. I recognize that and will gladly change my record as needed. Thank you for your grace, and perhaps, forgiveness.

During our Latin America season, I served alongside many people whom I respected and learned from. I also worked under a couple of very difficult leaders, some bull-headed ones, some insecure and wounded ones, a few immature and selfish ones—both expats and nationals. Over the years many of my Latin American colleagues and associates became friends, and our relationships have lasted to this day. Most of my former international students returned to their home nations to serve with integrity, others traveled far. I'm in contact with some of the children of these former students. Other students made bad choices, broke their vows and marriages; the detritus is tangible. Providentially, I'm in touch with some of their children also.

God recently reminded me of two stories from my Guatemala years that illustrate some of the challenges and conflicts with my senior missionary colleagues. During our first term I worked with a gifted but stubborn professor. We served in the same department, but every time I came up with an idea, he promptly shot it down. Finally, I lost it! "George, you are impossible to work with. So, from now on, I refuse to serve on the same projects. I'm done!" It wasn't polite nor very Christian, but it was effective. Yet, the Spirit was working, and in our second term the relationship was restored. He and his wife worked healthily with Yvonne and me on a very creative, new venture.

During our third term, I was appointed to new leadership on the Academic Executive Committee, serving with a select group of gifted men and women. Ah, then there was Peter. He had the gift of negativism, and every idea I recommended (some good, others perhaps not) was immediately neutralized, "We have *never* done it that way." That word, *never*, stuck in my craw. Peter took other digs at me, "Watch out what you say to Bill. Remember, his dad is our mission president." Frankly, he was close to the top of the list of colleagues I was glad to say farewell to when we permanently departed Guatemala in 1985. Our family returned to Guatemala for many summers. On one of those trips after I spoke in chapel, Peter came up to me, surprising me with the invitation, "Hey, later on could you drop by the office for a minute?" I arrived with trepidation. Surprising me again, he said, "Bill, during the years we served together on the ExCo I was your perennial thorn in the flesh. In conversations with our mutual friend Danny Carroll, he helped me understand what you had been trying to do for us as a seminary. I am sorry, Bill, and I ask your forgiveness." The *abrazo* was sweet and authentic, a new beginning. He said, "Well, an old dog *can* learn new tricks." Of course, there are other cases where I was to initiate reconciliation, and request forgiveness.

I was surprised, and perhaps encouraged, to read more recently about the young Elisabeth Elliot's intractable relationship with her translation colleague, SIL member Rachel Saint, sister of the speared pilot, Nate Saint.[2] These two were oil and water, total opposites, diversely gifted. Yet both categorically were convinced that God had individually called each one to live among the Waorani in the Ecuadorian rainforest. They separately dreamed of analyzing this unique tongue, of creating an alphabet and written language which would become the linguistic foundation for the translation of the New Testament into *Wao tedeko*. After many years, the relational smoldering volcano finally erupted; Elisabeth was forced to leave the Waorani, abruptly and forever, and soon after, she left Ecuador—returning to the USA to embrace a new calling as a writer and speaker. Eventually Rachel Saint would have to leave SIL, but she lived her last years and died in the rainforest. Reconciliation was impossible, and Elisabeth's life was launched into a radically different set of paths.

The historic, worldwide volunteer, self-supported mission cosmos particularly attracts entrepreneurs, dreamers (visionaries), and some

---

2 Long, *Gods in the Rainforest*, back cover.

lone rangers who dislike serving under authority or administrative structures. In the mission context, it is tough to build a consensus vision or a committed team ethos—unless those values are crucial DNA factors of the mission society and unless before joining, the volunteer knows what she or he is getting into. Our agency had both entrepreneurial and bureaucratic (in the best sense of the word) leader-members, in addition to many missionaries faithfully dedicated to their particular tasks. The composite created a singular (or peculiar) community. Tension existed between rural and urban members, the former considering themselves the real missionaries. A different strain emerged between those in institutions and the field people, between the seminary and other training centers. We had no clear agency leadership path nor visible leadership development values. Leaders just emerged over time and with different styles moved into different positions. I am not sure we ever were a team in Guatemala. It was a royal mélange! At times I did not know where Yvonne and I fit into this culture.

> The historic, worldwide volunteer, self-supported mission cosmos particularly attracts entrepreneurs, dreamers, and some lone rangers who dislike serving under authority or administrative structures.

Our family transitional years in Arkansas became a unique school with lessons, blessings, wounds, and scars. For three and a half years I tried to serve a congregation where opposition emerged from former best friends. At SETECA I had faced differences of personality, policy, and procedures with colleagues, but nobody had attacked my integrity or accused me of lying or being the root problem. Arkansas was different. I sat through elder meetings where members showed up to condemn me personally. I learned to be silent. And take notes.

A deacon formally accused me in an ecclesial elder court. I had considered him a thoughtful disciple whom I was mentoring—he asked me good questions. Little did I know he was building a case against me. When the elders convened that meeting, he leveled his charges against me. Any response was futile. When the board chair asked what outcome he sought, he stated, "Bill must step down from all leadership, submit to the discipline of the elders; and only if he truly changes his character and behavior can he be restored to eldership." I waited silently. The chair replied that this outcome was untenable, but they would take it under advisement. The accuser left. I sat stunned. At no time did anybody reference 1 Timothy 5:19, "Do not admit a charge against an elder except on the evidence of two or three witnesses."

Then the chair capped it off: "OK, I think that's all for tonight's agenda?" The meeting ended, I mumbled farewell and drove home with a younger elder. "Joe, please explain what happened tonight?" He said, "I really don't know. They left you sort of hanging, didn't they?" I said, "Yes, twisting in the wind." Much later, Psalm 55:12–13 helped heal the still-tender scar, "It is not enemies who taunt me—I could bear that; it is not adversaries who deal insolently with me—I could hide from them. But it is you, my equal, my companion, my familiar friend." Many years later, this younger elder asked forgiveness for his silence. Was it too little, too late? No.

That meeting commemorated my watershed—or was it a Waterloo? These elders, whom I had considered friends (one from before our marriage) had betrayed the relationship. It was symptomatic of a deep church dysfunctionality, a pathology corroborated by other spiritual leaders in town. Some members asked us to stay and start a new church. That would have been a devastating mistake. About a year after that watershed, I resigned as teaching elder effective December 31, 1989. On January 1, 1990, I transitioned full-time to the WEA-MC, and in September, 1990 we moved to Austin. Sadly, from afar we watched a progressive disintegration of the congregation. Some leaders walked away from marriage and others from orthodox Christianity. Our wounds healed slowly. But healing did come. God knows forgiveness has been extended. Yet, truth be told, my heart still feels bruised even while writing these words, and that's OK. I live with the acrid taste of strange ashes. The Russellville church was founded on unhappiness and a divisive spirit with endemic "viruses" in both congregants and leadership. Before those years I had never understood the New Testament passages on Satan's work in the life of a local church. We grew in discernment about demonic activity and warfare prayer.

Resurrection completed.

Too Close to the Top

I thank God for the leaders and colleagues who set good examples to me during my two years on the faculty of TEDS. They were gracious, expansive, aware that I was a DTS grad and a veteran of seventeen years in global mission with an earned PhD in two secular disciplines. They respected me as a person and scholar with the gift of teaching and a unique cross-cultural combination of insight, intelligence, study and experience. My second year, however, taught me more about the politics of academia, and I faced unexpected challenges. In one case I think I was played by a superior, but I refused to participate in that game. I also, sadly, witnessed a colleague's divorce due to conflicted priorities between family and academia.

During my thirty years with WEA, I was as close as possible to the highest levels of national and global evangelical leadership. I know my name was twice on the short list for its top leadership, but I knew that wasn't God's call on my life, nor a match for my gifts. I knew too much: the toll paid for excessive expectations from others was not worth the "glory"; I saw the subtle, lurking temptations of hidden addictions. It seemed that the higher one ascended, the scarcer the oxygen, the fewer the friends and rarer the accountable community.

> I saw the subtle, lurking temptations of hidden addictions. It seemed that the higher one ascended, the scarcer the oxygen, the fewer the friends and rarer the accountable community.

Over those decades it was disheartening to see how poorly some former global leaders transitioned after their high appointment into more prosaic, normal life and service. Was the drive to "get there" toxic in itself? Or did positions of fame and influence misshape them? Studying high level leaders, their gifting and charisma, their magnetic personality, their way with words, their diplomatic and administrative skills, their ability to raise big money, and in some cases, their veiled ambition, I thank God he kept me within the MC community.

Intriguingly, ambition emerged in our Lord's dissimilar apostolic team. We see them jostling for position, some much more than others. They misunderstood Jesus's Messianic destiny in the first coming, and wanted to rule so desperately that even a mother lobbies for her sons' position and glory. These stories teach us much, and Jesus and the Twelve become insightful instructors, positive and negative.

This chapter raises some intriguing thoughts on ambition. Some praise ambition and others condemn it. Is it a virtue or a flaw? If ambition is the focused desire to achieve power, status, influence, and fame, then it is dangerous for us in Christian leadership. Yet, if ambition is rooted and purified in a healthy way, then the restless dream to rise out of poverty, to overcome systemic family deficits, to provide for family, to acquire a valuable formal education and job, or to serve more effectively, I sense it is not wrong. At times it's difficult to discern the difference between holy dreams and desires or unhealthy and toxic ambitions.

What happens when you read a book on leadership and it suggests the idea of "growing your leadership from *good to great*"? Is that idea or motive legitimate, pure? What are the tricky ingredients of this human desire? How does this feed hidden addictions? Who will speak truth into your life about the dangers? What would Jesus say, the Spirit suggest, your spouse speak? What about unhealthy self-promotion, when people plot and scheme their way up the ladder—even in Christian organizations—when they become the architects of their own career, or covet that promotion or dream to sit on top? A good friend of mine told me of an Episcopal seminary classmate who as a student plotted his path to become a bishop. And he accomplished his goal! Recently I congratulated a young manager at my brother-in-law's memory care center on her promotion. "Good on you, Maggie!" Her response? "Thanks, but I'm after his job [pointing to the executive director's office]." Ironically, they both lost their jobs shortly afterwards.

> At times it's difficult to discern the difference between holy dreams and desires or unhealthy and toxic ambitions.

I have said to myself, "Beware, Billy Boy, of the pitfalls of self-attribution; never believe the press releases about you."

Difficult People I Worked Under, With, or Over

While writing this chapter I identified categories of people I have worked with. Most were gracious, gifted, and relatively secure, modeled healthy leadership, and were unafraid of emerging leaders. However, other good people were simply in wrong positions, exemplifying the "Peter-principle," a concept in management which says that competent people are often promoted to their "level of incompetence." They rise because of their abilities but can end up attaining leadership beyond what they are gifted to do.

Other leaders I worked with were "small," defensive, and insecure. Still others were toxic, as my English colleague, Rob Hay, described in conclusions emerging from his MC team research on attrition-retention issues. I served under and alongside very few of them, thank God. Toxic language was new but helpful in explaining some of my own experiences.

Regretfully, during my years with the MC we had to dismiss a few colleagues for violating our guidelines, ethos, and collegiality. One case was due to long-term adultery, another came after a marriage disintegrated due to constant travels—all trips in his mind as "crucial." I had warned him about his obvious travel addiction. Another three were released because they abused their MC leadership, using it for their own personal agenda and international platform, not the values shared by our missional community. We observed a few high-profile, charismatic international mission leaders circling around us, negotiating for more influence and status. God protected us. Very early in my MC years a well-known older leader told me, "I deserve to sit at the top of MC leadership because I am 'Mr. Missions' in my region of the Majority World." He never did.

A prominent, gifted, yet prickly leader joined the MC only to champion his focus on one of the lesser-reached religions of the world. I had hoped we could cooperate with him, but little could we have anticipated how he utilized the MC as his personal global stage, unilaterally launching initiatives without consultation. The final separation between the MC and this leader was exceedingly difficult. It was also imperative.

WEA and its parallel structures are challenging global entities to lead. A new Secretary General-CEO should best come from within the organization and not as the result of a headhunting group nominating an outsider. He or she must understand the staggering, if not impossible, challenges to build coalitions, to visit and strengthen the alliances, to balance the needs and drives of regional bodies vis-à-vis national ones, to engage with service units (e.g., commissions) of WEA, to raise funds, and represent evangelicals around the world to religious, NGO, economic, secular, and governmental authorities. This person must not be addicted to travel because it will inevitably be fed. I concluded that this position should be limited to mature empty nesters. The cost is simply not worth it. It was reported about one leader that "He thought he had accomplished his job when he got into his airplane seat." And always first class.

It grieves me to remember some individuals whom I did not enjoy meeting, yet they also imparted lessons as I observed them. A few loved their glittering self-images, their glamorous powers. Some were career climbers, manipulators, wounded and angry, or downright obnoxious. The most difficult people to work with were the narcissists. Their pathology was deadly. However, all in all, in significant ways even these problematic people taught me to beware of idols and called me to pray for leaders in those high-altitude, oxygen-deprived atmospheres.

Unhealed long-term wounds in leaders will ultimately show up in real-time, whether in family or ministry, but always in family and human relationships. Hidden secrets will fester and burst out of their fragile scar tissue, breaking out in the oddest, most delicate or dangerous moments of our life—even after death and the eulogies. For sure they will affect others, especially those we love the most or work the closest with.

Christian Leadership: Values and Sadness

Good theology, gifts, and charisma do not guarantee godly Christian leadership. Character is the crucial ingredient. The following ingredients profile Christian leaders with whom I most desire to work: tested spiritual maturity; healthy marriages; the fragrance of Jesus; tangible accountability; track record of suffering; cultural intelligence; servant heart and the grace of collegiality in team building; awareness of hidden addictions; gifted but humble; an intentional mentor; the maturity to know when to leave graciously. I know this may sound totally unrealistic and the Apostle Paul might possibly not make the cut. But I can dream.

Friendships are personal, tenuous, mysterious. They can be lost—some for good. Others can providentially be restored. This chapter forced me to review my entire life to see if there were shards of unreconciled relationships lying around. I hope not. In some cases, the Spirit stirred me to extend generosity and grace to some of the difficult people in my life and release them to God. However, when trust and relationship are broken, forgiveness extended and exchanged does not automatically require a return to the previous relational warmth. It does call us to release hurt and resentment, which generates peace and clarity. Paul's relationship balance and realism in Romans 12:18 encourages me, "If possible, so far as it depends on you, live peaceably with all."

Sadly, I have had to deal with the fallout from colleagues and top leaders whose moral failure destroyed their ministry and impacted so many others. In response to one tragic high-profile case, Jun Vencer, WEA's international director, tasked me to draft in 1994 what became *The Singapore Covenant*, an ethical declaration that we WEA (then

WEF) staff would affirm and sign. I researched the issue from various angles, personally interviewed key people, received some amazing documentation from eyewitnesses (i.e., the Billy Graham team), and drafted a document. We identified the pitfalls that can destroy us, our marriages, our ministries, our credibility, and our reputation. I personally was most shaped by the *Modesto Manifesto* crafted by Graham's first team that set out and then lived by those guidelines that ensured protection and purity. Sadly, the WEA *Singapore Covenant* was never referenced later in our history.

What issues require stepping down earlier than expected, voluntarily or involuntarily, from Christian leadership? Here are a few: loss of or absence of accountability, abuse of authority and power, financial mismanagement, sexual sin, marriage breakdown, major doctrinal departure, destructive hidden addictions, borderline inappropriate behavior, anger, narcissism, and general moral issues. Seldom is it just one cause, for they tend to converge in a combined, enmeshed maze of brokenness. One famous American pastor whose adultery was exposed, confessed afterwards to David Howard, "Dave, as I reviewed the case studies of other leaders who fell such as I, none of us were in significant accountability with others."

Can these people be restored to ministry? Yes, but only with authentic repentance and a long-term restoration process. We extend grace and mercy, but true brokenness must be genuine with time for deep healing. I'm dismayed by and distrust those who jump their discipline, claiming, "I have suffered enough, I'm forgiven, and the Lord's servant cannot deny the Spirit's gifts. It is time to return." Can a pastor, or mission leader, seminary professor or other head of a Christian ministry be derailed for adultery or other major cause of downfall, and then be restored to that ministry position? Some argue, "Yes, in time." Others say, "No, that person has lost moral and spiritual authority to return to the pastorate, or the classroom, or other public ministry." These brothers and sisters must first be deconstructed by God and only in that brokenness can the Spirit reconstruct them and perhaps guide them into a different ministry.

Happily, most of the women and men I served with or under during my six decades in cross-cultural service were people of integrity. I learned from them all. Their life and service shaped mine. Yes, not all were easy to work with but what's new? I did not always respect nor admire some of the people I worked with or under. In Spanish we would say, *"No es santo de mi devoción*," which translated means, "He is not a saint of my devotion." It's a subtle saying.

I am skeptical of any book that purports to impress us with inspiring stories about children of well-known Christian leaders. This is dangerous and deceptive; dangerous because it can fabricate hagiography as well as elevate expectations; deceptive because these stories tell only the good ones. My father told me that David Livingston's son, Robert, moved to America, took the name Rupert Vincent, fought in a New Hampshire regiment in the Civil War, was captured and died in the Confederate POW prison in Salisbury, North Carolina. He wrote his famous father to no longer consider him his son.

I know too many stories of children of well-known Christians. The narrative is mixed, sometimes heartrending, all complex. Stuff happens, parents make mistakes, and poor decisions can misshape families. Children born in the best of families (whatever that might mean) at times make wrong, sad, and even tragic decisions. I grew up in the home of modestly well-known leaders and have invested my life and career in the global evangelical world. That means I know too much and see too much dirty laundry. Who will tell the true story of a son or daughter who walks totally away from faith? What if the son becomes a Hindu or a convinced atheist? Children of Christian leaders are all under special attack. For many I pray and for some I weep as I pray.

None of us enter long-term vocational mission service to get wealthy. That doesn't come with the territory. However, other temptations arise, other hidden addictions. Ambition appears in different facades and disguises. Some trade wealth for power and influence that provide fleeting status in their support circles for their "high sacrifice." I've met some missionaries who somehow made "extracurricular money on the field." They gained the reputation of *personas metalizadas* (literally a metalized person, a money-making schemer). Their stories did not end well either.

Conclusion and Lessons

We have journeyed far and deep in this chapter. Reviewing my long years in cross-cultural ministry, I thank God for the men and women who set good and healthy examples of Christian ministry. I learned a few lessons along the way: first to seek reconciliation and restoration, but to do so with integrity and to ask God how even negative lessons can mold us for his good. I learned that some said I too was a challenge to work with. I discovered that I emulated many colleagues in my subconscious leadership development—only discerning this decades later. I discovered over time that my skill set and gift mix worked the best when I was part of a team. I also identified arenas where I was not to serve, or did not have the desire nor capacity to go beyond the levels of leadership that God gave me. I saw the price that some leaders paid who did go beyond where they should.

I thank God for the women and men with whom I served in Guatemala and in the three WEA decades who shaped me; they remain colleagues and friends. Yes, we had disagreements and hard situations to sort out. But it was worth it. Elements of this chapter deal with God undoing us to redo us, deconstructing to reconstruct. Hwa Yung nails it as he concludes a section on God's transforming process:

> First, like it or not, if we are to be used by God for his purposes, each of us will have to go through this breaking and transforming process. As noted earlier, sin has left all of us with varying degrees of dysfunctionality. Furthermore, growing up under the influence and pressures of the world around us, consciously or unconsciously we have imbibed much of the corruption and pride of which it boasts.[3]

Our MC staff and ExCo team met in Korea one year; and our host, the gracious and gifted colleague, Dr. David Tai-Woong Lee, took us to visit a "very important pastor." We twenty were ushered into the inner sanctum, a massive room, the pastor's office with his ornate desk and a huge table for key meetings. The walls were covered—yes, *covered*—with degrees, diplomas, certificates, ornate letters of gratitude, some art, and the like. I quietly drifted around that astonishing monument to hubris. The next day David and I sat in his own very small office, surrounded by his books. The contrast of spirit and simplicity was categorical. Give me David Lee anywhere and always. He, my beloved friend, started well, kept at it, and is on track to finish well.

The lessons I have learned here are imprinted with deep implications for finishing well. I learned from difficult people, as well as impossible people. I learned to ask for grace and space, as well as forgiveness. I had to extend the same, at times even reluctantly, but ultimately fully. And even while editing this manuscript, relationships have been restored. This is grace, God's grace.

---

3 Yung, *Leadership or Servanthood?*, 120.

All hail, Jesus our model par excellence!

Reflection Questions

1. What lessons have you learned from having to work with difficult people? Describe one case study.

2. Why does James warn us, "Not many of you should become teachers, my brothers, for you know that we who teach will be judged with greater strictness." Substitute "leader" for "teacher" and what it might imply. In what way is this true?

3. Why does Paul, writing on church leadership state, "He must not be a recent convert, or he may become puffed up with conceit and fall into the condemnation of the devil" 1 Timothy 3:6. Are these biblical norms applicable to vocational Christian ministry?

4. What else in this chapter has provoked your reflection?

13
Surprised by the Gifts of the Spirit

> But, as it is written, "What no eye has seen, nor ear heard, nor the heart of man imagined, what God has prepared for those who love him," these things God has revealed to us through the Spirit." (1 Cor 2:9–10)

> Perhaps what most distinguishes Christian leadership from any other form of leadership is the understanding that it is received from God as a gift. Leadership undertaken in any context is, for the Christian, a vocation, a sacred trust from God.[1]

Ancora Imparo—I Am Still Learning

Peter Drucker states, "We now accept the fact that learning is a lifelong process of keeping abreast of change. And the most pressing task is to teach people how to learn."[2] His insights underscore my personal heart's desire, to keep learning until the end. That vision has shaped this entire narrative and it's not yet completed. Recently, Yvonne and I discussed again the timing to transition into a smaller home (our "final" planet earth residence?), moving out of our museum-art-gallery-home packed with a life of memories and furniture and artwork and books, a grand piano, even an accordion. We are surrounded by remembrance and poignancy, celebration and sadness. Our walls talk to us. While that decision has been temporarily put on hold, how might we embrace the uncertainty of our latter laps?

Meanwhile, deeper reflections stir. My deepest "me" celebrates the reality and presence of a living and gracious Father God, and I as his son. He's neither candy man nor ogre; rather, he is good, gracious, unique, and just. He's sovereign over the universe, the nations, history, and my family and life. He holds supreme dominion over my life, and I rejoice that he still has a purpose for me in this lap.

I have embraced the vision of the foothills, that gentle yet firm Spirit word that my journey won't cross another mountain range but rather will

---

1 Parkinson, *Understanding Christian Leadership*, 252.
2 Drucker, *Leadership Now*.

conclude somewhere in the visible rises and bluffs where I will be laid to rest with my fathers and my people.

Renamed Again

What does renamed mean? How many times can you be renamed? The existential reality of renaming is mysterious and personalized. At times we rename ourselves, at times others do it, and God certainly can. I switched from Billy to Bill when starting high school in the American School of Guatemala. For seventeen years I was a *cross-cultural missionary* serving with my family in Guatemala, primarily a teacher. For some I was a *Latin Americanist*, thanks to my PhD. For years I lived in transition following our 1985 move to the USA. Around 1992 I heard the Father's whisper, "Bill, you are a *globalized servant leader*." It rang true, consonant with my new realities. The High One renamed me into a new expression of my core vocation.

> What does renamed mean? How many times can you be renamed?

Over the last ten-plus years I intuited a new future emerging, expressed in a triad: intentional mentoring, some teaching, and writing. TaylorGlobalConsult was birthed in 2010 as a legal platform to carry us into our final preferred future. Around then I started studying the three Hebrew terms for *elder*, *seer*, and *wise*. They drew me in. I mulled them over and they mulled me over. Yet I wasn't free to appoint myself to something new; it seemed wisest that others call me into a new name. And that happened. My first American mentoring cohort, Matt and Matt, Mike and Doug, led a "renaming" ceremony as they spoke words and laid hands on me as "sage." It came from the Spirit. That unique ceremony used language of father, mentor, elder, seer, Yoda, Obi-Wan Kenobi, and my favorite, St. Simeon.

What do these terms mean or point towards? The Hebrew term for *elder*, used in the Old Testament 171 times, comes from *zaquen*, with roots that literally reference the beard or chin. It speaks of the elderly, then identifies the group of seventy with governance authority to assist Moses. In Deuteronomy, elders are joined by the judges and the heads of tribes. Later the term applies to heads of villages. Essentially the term combines age with wisdom. Its equivalent Greek term, *presbuteros*, is used for the collegial leadership of new congregations, later modified through church history to present day.

The *seer*, from *chozeh*, intrigued me. It appears seventeen times in the Old Testament. It parallels and precedes the meaning of prophet; 2 Kings 17:13 unites them. 1 Chronicles 19:29 identifies Samuel as seer. Gad is David's seer, while Nathan is his prophet. Seers and prophets spoke the word of the Lord with authority even over kings. 1 Samuel 9:9 clarifies this transitional term presented as a parenthesis in the text: ("Formerly in Israel, when a man went to inquire of God, he said, 'Come, let us go to the seer,' for today's 'prophet' was formerly called a seer.") Seers were recognized as those with discerning insight into people, reality, and the future.

Chakam, used 133 times in the Old Testament, refers to the wise or skilled person. Perhaps the richest of the three terms, it references the shrewd, the wise-hearted, the wisest, the skillful—hence qualities that describe the sage. These descriptors marked Joseph, who became Prime Minister. It also identifies the artists, Bezalel and his team (Exod 28:3; 31:1; 36:1–2).

Someone asked me how this tripartite renaming manifested itself in my life. I'm unsure. In part it's a calling/dedication to impart wisdom and experience to younger generation leaders. In part it's expressed by mentoring or through Spirit-directed conversations of import. It envelops the spirit of fathering the mis-fathered-mothered or un-fathered-mothered, which is a particular curse on our contemporary societies. It also requires courage to speak truth. Yvonne and I are equal partners. A friend recently wrote us after days and hours of deep conversation, vulnerability, and prayer in our home: "Thank you both for your sacrifice of time and spiritual fathering and mothering." Intentional mentoring equips and embraces godly subversives to survive, even thrive, in a wounded and wicked culture. The worst is yet to come, so we must prepare for a tougher future, regardless of political and economic systems or religious persecution. The signs of the times forecast unprecedented evil ahead.

These three Hebrew terms encapsulate the essence of my newer name. I am who I have become and wish to be. Then, beyond those appellatives, and totally unexpected, I realized that God had bestowed three gifts on me. It was Yvonne who first used the right language, "Bill, God has returned some gifts to you, re-empowering some of your deepest dreams."

The First Gift

Unanticipated doors once again opened in my beloved Latin America to speak, teach, consult, mentor and partner—in Spanish. This gift embraced geography, the Spanish language and ministry. I have attended and been a part of all four of COMIBAM's decadal congresses: Brazil, Mexico, Spain, and Colombia. The SETECA workbook, *Misiones Mundiales*, is a new 2025 edition and expansion from the 1984 version. Thirty years later it has expanded to twenty lessons, with a robust missiology of God on mission. The workbook engages in critical contemporary issues, and every chapter can be applied to the local church. The Spanish on-line educational site, *Obrero Fiel*, now features the course. There are other plans for its expanded use.

In early 2013, two of SETECA's leaders, its then-president (*rector*), Argentine Carlos López, and his younger Chilean colleague, Gonzalo Chamorro, approached me about their dream to establish a new research center. This visionary concept drew me in and surprised me, "We want to name it after you." I asked why? "Though you have been gone twenty-eight years, you are remembered, your legacy continues, and we want to honor you." I asked time to mull it over, pray and talk with Yvonne, and I thanked God she accompanied me. As we discussed and sought God, the next morning I was released to say to my friends, "I am honored, but I will accept only if you include my elderly mentor-friend, Dr. Emilio Antonio Núñez in the title, with his name going first." They agreed and Núñez blessed the venture—perhaps his last ministry decision before dementia neutralized his mind. The Núñez and Taylor Research Center (*Centro de Investigación Núñez y Taylor*) was conceived.

The vision was crafted, the SETECA and TGC (TaylorGlobalConsult) boards approved the venture. Gonzalo led the core team, and immediately it began to serve the seminary and the wider church. Creative publications were released. SETECA provided office space and staff assignments and TGC raised funds for this strategic alliance, providing for a future building. Then, with stunning speed, the dream was torpedoed after a radically different president assumed power with no vision for the center and who had determined to erase Carlos and Gonzalo's legacy. The memorandum of understanding had been signed by TGC and SETECA's executive board and the new rector. But within days, he retracted his approval, forcing TGC to withdraw from the partnership. Gonzalo was pressured out of SETECA. The dream died. TGC had to recall much of its financial investment for fiduciary reasons. Strange ashes again. Bitter gall.

So, tell me, how do you process the death of a dream at age seventy-four? I had to embrace the grief, the blows; I had to pray the psalms of justice and hope my heart was pure—no easy task.

Just one year later and to my utter astonishment, Gonzalo shared a different dream with me. He envisioned a new apologetics platform with a unique agenda: to address the Latin American crises of gender and family, Christian ethics, and the Christian mind. It was a God thing. We researched other similar groups and institutes around the world; we were not alone but there was nothing like it in Central America, perhaps on the continent. God birthed a creative team of five to discuss, envision, dream, and pray. That June of 2018 we convened a think tank of twenty-five evangelical leaders. They listened critically, asked hard questions, made wise suggestions, and prayed. By the end of the day, "It seemed good to the Holy Spirit and us" that the project was to be pursued.

Over the next year the core leaders hammered out critical issues, vision and mission, services, leadership, and governance. We needed a Guatemala-authorized NGO under which the new venture could flourish, a daunting project. What would we call this new creation? The concept of "Institute" was introduced. After weeks of discussion, its international usage led the team to adopt it. One night, in a waking dream, the term, *CRUX*, came to me, evoking the intersection of roads and ideas and the cross. Another miracle: a new but dormant Christian Guatemalan foundation, *Fundación Buen Arbol* (Good Tree Foundation) offered its legal and financial platform to embrace, launch, and support the CRUX Institute. In May 2019, the ministry was publicly inaugurated. Since then, the team has grown, staffed by some of Gonzalo's restless and creative former students at SETECA, funded locally and in partnership with TGC.

Who would have guessed that nine months later, the world would be attacked by an evil, illegitimate virus called COVID-19? The pandemic radically changed the 2020 CRUX Institute programs and services. Days prior to the lockdown, the team had convened its first experimental apologetics camp of thoughtful youth who helped identify key questions. Amidst this cauldron and Guatemala's own governance calamity, the team pivoted with a series of Zoom and YouTube panel discussions on the pandemic. It produced a unique book authored by Latin Americans with both electronic and print versions, *Dialogues in Times of Crisis: Reflections from the Pandemic*.[3]

Gonzalo's vision, passion, giftedness and leadership led the way. The team of Latin millennials is solidly undergirded by the viable and visible executive board. I am honored to serve with those colleagues, Carlos López, Frank Saenz, and Hugo Morales. The Spirit reminded me

---

3 Chamorro and Estrada, *Diálogos en Tiempos de Crisis*.

again, "Resurrection requires and only follows death." CRUX was birthed only after the death of the NTRC. Yet, in the nutrient-rich mixture of those ashes God created something unexpected. Who would have dreamed of an *Instituto CRUX*? Nobody. Operating out of Guatemala, it radiates to the global Spanish-speaking world.

It was a memorable first meeting of our two boards. Late in 2018 the CRUX and TGC boards met in Austin to determine the relationship between the two organizations and how TGC could serve CRUX. Gathering around the table, our chair, Howard Morrison, formally began the welcome that would lead to prayer. To my surprise, David Ruíz, my long-time friend and colleague, interrupted, saying, "Brothers, I would like to say something at the very beginning. May we be clear? We came from Guatemala to meet you, to get to know you, to learn how to walk together. We really are not that interested in your financial resources; we want to understand your hearts and know something about your personal lives. We want to walk together. Could we begin with this kind of exchange?" I stopped breathing, knowing that David himself had dealt with major USA donors who freely exercised the "golden rule" of international partnership: he who controls the gold, rules.

A Spirit-led Howard immediately pivoted, saying, "David, a brilliant idea. May I start with my own story," and thus began a unique experience for all as the North American members shared family challenges, unanswered prayers, the mystery of God somehow at work in their lives. The Latins reciprocated in like-spirit and vulnerability. I honestly forgot the rest of that seminal board meeting, but I know that Jesus knitted our hearts together in suffering and grace, in pain and expectations. Financial matters did emerge, but they were discussed in the context of transparent, mutual partnership.

Yet not all died in the *Centro de Investigación Núñez y Taylor* dream. SETECA's new leadership has revived it, staffed and budgeted it, opened space for it to send new roots, to lead the way in special events, and to produce new publications. Quietly it began to take new shape. An unexpected aftermath of ashes? Another death and resurrection?

Latin American Bonus Gift

In 2014 a unique facet of the Latin American gift came when I began the process to acquire Costa Rican citizenship. For years I had tossed that option around. Why? Well, honestly, I'm not sure. I think it was related to my roots—that my conception, birth, and early childhood were grounded in that cultural soil. Was it another sign of the poignant

Portuguese term, *saudade* (that deep nostalgic longing for something or someone absent) common to Third Culture Kids?

I called the Costa Rican consulate in Houston to initiate the process. In God's providence, my father (what possessed him?) had kept my legal birth certificates (both Costa Rican and USA embassy versions). But the next roadblock was unsurmountable: I needed two eyewitnesses of my birth on November 7, 1940, in the *Clínica Bíblica* in San José, Costa Rica. I told the consular officer there were none, to which she responded, "But surely you have some siblings or cousins or other family who could vouch for you?" I said I was the only one. She would consult with her Ministry of Foreign Relations and call me with the official word.

Her email arrived three weeks later, "The Ministry says that all you must do is to find two people in Costa Rica today who would vouch legally that you are who you say you are. With those witnesses, your Costa Rica birth certificate, and other documents, we can finalize your process." My two witnesses signed the official papers, I drove to Houston to sign the final documents, then waited for their notification to acquire my national citizenship card (allowing me to vote in Costa Rica elections) and my coveted passport.

That final trip to Houston released an emotional whirlpool, and David accompanied me to the consulate. Costa Rica has singular official photograph requirements: "Turn your head to the right. Do not smile." I was also required to produce a unique, illegible signature, recalling how Latin children create their own signature, a fingerprint peer. I practiced in front of the consular official until he said, "I think that one will work." I am incapable of reproducing that signature.

I write these lines gazing at my Costa Rica passport to my right, issued on April 16, 2015, along with my *Cédula de Identidad* (national ID card) from the *Tribunal Supremo de Elecciones*. I am an official citizen of Costa Rica and of the USA, and by residence and marriage also of the Autonomous Republic of Texas. On planet earth I am a resident alien. Along with my citizenship in heaven, that should keep me covered through time and eternity.

The Second Gift

After leaving Trinity Evangelical Divinity School in mid-1986, I anticipated another profound loss: I would no longer teach in the formal academy. I would no longer hone my lifelong craft in the classroom. Teaching had been my core gift and passion. Yet I sensed the Spirit's whisper, "Bill, I asked you to die to Latin America in 1985 and now in 1986 you must die to formal teaching. A preferred future will come, and you will flourish." That Spirit-impression salved the sting. While on one hand the Arkansas church experience was bitterly discouraging, my expanding global reality with the WEF Mission Commission catapulted me into a radically new cosmos. New gifts were required, all my cross-cultural experience would now be stretched to build qualitative relationships with sisters and brothers from so many nations of Asia, Europe and Africa, the America's, South Pacific, Middle East, the Caribbean. Increasingly globalized, founded on the seventeen years in Latin America, I embraced a unique convergence of gifts, passions, and greater maturity.

But teaching? Ah ... My journey during those MC decades challenged me to study the place and power of nonformal education, a modality not needing heavy educational structures, residential study, examinations, rites of passages, tenure, expensive campuses, library and faculty, nor the perennial demands of secular and Christian accreditation requirements. However, nonformal education can be intentional and designed, with tangible outcomes and expectations, focused on self-discovery and less teacher centered. Around the world, our MC team posed critical questions: How might we best equip-train-prepare men and women in context for cross-cultural ministry? How would we design a novel equipping program from zero? How can creative educational contextualization conceive and give birth to new missionary training centers around the world? Will the formal educational system accept nonformal graduates? How do the terms, *excellence* and *access* apply? It had to be open to all who qualified for longer-term cross-cultural service. Excellence for us didn't equal academics nor accreditation but rather the outcome: graduates would serve with integrity of Christian character, equipped for their challenging work. I am indebted to Jon Lewis, Rob Brynjolfson, Bayo Famonure, Bob Ferris, Lois Fuller, Rudy Girón, David Harley, Steve Hoke, David Lee, Titus Loong and Ray Windsor. Through them, Jon especially, I understood nonformal education and its application to effective ministry equipping in all dimensions. Approaching the conclusion of my WEA years, God returned the unexpected gift—classroom teaching.

Ancora Imparo

New doors opened to teach again in formal schools, starting with SETECA in the DET (*Doctorado en Educación Teológica*) program in 2008, designed to equip key theological educators for Latin

America. I inherited Dr. Núñez' course, "The Contextualization of Theological Education for Latin America." As I shaped the course, it gained a reputation for theological and educational rigor, but also for an innovative, fundamental focus on the spirituality of theological education. This academic cohort started every three years, allowing time to prepare, revise, and recover. My SETECA colleague and coinstructor, David Suazo, graciously assumed grading. The Spirit released me from teaching in 2021. Another professor would now reshape the class.

However, never would I have imagined that in early 2023, SETECA would surprise me with a *Doctor Honoris Causa en Educación Teológica*. The words of affirmation and honor, both in the diploma and in its presentation by Drs. Paul Branch and David Suazo underscored the mutual love and respect we share. Yvonne's presence was especially meaningful to share the surprise. My 1970–2024 relationship with SETECA, from the novitiate professor to these latter opportunities, has provided singular personal highlights.

In 2010, TSM (Trinity School for Ministry—the Anglican seminary in Ambridge, PA) invited me to teach their DMin class in missiology, starting in 2011. The challenge was to create a thirty-hour credit course taught in five intensive days. Significantly, it reflected a massive expansion of *Misiones Mundiales*—now contextualized and translated to a different audience and academic level. I was blessed to teach at a seminary where Morning and Afternoon Prayer frame each day, with Eucharist each Wednesday, which significantly strengthened my Anglican pilgrimage. Also in 2021, after eleven wonderful years teaching the course, it was time for me to step down.

The CRUX Institute opened a novel series of Zoom webinars, teaching events, and blogs, allowing me to utilize my Spanish in a variety of contexts and content. In summary, the gracious Father released me at this latter stage to reembrace my first ministry love—teaching—exercised in diverse educational contexts around the globe. I invested twenty years in formal education, another thirty in nonformal education, and at the end I taught in both modes. These latter teachings were nourished and saturated with stories and experiences, maturity and missiology, a vision of new programs and new methods, including the value of nonformal and formal education, and the role of virtual learning vis-à-vis residential education (a context where community is developed and experienced). In all new methods there is a focus on spirituality and perspectives from the global arena. Of course, the pandemic challenged all training assumptions, and I am convinced we are the better for the creative but needed modalities, especially distance education.

For this multifaceted gift, I am a grateful man.

The Third Gift

When I began vocational ministry, we *discipled*, a term with currency lasting for years. During our years in Latin America, terminology shifted. Today, the terminology includes *mentor, mentee, mentoring*, which intersects with discipling yet brings in a different ministry genre. I think I was born, shaped, called, and gifted to mentor. I also honed this gift. In that space my passions for transformational discipleship took place, but now intentionally. This life-on-life dynamic combines a relational cluster of terms: "example," "model," "teacher," "disciple," "mentor." Mentoring seems to require the gift called "the word of knowledge" and "the word of wisdom." We owe a great debt to Dr. Bobby Clinton, and later his son, Richard, for the broad spectrum of reflections, writing, exercises, and courses on this crucial theme. I encourage you to probe those resources.

Samuel Escobar articulates my feeling about mentorship:

> That someone would be interested in you as a person, that he or she would know you by name, that they would bring you into their sphere, opening opportunities to teach, to counsel, to lead, someone who will reprove or exhort you when needed without losing sight of the dimensions of affect and trust; that is the first and primal experience of pastoral care that will mark you and will awaken a vocation in the person. That, no book can teach you.[4]

During recent years I developed my *mentoring markers*: intentionality, community, collegiality, continuity, longer-term commitment, vulnerability, honesty, confidentiality, confession, a safe space for laughter, tears and repentance, courage to speak and reprove, extended times of silence, Lectio Divina, evening compline, speaking healing words and touch, encouraging them to dig deeply into their private and secret lives, to study how their family system has shaped or misshaped them. I have developed the ability, and need, to discern when to conclude a relationship or cohort. God has allowed me to be a mentor to individuals as well as groups—two very distinct categories.

---

4 Samuel Escobar in personal conversation with the author, 2020.

In some cases, I have invited a few people to form a small community. I clarify the guidelines, asking them to pray for a season and then inform me if they accept them for this off-grid, anonymous group. In the process, God birthed six groups, three in the USA and three in Latin America. Each *Community of the Cross* participant receives a small Costa Rican hard-wood cross and a notebook to journal reflections and conversations. Each gathering has reading requirements that are central to our prime theme. They must be present for the full yearly gathering. We initiate our community with extended times for personal narrative and dialogue, prayer, and laying on of hands. The Latin American colleagues (all in vocational ministry) received a shepherd's staff as a symbol of their identity and role. We read the evening compline service, as I slowly introduce them into sacramental liturgical disciplines. We have learned how to write Collects, psalms, and "Letters to the church." I desire that they finish well, that I will model graceful aging as well as how to die well. These are heavy challenges. We concluded with Holy Communion.

I learned the power of blessing, and the surprising power of withholding blessing. Mentees have spoken prophetic words into my life, and I into theirs. I have asked forgiveness in those bands. While not easy, I was wise and courageous enough to bring closure to a group when its divine assignment ran its course.

In both cultural contexts, I have been gratified at the level of vulnerability, truth-telling, and honesty of the men. In Latin cultures some values operate more subtly, and I pick up only some of them. My cultural intelligence skills are stretched! But even very private topics have emerged in those contexts. In the USA cohorts, I mentor men primarily in the marketplace, discerning the common and yet unique values of their calling into singular vocations.

The Holy Spirit has opened many cases of one-on-one mentoring, especially during the decades with the Mission Commission. Just now I listed forty names of individuals who have called me *mentor*. In some cases, I had no idea they saw me as a nonformal mentor. Others in an earlier intentional relationship are now released as my assignment with them is completed. Intriguingly, some of them return after years of gracious separation.

A memorable life-on-life experience took place in mid-2019. I had traveled to South Africa to speak at the thirty-year celebration of a key ministry founded and led by my friend and colleague, Willie Crew.

Afterward, Adriaan Adams and his close friend, Tertius Nieuwoudt took me on a seven-day road trip through Botswana. We stayed at the inimitable Elephants Sands camp, then traveled through Zimbabwe into Zambia to visit Victoria Falls and the monument to David Livingstone (the final leg to my "Big Three Waterfalls" experience—Iguazzu, Niagara, Victoria). We drove through Namibia and then back to Botswana and South Africa. The life sharing was vulnerable, rich, mutually nourishing, I the elder and they the younger, conversing nonstop (a marvelous ongoing exchange about the concepts of "liminality," and of the richness-challenge of both gathered and scattered church). I slept too close to a hippo one night. That extended opportunity shaped my own life and worldview. God met us on the road and on paths, as we ate and drank, observed creation, prayed, conversed, wept, and slept. I love spending my life that way. Those younger men poured their lives into mine. I am who I am because of them also.

I've been honored to sustain peer-mentoring relationships with colleagues and friends around the world. That genre is very different but also powerful. It folds into accountability, which, when absent in a leader's life, inevitably leads to hidden addictions, sadness, brokenness, and many times into career-ending sin. A final comment on these life-on-life relationships: I am surprised and concerned at the number of women and men in Christian leadership who don't mentor. Is it a unique gift, a calling, a commitment that only falls on a few? Why don't they mentor? Why is it not on their screen? I am puzzled.

Conclusions and Lessons

Yes, these three gifts surprised me. I never dreamed they would come so many years after departing Latin America. And they arrived after a lifetime of service, and after the thirty years of the WEA-MC leadership crucible. Was the best wine saved for the latter segment of the wedding?

I walk slower now, a unique feature of my age and health, current life, and calling. I also walk with an internal limp, trophy of diverse battles.

> **I embrace the expanding dimensions of my renamed identity.**

I embrace the expanding dimensions of my renamed identity. I will continue reading, learning, engaging, disagreeing. I want to understand contextualization not only in its cross-cultural dimensions but in my city, Austin, Texas, where God has planted me. I want to mull God over more, explore his Word deeper, experience his Spirit more intimately and his church more relationally. I am troubled by racial and ethnic conflict and violence, tribalism and migration, and the growing antagonism to true Christianity in a shredding American society. I want to think missionally and missiologically. I want to continually grow as a reflective practitioner. I continue to probe the forces and factors that bring people together in cooperative ventures, whether secular or Christian, whether in networks or alliances or federations or combinations of these.

I am leaning into the singular seasons of the last lap. I am seriously committed to simplify, to dispose of things and books and more, to reduce our "stuff," and to prepare for the next season. I am still learning. That spirit captivates my imagination. I wear my own old shoes, themselves now aging and cracked. I am a man grateful for the latter gifts of my latter life. I want to finish well.

Reflection Questions

1. What does it mean to be renamed in the latter laps of life?
2. In what ways have you already been renamed?
3. What do Bill's late-coming gifts reveal about the nature of God?
4. What are some of the main challenges of aging and simply being old? How can they be reframed? What are the challenges that must be faced?
5. What does it mean to finish well?

Into the Present

Family in Orlando, Missio Nexus Award

Dr. Ted Esler, Missio Nexus, 2018

50th Wedding Celebration, Antigua Guatemala, 2016

Yvonne: Reflections of Beauty

Bill, Trinity School for Ministry

Adriaan and Tertius, South Africa, 2019

Community of the Cross I, 2023

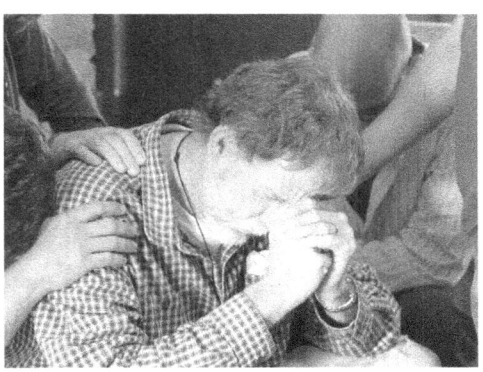
Pray for one another

Community of the Cross II, 2023

CRUX Institute Staff Team, 2024

Gonzalo Chamorro

Speaking at SETECA Graduation, 2023

Ancora Imparo

My Father's Shoes

St. Simeon

Conclusion

Leading and Finishing Well

I leave you with the image of the leader with outstretched hands, who chooses a life of downward mobility. It is the image of the praying leader, the vulnerable leader, and the trusting leader. May that image fill your hearts with hope, courage, and confidence … [1]

I would have lost heart, unless I had believed that I would see the goodness of the LORD in the land of the living. (Ps 27:13, NKJV)

"I Have Come"

Late one Guatemalan night in March 1972, the doorbell jolted Yvonne and me. We were under a military curfew. Peering through the triple-locked garage gates, I recognized someone I knew and cherished, the president of our mission agency; but he lived in Dallas, not Guatemala. Perplexed, I asked, "What are you doing here?" His brief and never-explained response: *"I have come."* I unlocked the gates and followed him up the stairs into our small home.

He showed up in one of my worst moments, when I was bruised by unresolvable conflict with my direct field leader, an immensely gifted man but in my case, difficult to work under. During those early months of 1972 I was devastated, my dreams shattered, I felt on the cusp of failure. I could not understand that the Spirit had cast me into my *first* fiery deconstruction, I was in a furnace with no controls and no exit. I was tasting the bitter ashes of possible career failure, on the verge of becoming an attrition statistic. I was gutted. How would I explain my failure to family, colleagues, supporters, or even to myself? What in God's name would I do back in the USA, a castoff? I didn't even like the USA.

Then he arrived late that night. He peered into Christine's bedroom, blessed her, and then came back into our small living room and sat down. He gazed at us (Yvonne eight months pregnant with our son, David) and simply asked me, "How are you doing?" I uncontrollably dissolved into sobs. I knew that he loved me deeply. I felt safe with him.

---
1 Nouwen, *In the Name of Jesus*, 71, 7 3.

Haltingly, I attempted to explain the issues. He listened, interacted. Much later, he affirmed, gently, "Bill, there is a place and role for you in the Lord's vineyard. We will find it for you. Can you last four months until you leave for your doctoral studies? You have time." A long, healing conversation began as he sat quietly, listened, commented, asked questions, prayed.

Significantly, Yvonne was not in crisis at that time, though she experienced much greater culture shock and adjustment than I. Mysteriously at peace, she identified with my own pain and became a rock of stability to my spiritual, vocational, relational, and emotional struggles. Our visitor took his leave and slipped out into the night. To this day I have no idea why he flew to Guatemala, how he arrived at our door that night in my time of watershed crisis, nor with whom he left. He just showed up, unexpected. I've even wondered if he was an angel unaware. We never discussed that encounter. That night I slept in peace. Hope had returned. Only decades later I would discern how that visitor subtly shaped my leadership vision for the rest of my life.

That man, Dr. William Harris Taylor, was president of what was then CAM International (later Camino Global, now merged into Avant). I've referenced him earlier and his puzzling resignation from the presidency of the mission at the peak of his leadership and influence. My father, Dad, a mystery. An angel?

Interpreting the Story

Neither Dad nor Mom had visions or aspirations of leadership. They were in love with Jesus, passionate about the gospel and the lost. Jesus was coming soon. Dad would learn the Spanish language with excellence, including its subtle subjunctive mood. He was a master storyteller. He and mother and thousands of others of their generation also took steam-driven ships across the world with the weight of those without Christ on their hearts and the certainty of the Second Coming of Jesus as an imminent historical event. The old hymn called out, "Bring them in. Bring them in. Bring them in from the fields of sin." They were willing to pay any price, a lifelong price, persecution, and if called upon, martyrdom. My farm-girl mother and city-bred father could not have originally imagined their lives as global representatives of that Great Generation, whose greatness traveled into the farthest reaches of the world. They purposed to be long-term missionaries from start to end. Their reward is great, and they are now Home.

Did Dad have an inkling in 1938 that he would become a field leader, then a regional leader, then the president of the mission? I am positive he did not. It was not his character. His story describes someone who was not looking for leadership but did not shirk from it when the seeking Spirit called him into it. His path into leadership was not the normal, expected one. But then, what paths are normal? He modeled "leadership from below" to me.

That late night visit shaped me irrevocably; I have not forgotten it. It exemplified the pastor leader, the listener, the one who cast a new vision of my future, who knew there was a place for me in the kingdom of God, who saw what I could not see, who challenged me to knuckle down and finish that first term well. Only afterwards would the Spirit open new doors and unexpected vocational possibilities to me. Dad's personal leadership that night was not focused on attrition reduction, nor problem solving, nor the drudgery of spending time with an immature new missionary. He was the shepherd and I the younger vulnerable sheep.

Billy from Costa Rica

Little did this carrot-topped, hazel-eyed MK born in Costa Rica some eighty-four years ago dream what his life would turn out to be. But then, who does? I grew up unevenly, but God was there. I was shaped by loving yet passive parents, but God was there. I grew up in a fundamentalist separatist world, but God was there safeguarding me from its extremes. Thank God that my parents, while working within that worldview, were not driven by its excesses. That grace led me into freedom, then into a secure self-understanding of who I was in the Father's eyes. I grew up on the dirt streets of Turrialba and Guadalupe de San José; my youth was spent in two Guatemalan cities. In God's proactive providence, I lived most of my adult years in worldwide arenas. I was shaped to wait. James and Peter's words echoed repeatedly, "Humble yourself in the sight of the Lord and he will lift you up." Today this global pilgrim paces his latter life laps with a modest gait, at times with a metaphorical limp.

In these latter years my life task invites me to release most positions, titles, and roles; to step back, opening space and investing in younger generations, rejoicing in their formation and success, their challenges, and some failures. This long journey through its variegated paths has not been without pain, suffering, loss, nor without unanswered prayers.

In the first stirrings of discernment of my vocation I did not know what I was being called into. Who does? Three crucial decisions irrevocably shaped me: my childhood conversion, my invitation into mission at age nine, and receiving God's gift of Yvonne as my life partner at age twenty-six. Those decisions turned me around and made me.

Dad's old shoes—sitting on my office shelf—remind me of his embodied example. They became both metaphor and model. He also released me to make my own journey, to run the race in my own shoes. That freedom carried me beyond the narrow worldview and community I grew up in. I accepted the good gifts of that fundamentalism, but I was irrevocably transformed when the Spirit led me into global evangelicalism. The Spirit reworked my theology and praxis, my spirituality, missiology, and ecclesiology.

> Dad's old shoes–sitting on my office shelf–remind me of his embodied example. They became both metaphor and model. He also released me to make my own journey, to run the race in my own shoes.

Leadership Lessons and Finishing Well

Crafting the final draft of this manuscript, the Spirit led me to let it marinate for much of 2023. During that season I discerned three distinct truths: First, in peculiar yet specific ways the seventeen years (1968–1985) based in Guatemala granted me a unique arena in which to begin exercising leadership. Spaces and places and opportunities opened to exercise leadership giftings and skills, though I sought none of them. There and then I made many mistakes, some that embarrass me to this day. But grace was extended. Challenges stretched and grew me. My teaching vocation was exercised and we became church planters also. My children were born in Guatemala, and we became an internationalized TCP family. That season was enormously valuable. But little could I have imagined how they would prepare me for thirty years (1986–2016) in the global arena with the World Evangelical Alliance Mission Commission (WEA-MC). Second, the transitional season of three deaths and resurrection was an imperative rite of passage for me and my future. Third, there was a Hand over my life, protecting me, overruling me, guiding me, empowering me, releasing me for the Spirit's purposes in my life.

In 2010, on my seventieth birthday, my son David gifted me a disquieting set of books on aging and dying, with unsettling titles.

"Why these books, David"? He said, "I want you to prepare for this season and the end." Those cryptic, poignant words struck home. And I prepared, ultimately reading a shelf-full of works on aging and dying, autobiographies and memoirs, from well and less-known Christians and seculars. Each speaks wisdom, some at times a bit ego-centric or photoshopped, others vulnerable and authentic; but in all I discovered value. They sit in front of me on my desk in a long row of other resources I read during this writing journey. I now want to lean into that ancient understanding, *ars moriendi*, "the art of dying well."

Am I finishing this latter season well? Did I finish my previous life seasons well? My mission colleague and friend, Paul McKaughan, pointed me years ago to Jeffrey Sonnenfeld's thoughtful work, *The Heroes' Farewell: What Happens when CEO's Retire*.[2] I read it carefully in 2006 when the MC leadership was transitioning to Bertil, and it called me to seriously examine leadership transitions. I was struck by the categorization of departed CEOs who plotted a coup to return and "rescue the company," often called "founder's syndrome." I most identified with the "governor" and the "ambassador" categories of exiting leaders. They seemed to fit my own desires and trajectory, as both categories are portrayed as graciously seeking to move into different arenas of life. Dad chose that path, returning to his church planter roots.

I was surprised when reading the more recent books on leadership that very few of them developed the category of finishing well. I just discovered John Stott's last book, *The Radical Disciple*, a refreshing exception.[3] This small book became a final challenge to learn what it means to finish well ... which Stott certainly did. This theme is missing even in Ian Parkinson's *Understanding Christian Leadership*, my motherlode resource.[4] Most books on aging and death rarely talk about finishing well. This has been a disturbing discovery in evangelical literature. Finishing well is far from easy, and the battles at this latter stage are fierce and unrelenting.

As I pondered this final chapter, David asked me, "Dad, if you were sitting in a circle of younger emerging leaders or veterans, and they said 'Bill, summarize your prime leadership lessons learned over a lifetime,' what would you tell them?" This pointed question challenged me to

---

2 Sonnenfeld, *The Hero's Farewell*.
3 Stott, *The Radical Disciple*.
4 Parkinson, *Understanding Christian Leadership*.

encapsulate my reflections, the crucial conclusions emerging from the tutorial of life, based on my own definition that "The leader is one who provides a vision of a preferred future and invites-gathers-empowers others to participate in that vision." Leadership combines natural skill sets with spiritual gifts, training and intentionality, the casting of creative vision, and the invitation for followers to join that venture.

First, accept leadership roles as they come. If the Spirit has qualified you for any arena of leadership, it will come to you. Do not seek or jockey for it. For years I never self-identified as a leader. I was reluctant to use the term even into my early WEF season. When others identified me as such, I shied away from it. Why? I really don't know. Was it false modesty or weak humility? No. I honestly never thought I would emerge with leadership gifts. I was a team player, a follower of more gifted people. However, as I have reviewed my life, I realized that when I was invited into a special arena to perform a specific task, I was able to sense that I was to accept it. I did accept, but then would return to my *follower* identity. I had inklings of leadership: I experienced them in seminary, on IVCF staff, and then, SETECA. Can the Spirit of God empower a reluctant leader? Yes, he can. He did.

During our first term in Guatemala, our prime assignment was to learn language and culture and to create life and family in a different context. I began formal teaching as a novice, making my generous collection of mistakes. But I loved my job, honing my teacher craft. In retrospect I think I was a teacher-pastor at heart. Leadership showed up indirectly as advisor to the IFES student group in Guatemala and as a discipler of a few guys. One of those men is the oldest member of one of my Latin America mentoring groups. In our second term, evident leadership emerged when I became a very young, thirty-three-year-old elder in our newly founded church.

Intriguing biblical case studies on leadership reveal that God's anointing for future roles takes place long before entering the public arena. Study Joseph, Moses, David, Jesus, Paul. Therefore, we wait and serve, many times not understanding God's timing. The contrast, obviously, is the leader launched like a celebratory rocket, whooshing high into the sky, brilliantly illuminated, and then plummeting down, a spent shell. I've seen my quota of these. Beware of ads, like one touting a new MBA program, "The road to success has a fast lane." Another Christian school promises "impact metrics."

Which brings up the issue of charisma in leadership. Rick Warren famously stated, "Charisma has absolutely nothing to do with leadership." But is that true? I don't think so. The term is hotly debated in secular and Christian sources, many returning to Max Weber's original thinking. "For Weber, the essence of charisma was a leader's forceful personality that compelled others to follow."[5] Personality obviously plays a critical role, but in authentically Christian leadership it must be controlled by the Giver of the charism, the Spirit.

> Successful leadership depends upon charisma in the larger, biblical sense of the word. It is a gift that God grants through his Spirit. Leadership abilities, as well as the leaders themselves, are given by God today, just as they were in the Bible. They are as varied in their personalities as any of the leaders we read about in the Bible and just as imperfect ... We are longing, I think, for a movement whose only impetus comes from the Spirit rather than as a response to someone's personality. Such a thing is certainly possible, but it is not the norm. Most of the time, God works through people. Where there are people, personality is always a factor.[6]

At the end of the day, strong charismatic missional leaders (from many nations) tended to establish, grow, found, and serve their own organizations for a long time—perhaps until death. They might be guest speakers at major events, and even "loan" their name on occasion for some kind of value-added negotiation. But they are not team players, they find it hard to serve under accountability. We have witnessed too many who have resigned in shame or ended their service with serious shadows. Charisma is a tricky gift.

I was shaped by my own father's personality and development as a leader. I discovered much in his early journals and in my years of observing him. While he never sought leadership, he didn't turn away from invitations to lead, nor was he hesitant to step into leadership vacuums or into spaces lacking in vision and guidance. He learned the cost and importance of calling a spade a spade and not backing away from speaking hard truths to some colleagues and missionaries.

---

5 Koessler, "Charisma Has Fallen," 60–66.
6 Koessler, 63.

Second, measure your mentors by how they model the style of Jesus. Blessed is the emerging leader who matured under those who truly modeled the Jesus style. For Jesus, leadership was not primarily about results; it was the peripatetic transformational learning journey with him, the path to the cross, the resurrection and ascension, the Spirit's arrival, and then global mission. The inimitable Paul Little shaped me as my IVCF staff director. In Guatemala I served under a variety of leaders with very different styles, some healthy and more collegial though unafraid to make hard decisions. Yes, a few of my leaders were difficult people, but I also learned how I did *not* want to lead, and I still served them. During our first six years in Latin America, Dad was the mission president, and I saw up close how he envisioned, served, and shepherded, how he organized, administered, and guided a lethargic agency into new arenas and geographies. I also encountered early judgment simply because I was "the president's son." We learn how to lead from positive and negative examples.

Third, serve in diverse arenas. Working in three radically different ministry arenas taught me a lot. The first was the academic world with its more structured boundaries, vertical hierarchy, systems and histories, rites of passage, bylaws and governance, educational requirements, and its academic and promotional categories. The second was the volunteer society with its fuzzy boundaries: mission agencies, networks, and alliances, areas where financial matters and direct accountability had little influence over commitment and participation. It was in this latter world that I developed my understanding of leadership from below, marked more by collegiality, flat structures, with personal relationships in the global community and in shared passions. I also embraced the challenge within the MC of leading independent leaders from some fifty nations, women and men with diverse cultures and mother tongues, and many different organizations and structures. The third was the local church with its challenges of ecclesiology and polity, of personality and cross-generational relationships, of die-hard commitment to the past or passionate embrace of the unknown, and the confusing success metrics that Christian and secular culture imposes on churches.

As I transitioned into new arenas, God's Spirit gradually empowered me with new skills and gifts. I was growing into leadership, energized, and equipped by God. Some of these gifts might have been latent; others were new, given, revealed, and exercised. Each invitation to a new service was to be examined and prayed over. Sometimes I was invited to the threshold of an invitation, to evaluate a new opportunity, but not necessarily to walk through. Not every open door is one we must enter.

I was privileged to serve within WEA, an historic evangelical body with a global constituency, constitutional governance, commitment to continuity, and rooted relationships to its national and regional alliances and commissions. At times WEA's global identity, role, and impact seemed uncertain; at other times it was more settled and encouraging. At times it seemed we had to learn to be leaders on a tight-rope act. One thing we learned for certain: in the long term there is no conductor-less orchestra. Leadership is rooted in the Trinitarian community, central to the DNA of creation and the churches. Both man and woman are mandated as stewards of creation and culture.

Fourth, be aware of temptations. Upon our return to the USA in 1985, first teaching at TEDS, then part-time pastoring an infirm church, and finally transitioning into the global evangelical arenas, I came face to face with the power of seductive leadership temptations. While WEA was international in scope, a good percentage of its structures had been formed in the Western nations with its hidden addictions and glittering images. But I discovered a trickier reality.

Every culture in the world and every church in every culture struggles with issues of power and influence, money and sex, abusive and toxic leadership, and particular styles of leadership. Some of my African colleagues operated from the tribal chief presupposition—for them it meant no term limits. Latin cultures had their *caudillo*, the strong man. Asian cultures deal with power control issues by the elderly, in addition to shame and honor values, which affect leadership. Most Western styles seemed to model leadership from above.

Some temptations swirling in the MC world came from conflicting leadership styles and priorities; doing measurable research; operating from a numbers and end-date game; temptations to compromise our proposals to the donors with capacity to invest generously in our assignments; and the passionate desire to "complete the Great Commission." The MC eliminated one status symbol in all our gatherings, roundtables, and consultations: our name tags only gave names plus country of origin or service. No titles: we leveled the ground. Not all WEA units followed suit.

It is encouraging to read that while the Evangelical Council for Financial Accountability (ECFA) has primarily set standards related to governance and fiscal integrity, "This year, the organization announced plans to add a new requirement to address the integrity and character of a ministry's leaders. It's the biggest change to ECFA's standards in forty-five years."[7] Whether this will reduce the crises of not finishing well waits to be seen. But it does charge boards with a powerful new dimension to consider.

Fifth, discern your personal gifts. I had to learn what vocational ministry was best fitted to my skill set and gift mix. Having tried several ministries, thank God I discerned where I was not to serve. My primary calling/gifts are not as church pastor, board member, president of an agency or educational institution leadership. I don't think I'm a project or program manager either. Once during seminary years, as I cut the grass at our mission offices, a former agency president came out to chat with me. Out of the blue he said, "Bill, some day you will be the president of our mission." Incredulous, I just looked at him; I might have said, "Hmmm, I rather doubt that." Over the years, I saw myself as a middle-level leader, which fit me in the Mission Commission. I never submitted my name for WEA's top position.

I also learned leadership in the global arenas by studying the kinds of people who sought, were appointed, or elected to higher positions. Each role requires a singular kind of leader, whether it's a mission agency and its top executive team, or the mission field director, or the loosely structured flexible missional network, or the strategic cooperative initiatives, or other global entities. Many bigger organizations are denominational, tending to operate top-down. Others represent worldwide alliances like WEA. Some global networks, like Lausanne, focus on integral evangelism, the global church, a host of interest groups, and they often have some kind of national or regional organizational structure. Lausanne seems to draw the entrepreneurial leader—from many cultures. Other arenas emerge, leaders of prayer networks, or teams focused on research and statistics, or strategic alliances, or "finishing the task." Each needs a certain kind of leader. It would not be wise to promote a leader in one field of expertise into other positions that require different sets of capabilities. I learned the difference between managers and leaders.

---

7 Evangelical Council for Financial Accountability, 2024.

Sixth, learn from leaders who are unafraid to mentor younger men and women, who open space for them, who are not threatened by those with greater gifts and potential. It still befuddles me how few mission leaders mentor. Are they not gifted for it? Don't they see the need for it? Mentoring just seems to be a Jesus thing, a Barnabas thing, a Paul thing.

Part of the joy of working with younger leaders comes from observing their development as they gain experience by error and grace and face challenging situations. Some would remain at a lower level of leadership, for that is the Spirit's place for them. Others emerged into middle positions. Yet others will be assigned to higher arenas of responsibility. If we have played even a small role in their development, does that not bring joy? Finally, as I engaged younger leaders in the Mission Commission, they taught me skills I did not have. I thank God for Jon Lewis and Bertil Ekström, Ray Windsor, and Rose Dowsett, my master teachers.

I observed a diversity of leadership virtues and styles emerge before me in our MC community. We had the servants and proactive leaders, organizers and managers, volunteers, and invisible ones behind the scenes. We observed the more collegial styles engaging with the top-down people, the emerging leaders with people of current influence. But it was a special delight that at all MC events, their name tags gave no titles!

Seventh, long-term service enables greater perspective. My long-term service with the MC gave me the benefit of observing the gradual growth of a ministry and its emerging influence. At times this element was mysterious—there was a *Hand*—particularly in the purposeful development of the MC as a global community, our global practitioners. The MC, as well as WEA and other groups, had a singular capacity and power to convene, to communicate, to influence, and to coordinate. And personal longevity has allowed me to follow the journeys of so many former friends, students, disciples, mentees, and colleagues, tracking their lives, rejoicing in God's blessings on them, praying for many. A liability of leadership longevity is that we witness some colleagues derailed by hidden addictions, open sin, unfaithfulness and more. It's a peculiar sweet-sour taste in the mouth.

Eighth, learn all you can about leading from below. I am thankful God-designed me to follow those who lead from below. I think I was wired for this style, but I also grew it in different contexts. Clearly, I wish I had done some things differently. That's life. Leading from below requires Spirit-guided leaders to serve collegially, from the servant heart, sharing the downward path of the cross. It's a call to vulnerability, to sacrificial service where there is no apparent value-plus benefit, an invitation to serve with wounds and scars, by a life marked with suffering and unanswered prayer. "Jesus, to whom else would we go?" And yes, these lessons are learned and exercised in the context of the crucible of global mission. Crucible: vat, hot kettle, place of trial, affliction, suffering, purification.

Leading from below includes acknowledging my own leadership shortcomings and mistakes and what God and life taught me through those experiences. And I made mistakes, not just early on. I learned to highly respect my colleagues and friends who led within the realities of personal suffering.

Ninth, respect leaders with honest wounds and scars, yet who don't boast in them. This also is in the DNA of finishing well. I don't trust high-flyers where everything they touch seems to turn to gold; they are enamored with glittering images and glamorous powers.

Over the years, Yvonne and I have found ourselves attracted to and respectful of those who themselves have been broken by life's blows, the price they paid to follow Jesus. They have suffered greatly; yet despite it all they continue to love Jesus. Having faced loss and grief, their discipleship is steadfast and transformative. Regretfully, too many missionary letters ignore and spin these realities. A twisted theme within cultural evangelicalism seduced some believers with sub-biblical goals, conflating them into the "American (or Korean, Nigerian, Brazilian) Dream" where a painless as possible, comfortable, and successful ("everything turned out well") life is the goal. But we are called by Christ to walk the path overshadowed by the cross. Yvonne says it well in her chapter, "Embracing the Invitation to Brokenness and Deconstruction" in *Spirituality in Mission*: "God fashions his saints in the crucible of suffering."[8] Those we have known who chose that path are beautiful to behold, and we are privileged to count many as friends.

Our most recent battle with deep suffering came in the context of my daughter's near-death accident in April 2018. Christine fought a life and death war for six days; then God miraculously brought her back—from traumatic brain injury and subdural hematoma, a punctured lung, dissected carotid vertebral arteries, pan-facial fractures (literally dozens, requiring a facial reconstruction), a split liver, seven broken ribs, and broken bones in her feet. *Talitha cum* (little girl, arise) was prayed by

---

8 Taylor, *Spirituality in Mission*.

believers around the world. Amazingly she recovered, though now years later, her capacity is still around half of what it was. How does a mother and father pray and trust a good God?

We personally love and know five couples who, called into long-term cross-cultural service in tough areas of China, battled inordinately difficult health crises in their own lives or in their children's lives. Cancer, deformed babies in womb (one told to go down the hospital hall to room #200, get the abortion and return; another whose equally handicapped child was healed in the womb). Three with disabled children. Demonic? Urban pollution? Random? Suffering beyond bounds? Yes.

Henri Nouwen again:

> The way of the Christian leader is not the way of upward mobility in which our world has invested so much, but the way of downward mobility ending on the cross ... Powerlessness and humility in the spiritual life do not refer to people who have no spine and who let everyone else make decisions for them. They refer to people who are so deeply in love with Jesus that they are ready to follow him wherever he guides them, always trusting that, with him, they will find life and find it abundantly.[9]

Finally, my good friends, always seek to grow. Love Jesus, emulate Jesus, study Jesus. Study Scripture. Study history. Study culture. Learn to lead as you observe gifted women and men. Discern the gifts the Spirit has given you. Cast vision, retrain yourself, invite others to dream with you on this journey. We are coleaders with the Triune God. Accept the challenge: lead from below.

Conclusions, Gazing Towards the Foothills, Finishing Well

"Little did I know." This phrase kept returning to me over the course of these narratives. How could I have known or dreamed? Nobody has that kind of prophetic insight. So, I simply affirm, "But God knew, and knows." This conviction reassures me. I muddled through my early life. I did not seek a *career path*. I now walk into my mid-eighties with a hope, anticipation, even wary excitement to discover the last bits of this long-term

> "Little did I know." This phrase kept returning to me over the course of these narratives. I simply affirm, "But God knew, and knows."

---

[9] Nouwen, *In the Name of Jesus*, 62–64.

journey—that "long obedience in the same direction" which Eugene Peterson folded into our evangelical language and experience. The deepest, truest memory of my life will be seen and understood after my *Permanent Change of Address*; the testimony of life. For me that will be Home; for others, here.

Early on, I sensed God impressing upon me the commitment to finish well, regardless of the season and assignment given to me. Again, Dad set the tone by what he did and didn't do. Remember the young Solomon. He did not ask for money or fame, but rather wisdom. Yet God gave him all three, which he squandered and thus left us a mixed legacy. Steward carefully God-given gifts. I have had to grapple with profound disappointment, even betrayal, of leaders whom I have trusted, who proved untrustworthy. For some I pray today for brokenness, repentance, and restoration.

In recent years I've read and pondered many stories of men *and* women in high leadership who have been removed from leadership, have resigned in disgrace, or who have been exposed as power abusers (living or shortly after death), so many times linked to sex and influence, money, and fame. Other forces can derail us: self-pity, loss of self-value, doubts that destroy, coasting at the end, too many "what ifs," bitterness, disappointment with God, unhealed wounds and truncated dreams. For better or worse, the decades with WEA meant that I learned of sad cases around the world, regardless of nationality or culture. Some were personal friends. I grieve. Finishing well is not easy. Aging is tough.

I have asked myself: Can good leaders *not* finish well? Or does good leadership implicitly imply finishing well? I am puzzled by some cases where someone I had thought of as a very good leader ended up disappointed in life, running out of steam, coasting, deciding not to grow or learn. So, I conclude that good leadership does imply finishing well.

"Retirement," stares at me. Rejecting its secular or spiritualized iterations, this season must be marked by courageous self-examination, down-shifting, embracing less-is-more, releasing. I want to love and pray as never before, to mentor and write as never before. Biblical passages reference age, the aged, the gray head, the wise, the elder. Levites relinquished some duties at age fifty. But latter life season is, as we understand it today, a modern construct requiring us to repurpose it with Christian values. Jeff Haanen's *An Uncommon Guide to Retirement— Finding God's Purpose for the Next Season of Life*, is excellent.[10]

---

10 Haanen, *An Uncommon Guide to Retirement*.

Just recently I discovered Alice Fryling's insightful gem, *Aging Faithfully: The Holy Invitation of Growing Older*, and have discovered some of the most helpful wisdom at this stage of my life.[11]

Engaging life now, I want to release younger leaders. I want to be a sage, by God's grace. I desire to see visions and dream dreams. And interwoven through all is the passionate drive to finish strong and well. The essence of what this means is encapsulated in my chapters in the last MC book I helped edit and produce, *Spirituality in Mission: Embracing the Lifelong Journey*.[12]

Three central passions guide me as I gaze at these foothills before me, lacing up my shoes. First, to die having been faithful to my marriage vows with Yvonne, assured of my oath. Second, when my children carry my coffin to the opened Texas soil, I hope they can say to each other, "Dad did not sacrifice us on the illegitimate altar of his own ministry." Finally, I want to die in faith, sure of the core truths I attempted to follow and believe: the Triune God on mission, the uniqueness of Jesus, the authority of Scripture, the mission of the church, the return of Christ in power and glory. I appreciate and hold with respect the historic affirmation of orthodox Christianity as expressed in the Nicene Creed. The words of Jesus in Luke 18:8 disquiet me, "When the Son of Man comes, will he find faith on earth?" As I see Christians walking away from Jesus around the world, including from my own circle of friends, I now understand that passage better.

I do not want my narrative to smack of missionary hagiography, with airbrushed tales of super-holy, unusually gifted, always-exemplar people, the ones "God really loves and rewards, who learn language and culture rapidly and never get sick and all prayers are answered." God knows that's not my reality. My personal story has significance primarily to my family, friends, and colleagues.

> **Three central passions guide me as I gaze at these foothills before me, lacing up my shoes.**

The broader brushstrokes are told in the context of larger templates of my life. My multi-generational family represents but one case study of thousands of cross-cultural servants who traveled far from home for the sake of the gospel, regardless of the specific assignments they accepted. And superseding it all, ours is the Epic Story of God in Christ, Creator,

---

11 Fryling, *Aging Faithfully.*.
12 Amalraj, *Spirituality in Mission*.

Redeemer, Crucified, Resurrected and Returning Judge. True honor and glory ultimately and imperatively belong to our majestic Triune God.

That gives perspective to the question, "Were these choices costly?" Yes, Jesus told us it would be so. Yes, many tough, challenging and heart-wrenching things have come to me. Some I provoked. Others I did not. But all contributed toward shaping me in the image of Jesus, the only icon worth emulating.

I simply want to finish this current season of my life well. I do not know when or how (in the language of the Old Testament patriarchs) I will be "gathered to my people." A few years ago, Yvonne and I purchased our funeral plots in a small-town Texas cemetery. We have paid for our funeral services. Our caskets will be made of simple pine, crafted in an Orthodox monastery whose craftsmen pray over those who will rest and turn to dust in these boxes. We have a "travel insurance" policy that guarantees our remains can be repatriated to Austin. We have written our final service directives, entrusting David to coordinate those remembrances and rites. Our children know where the crucial information and passwords are. They know the essence of our wills. While Yvonne and I would love to go Home together, God alone coordinates that timing. Ironically, I just renewed my driver's license and my passport, suspecting this is the last renewal. Poignant act.

Facing my own death, whenever it comes and unless our Lord returns first, is not something I really fear. What I least desire is the slow-motion erasure of the memory of love and life because of Alzheimer's, stealing my brain and true self. God, please deliver me! But at the end of the day (and life), it's not my choice how I will "permanently change my address," quoting Dad. The future will be immeasurably transformed into glory. I have a list of people in heaven with whom I want to spend time and ask questions, many found in Scripture and so many others throughout history. Eugene Peterson's, *The Message*, translates Philippians 1:22–26 so beautifully, even as I also await that day when we "break camp."

During this narrative on leadership, a bit over eight decades has been spaded up and sifted in that search. My personal story parallels thousands of other Third Culture Kids who strove to follow God and his mission. Did any of us really and fully understand our eternal Trinitarian community at work in our lives? No. In my case, the Father revealed his love to me; the Son's completed work redeemed me and modeled humanity and integral mission to me; the Spirit wooed me, convicted me, disciplined me, empowered me with gifts, and set before me a vision of his person, power and presence. And they all entrusted me with leadership. This is my final convergence of life and gifts.

Throughout this writing experiment my father's shoes have continually gazed at me, spoken to me, encouraged me. While I wear my own shoes, Dad's old pair reminds me to walk and persevere, to rejoice and laugh, to lead well, and to finish strong and well.

I conclude these narrative reflections on leadership and on finishing well. Today, lifelong streams of memory and gratitude flood over me. Eugene Peterson taught me to accept life with a new "friend" named "Anonymity." While my end may not be imminent, I prepare for its arrival. Do I detect a Hand over my life? Are there fragments of an overarching meta-story line woven into my story? Yes, it is the portrait of a life chronicle shielded by the quiet, steady presence of the Spirit—empowering, protecting, preserving me.

> While I wear my own shoes, Dad's old pair reminds me to walk and persevere, to rejoice and laugh, and to finish strong and well.

Thank God for my family, friends, and close colleagues for traveling with me on this journey. Caleb's courage and request when he was eighty-five encourages me (Josh 14:6–15). Jesus finished well, but it required the downward path to the cross—then resurrection. Thankfully, on that Great Final Day, none of us will be evaluated on performance but rather on integrity and faithfulness. Accompanied by kingdom friends, I press on, "farther up and farther in."

Reflection Questions

1. What does Henri Nouwen teach us about leadership? In what ways is this a challenge to modern leadership thinking and style?

2. Which of the "lessons learned" resonate the most with you? Why so?

3. What does "finishing each season well" mean to you?

4. What's the difference between retirement and finishing well?

5. How would you contrast "leadership from above" with "leadership from below"? How might God use both styles?

A Collect

God's Heart for the World's Peoples

O Lord, you from whom every family in heaven and on earth derives its name, bless the nations this day, we pray, and use us to bear witness to your glory in all the peoples of earth, so that your ways may be known upon the earth and the nations be glad and sing for joy. We pray this in the name of the One around whom representatives from every tongue, tribe and nation gather in praise. Amen. (W. David O. Taylor, 2022)

Afterword

The Next Generation

Walk through the front door of the grand old house at Easneye Estate, on the rural outskirts of Ware, Hertfordshire, and you will see a wide staircase at the far end of the large reception room. Skip across the polished floor flanked by a sandstone fireplace and the stairs sweep you around to a glass encased lounge, locked to the general public. To this day the lounge serves as the conversation space for Master of Arts students at All Nations Christian College (ANCC). I first encountered Bill and Yvonne Taylor there, in the spring of 1998.

I cannot remember how the meet was set up, but I do remember my MA research was intended to refute the way my mission organization (at the time) was applying the Mission Commission's 1997 book, *Too Valuable to Lose: Exploring the Causes and Cures of Missionary Attrition*—the report of the (first) REMAP study on missionary attrition. Based on those findings, our agency was developing a narrative that the new generation of missionaries just did not have the mettle to endure the rigors of missionary life. As one of this new generation, and an early adopter of mobilization as an emerging missions activity, I was incredulous. "No, no" I thought, after reading the conclusions myself and recalling the conversations I was having with my age-cohort bouncing out of the institution. "It's not the missionaries, but rather the missions structures that are to blame" ... and maybe also the editor of the book for presenting the findings in such a way that such erroneous conclusions could be drawn. Now, here was my chance to have it out with that editor! I was thirty years old, and my wife and I had been serving in missions for all of three years.

Charged with enthusiasm for my cause, I arrived for my appointment with Bill and Yvonne. Upon arrival, I immediately forgot why I was there. Before me sat an older US American couple looking somewhat counter-cultural after a Celtic fashion, with no hint of the air of authority I had come to expect from missions leaders. Soft-speaking, with eyes that searched the soul, I was immediately disarmed. They asked about me and my interests and actually seemed to listen to my over-inflated opinions. Furthermore, they seemed enthusiastic about what I understood to be my generation's perspectives and concerns. This grace was highly unusual. We are GenX. We were used to being ignored, overlooked, and underestimated. These veteran mission leaders were endearingly peculiar.

Furthermore, Bill shared with me a vision for a Holy Island Roundtable of younger missions thought-leaders to explore the future of missions for the next generation, and invited me to consider attending. I never expected to get an invitation, but I felt honored in the moment. To my surprise the invitation did come, but I had just been appointed the director of another organization and my first international meeting clashed with the Holy Island dates. That gathering resulted in the book, *Postmission: World Mission by a Postmodern Generation*, edited by fellow GenXer and convenor of the Roundtable, Richard Tiplady.

My wife and I met Bill again in 2004 on the shores of Lake Taupo in the middle of the North Island of Aotearoa New Zealand. He was the keynote speaker at the Missions Interlink (NZ) national missions conference. I was four years into what was to become a fifteen-year missions leadership role, mobilizing, recruiting, sending, caring, and reentering missionaries, mostly GenX, from Aotearoa New Zealand to the world, guided by principles drawn from my ANCC MA research. Bill's keynotes at that missionary alliance event are etched into our memories. If Bill were any more laid back, he would have been horizontal. Backward leaning, in his inimitable thinking-speaking style, he spoke of downward mobility. He flipped the script on leadership expectations and success metrics and drew us toward the heart of our self-giving God. Those thoughts, that were seemingly downloaded from heaven in real-time beside the shores of that volcanic lake, are expanded upon in this volume after almost two decades of further development and practice. Simmering and ready to erupt afresh.

In 2007 Bill reached out and invited me to consider becoming a researcher in a project with global scope that would investigate reasons for people becoming involved in missions (whatever they understood missions to be). That research informed the 2016 book, *Mission in Motion: Speaking Frankly of Mobilization*, that I coauthored with sociological professor Malcolm Gold. Having completed one book, Bill figured I knew the ropes enough to take over from him as Publications Director for the MC. While I negotiated the publishing of the next book, *Spirituality in Mission: Embracing the Lifelong Journey* (2018), Mission Commission Executive Director David Ruíz (2016–2018) invited me to join his team of Associate Directors. A couple months later, David announced his resignation.

Twenty-two years after meeting Bill and Yvonne Taylor in that ANCC lounge, I was invited to take responsibility for the leadership of the very community that Bill represented so well. During my previous thirteen years' involvement I learned much about the World Evangelical Alliance's Mission Commission and the caliber of its other leaders, warmly introduced by Bill in the previous pages. Each leader's casual humility and generosity of spirit spoke volumes about the ethos of the MC, exemplified by Bill and Yvonne's commitment to lead from below. As I write, I am in the throes of administering the MC's next Global Consultation (Chiang Mai, Thailand 2023), the first without Bill's presence. It also marks the beginning of a new era—a new generation of reflective practitioners are carrying the vision forward. The vast majority of consultation participants were born between 1965 and 1982, so GenXers now carry the responsibility to rally participation towards a desirable shared vision.

The MC continues to be a community of reflective practitioners, drawing together established and emerging global leaders to share from their missions experiences. Humility, mutuality, and service remain core values, among others. Promoting missions perspectives from the Majority World, in concert with established and creative views from traditional missionary sending nations, is an ongoing commitment. Discerning the movement of God's Spirit to help the global church and its missions communities navigate our way into the future of God's mission is our central activity. All for the glory of God in all nations.

With the change of generations, we move from a "Globalization of Mission" focus (which generated a series of MC books, from 1997's *Too Valuable to Lose* to 2018's *Spirituality in Mission*) to a "Future of Mission" focus—beginning with this volume. My people, the Māori of Aotearoa New Zealand, have a saying, "*Ka mua, ka muri.*" Roughly translated, it means to "walk backward into the future." It carries with it the assumption that we look to our past to understand how we got to where we are and to determine where we are going. We never forget our roots. Our elders always remain with us, and we live to honor their contributions to our wellbeing today. I am committed to honoring those who have led before me as I now carry the metaphorical mantle and the literal South African wooden mace of leadership for the MC.

Even now, I am looking for the emerging leaders who will be among the choices for my successor—leaders who will hopefully be influenced by my leadership from below as I was influenced by Bill and Yvonne's. But if I fail, as has been my experience at times, at least they will have this book from which to learn. I commend it to every person who desires to walk the narrow way of Christ, the way of kenosis in service of the will of God (Phil 2:5–11). A way that is navigated by using two words: "Yes, Lord."

Jay Mātenga, May 2024
Director, Global Witness Department
Executive Director Mission Commission
World Evangelical Alliance

Bibliography

Acemoglu, Daren, and James A. Robinson. *Why Nations Fail: The Origin of Power, Prosperity, and Poverty*. New York: Crown Currency, 2013.

Amalraj, John, Geoffrey W. Hahn, and William D. Taylor. *Spirituality in Mission: Embracing the Lifelong Journey*. William Carey Publishing, 2018.

Augustine, Saint. *Confessions*. New York: Dorset Press, 1986.

Austen, Lucy S. R . *Elisabeth Elliot: A Life*. Wheaton, IL: Crossway, 2023.

Barna, George. *Master Leaders: 30 Leadership Greats. 16 Keys to Success. One Amazing Conversation*. Carol Stream, IL: Tyndale House Publishers, 2009.

Buechner, Frederick. *Telling Secrets: A Memoir*. San Francisco: Harper, 1991.

Carroll, Lewis. Illustrated by John Tenniel. *Through the Looking Glass*. Orinda, CA: SeaWolf Press, 2019.

Chamorro, Gonzalo, and Josué Estrada, eds. *Diálogos en Tiempos de Crisis: Reflexiones a Partir de la Pandemia*. William D. Taylor House, 2020.

Christian and Missionary Alliance in Canada. Accessed February 7, 2024. https://thealliancecanada.ca/beliefs/.

Drucker, Peter. *Leadership Now Remembers*. Accessed May 14, 2024. https://www.leadershipnow.com/druckerremembered.html.

Evangelical Council for Financial Accountability. Accessed May 24, 2024. https://www.christianitytoday.com/news/2024/.may/ecfa-evangelical-accountability-leader-integrity-standard-m.html.

Elliot, Elisabeth. *Furnace of the Lord: Reflections on the Redemption of the Holy City*. Hodder and Stoughton, 1969.

Elliot, Elisabeth. *No Graven Image*. New York: Harper and Row Publishers, 1966.

Elliot, Elisabeth. *The Savage My Kinsman*. New York: Harper and Brothers Publishers, 1961. (First edition a coffee table size, with full color photographs. Subsequent editions were paperbacks with black and white photographs.)

Elliot, Elisabeth. *Shadow of the Almighty*. New York: Harper and Brothers Publishers, 1958.

Elliot, Elisabeth. *A Slow and Certain Light: Some Thoughts on the Guidance of God*. Word Books, Publishers, 1973.

Elliot, Elisabeth, *These Strange Ashes: Is God Still in Charge*? New York: Harper and Row Publishers, 1975.

Elliot, Elisabeth. *Through Gates of Splendor*. New York: Harper and Brothers Publishers, 1957.

Elliot, Elisabeth. *Who Shall Ascend: The Life of R. Kenneth Strachan of Costa Rica*. New York: Harper and Row Publishers, 1968.

Foxe, John. *Foxes Christian Martyrs of the World*. Chicago: Moody Press, no date.

Franklin, Kirk. *Towards Global Missional Leadership: A Journey Through Leadership Paradigm Shift in the Mission of God*. Oxford: Regnum Books International, 2017.

Fryling, Alice. *Aging Faithfully: The Holy Invitation of Growing Older*. Colorado Springs, CO: NavPress, 2021.

Fuller, Harold. *People of the Mandate: The Story of the World Evangelical Fellowship*. Ada, MI: Baker Book House, 1996.

Haahnen, Jeff. *An Uncommon Guide to Retirement—Finding God's purpose for the Next Season of Life*. Chicago: Moody Publishers, 2019.

Hitt, Russell T. *Jungle Pilot: The Life and Witness of Nate Saint*. New York: Harper and Brothers, 1959.

Hoke, Steve, and Bill Taylor. *Global Mission Handbook: A Guide for Crosscultural Service*. Westmont, IL: InterVarsity Press, 2009.

Howard, David M. *The Dream That Would Not Die: The Birth and Growth of the World Evangelical Fellowship, 1846–1986*. Exeter, UK: Paternoster Press, 1986.

Howard, David M. *Hammered as Gold: A Poignant Drama of Human Suffering and New Hope Among the Evangelical Christians of Colombia*. New York: Harper and Row Publishers, 1969.

InterVarsity Christian FellowshipP Staff. *Quiet Time: A Practical Guide for Daily Devotions*. Westmont, IL: InterVarsity Press, 1976.

Koessler, Kohn. "Charisma Has Fallen on Hard Times in the Church." *Christianity Today* (May–June, 2024): 58.

Lane-Gay, Julie. *Common: Fifty Reflections on Everyday Life*. Vancouver, BC: Regent College, 2021.

Lawhead, Stephen. *Byzantium*. New York: Harper Prism, 1996.

Lederleitner, Mary T. *Women in God's Mission: Accepting the Invitation to Serve and Lead*. Westmont, IL: InterVarsity Press, 2018.

Lidstone, Julyan. *Give Up the Purple: A Call for Servant Leadership in Hierarchical Cultures*. Carlisle: Langham Global Library, 2019.

Lingelfelter, Sherwood G. *Leading Cross-Culturally: Covenant Relationships for Effective Christian Leadership*. Ada, MI: Baker, 2008.

Long, Kathryn T. *Gods in the Rainforest: A Tale of Martyrdom and Redemption in Amazonian Ecuador*. Oxford: Oxford University Press, 2019.

Mathewes-Green, Frederica. *Facing East: A Pilgrim's Journey into the Mysteries of Orthodoxy*. New York: HarperOne, 1997.

McKelvey, Douglas Kaine. "A Liturgy for Those Who Have Not Done Great Things for God." *Every Moment Holy, Vol. 1*. Nashville: Rabbit Room Press, 2019.

The Modesto Manifesto. Accessed May 14, 2024. https://www.billygraham.ca/stories/the-modesto-manifesto-a-declaration-of-biblical-integrity/. 2016.

Moody Bible Institute. *Demon Experiences in Many Lands*. Chicago: Moody Press, 1960.

Nouwen, Henri J. M . *In the Name of Jesus: Reflections on Christian Leadership*. Spring Valley, NY: Crossroad Publishing Company, 1990.

Núñez, Emilio Antonio, and William Taylor. *Crisis and Hope in Latin America: An Evangelical Perspective*. William Carey Publishing, 1996.

Núñez, Emilio Antonio, and William Taylor. *Crisis in Latin America: An Evangelical Perspective*. Chicago: Moody Press, 1989.

Overstreet, Jane. *Unleader: The Surprising Qualities of a Valuable Leader*. Westmont, IL: InterVarsity Press, 2011.

Parkinson, Ian. *Understanding Christian Leadership*. London: SCM Press, 2020.

Pleuddemann, James E. *Leading Across Cultures: Effective Ministry and Mission in the Global Church*. Westmont, IL: InterVarsity Press, 2009.

Pollock, J. C. *Hudson Taylor and Maria*. New York: McGraw-Hill, 1962.

Poverty and Justice Bible. Philadelphia: American Bible Society, 2009.

Saldívar de Escobar, Dina, and Guillermo David Taylor. *La Pirámide del Amor*. 2nd ed. Puebla, MX: Ediciones Las Américas, 1993.

Smith, Gordon. *Consider Your Calling: Six Questions for Discerning Your Vocation*. Westmont, IL: InterVarsity Press, 2016.

Smith, Gordon. *Courage and Calling: Embracing Your God-Given Potential*. Westmont, IL: InterVarsity Press, 2011.

Sonnenfeld, Jeffrey. *The Heroes' Farewell: What Happens When CEO's Retire*. Oxford: Oxford University Press, 1998.

Stetzer, Ed. Accessed May 13, 2024. https://www.linkedin.com/pulse/defining-leadership-what-why-does-matter-. July 8, 2021.

Stott, John. *The Radical Disciple: Wholehearted Christian Living*. London: InterVarsity Press, 2010.

Taylor, Guillermo D., and Sergio Mijangos. *La Familia Auténticamente Cristiana*. 2nd ed. Grand Rapids, MI: Portavoz, 2002.

Taylor, Guillermo D., David D. Ruíz, and Eugenio Campos. *Misiones Mundiales*. Guatemala: Estudios CLASE, 2025.

Taylor, W. David O. *For the Beauty of the Church: Casting a Vision for the Arts*. Ada, MI: Baker Books, 2010.

Taylor, William D. *Global Missiology for the 21st Century: The Iguassu Dialogue.* Ada, MI: Baker Academic, 2000.

Taylor, William D. *Too Valuable to Lose: Exploring the Causes and Cures of Missionary Attrition.* Pasadena, CA: William Carey Publishing, 1997.

Taylor, William D., Antonia van der Meer, and Reg Reimer. *Sorrow and Blood: Christian Mission in Contexts of Suffering, Persecution and Martyrdom.* Pasadena, CA: William Carey Publishing, 2012.

Taylor, Yvonne Christine DeAcutis. "Embracing the Invitation to Brokenness and Deconstruction." In *Spirituality in Mission: Embracing the Lifelong Journey*, John Amalraj, Geoffrey W. Hahn, and William D. Taylor, 135–42. Pasadena, CA: William Carey Publishing, 2018.

Vaughn, Ellen. *Becoming Elisabeth Elliot.* Nashville, TN: B&H Publishing, Pasadena, CA: 2020.

Vaughn, Ellen. *Being Elisabeth Elliot.* Nashville, TN: B&H Publishing, Pasadena, CA: 2023.

World Evangelical Alliance on "Evangelical." Accessed May 20, 2024. https://worldea.org/who-we-are/who-are-evangelicals/.

Wright, Christopher J. H. *The Great Story and the Great Commission: Participating in the Biblical Drama of Mission.* Ada, MI: Baker Academic, 2023.

Wright, Christopher J. H. *The Mission of God: Unlocking the Bible's Grand Narrative.* Westmont, IL: InterVarsity Press Academic, 2006.

Wright, Christopher J. H. *The Mission of God's People: A Biblical Theology of the Church's Mission.* Grand Rapids, MI: Zondervan, 2010.

Wright, Christopher J. H. "An Upside-Down World: Distinguishing Between Home and Mission Field No Longer Makes Sense." *Christianity Today* (January 18, 2007): 42.

Yung, Hwa. *Leadership or Servanthood? Walking in the Steps of Jesus.* Carlisle: Langham Global Library, 2021.

Spirituality in Mission:
Embracing the Lifelong Journey

John Amalraj and Geoffrey W. Hahn, editors

Authors from eighteen countries give us their perspectives on biblical principles and cultural expressions of spirituality. Mission without spirituality will only be a human effort to convince people of religious theories. Spirituality without a missionary involvement of the church will not express God's desire that the transforming gospel reaches every person. This book will help you rethink your understanding of what is spiritual and revisit your own spiritual journey.

Sorrow & Blood:
Christian Mission in Contexts of Suffering,
Persecution, and Martyrdom

William D. Taylor, Antonia van der Meer, Reg Reimer

This book is the product of the Mission Commission's global missiology task force. Some 62 writers from 23 nations have collaborated to generate this unique global resource and anthology. Ajith Fernando of Sri Lanka and Christopher Wright of the UK each wrote prefaces to the book. This latest WEA volume has the potential of profoundly shaping our approach to mission in today's challenging and increasingly dangerous world.

Learning to Lead at the Feet of Jesus:
Encounters with Grace and Truth

Todd Poulter

No matter how lofty our title, status, or renown as leaders, we can never rise higher in the kingdom than to the feet of Jesus. This book highlights the rich relational setting in which Jesus exercised leadership and developed his followers into leaders. In the context of his intentional "with-ness," Jesus generously shared his life and authority with the Twelve. Poulter invites leaders to a refreshing journey of discovery, intimacy, and transformation.

www.ingramcontent.com/pod-product-compliance
Lightning Source LLC
Chambersburg PA
CBHW052137070526
44585CB00017B/1862